Computer Applications in Electrical Engineering (ZKwE'2018)

ITM Web of Conferences Volume 19 (2018)

Poznan, Poland
23 – 24 April 2018

Editors:

R. Nawrowski
J. Lorenc
Z. Nadolny
A. Tomczewski
J. Jajczyk
L. Kasprzyk
A. Bugała
K. Budnik

ISBN: 978-1-5108-7182-3

Printed from e-media with permission by:

Curran Associates, Inc.
57 Morehouse Lane
Red Hook, NY 12571

CURRAN ASSOCIATES INC. proceedings.com

Some format issues inherent in the e-media version may also appear in this print version.

Printed by Curran Associates, Inc. (2018)

For additional information, please contact EDP Sciences – Web of Conferences at the address below.

EDP Sciences – Web of Conferences
17, Avenue du Hoggar
Parc d'Activité de Courtabœuf
BP 112
F-91944 Les Ulis Cedex A
France

Phone: +33 (0) 1 69 18 75 75
Fax: +33 (0) 1 69 28 84 91

contact-edps@webofconferences.org

Additional copies of this publication are available from:

Curran Associates, Inc.
57 Morehouse Lane
Red Hook, NY 12571 USA
Phone: 845-758-0400
Fax: 845-758-2633
Email: curran@proceedings.com
Web: www.proceedings.com

TABLE OF CONTENTS

Statement of Peer review

In submitting conference proceedings to *Web of Conferences*, the editors of the proceedings certify to the Publisher that

1. They adhere to its **Policy on Publishing Integrity** in order to safeguard good scientific practice in publishing.
2. All articles have been subjected to peer review administered by the proceedings editors.
3. Reviews have been conducted by expert referees, who have been requested to provide unbiased and constructive comments aimed, whenever possible, at improving the work.
4. Proceedings editors have taken all reasonable steps to ensure the quality of the materials they publish and their decision to accept or reject a paper for publication has been based only on the merits of the work and the relevance to the journal.

Title, date and place of the conference

Computer Applications in Electrical Engineering, ZKwE 2018
23 - 24 April, 2018
Poznan, Poland

Proceedings editor(s):

Ryszard Nawrowski
Józef Lorenc
Jarosław Jajczyk
Artur Bugała
Zbigniew Nadolny
Andrzej Tomczewski
Leszek Kasprzyk
Krzysztof Budnik

Date and editor's signature

30.08.2018

17, avenue du Hoggar - PA de Courtabœuf – BP 112 - 91944 Les Ulis Cedex A (France)
Tél. : 33 (0)1 69 18 75 75 - Fax : 33(0)1 69 07 45 17 – www.edpsciences.org

The forming and emission of high power electromagnetic pulses

Kazimierz Jakubiuk[1,*], *Daniel* Kowalak[1], and *Mikołaj* Nowak[1]

[1] Gdańsk University of Technology, Faculty of Electrical and Control Engineering, Narutowicza Str. 11/12, 80-233 Gdańsk, Poland

Abstract. An impulse energy source, a power conditioning system and an electromagnetic field emitter are essential to generate an electromagnetic field pulse (EMFP) with a specific frequency bandwidth. Selected simulation results for a power conditioning system consisting of a fuse opening switch and a paraboloidal electromagnetic emitter have been presented in this article. The synthetic system examined in the simulation is powered by an impulse capacitor instead of a flux compression generator (FCG) used in practice. The obtained results confirm that pulse generation and emission of high-power EMFP is possible.

1 Introduction

Generation of bandwidth-specific (e.g. in the order of MHz [3, 4]) high-power electromagnetic field pulse (EMFP) is essential in various technical applications. FCG are the most widely used energy sources in such systems [4]. They generate current pulses with the duration of several or tens of µs (substitute frequency in the order of hundreds of KHz) [4]. In order to decrease the duration of such pulse to the fraction of a µs (substitute frequency in the order of several MHz) it has to be properly formed. It is possible to accomplish this with a system incorporating fuse opening switch [4] or Blumlein transmission line which in turn provides the properly formed current pulse for the EMFP emitter (Figure 1). The used emitters must have the features of a mono-pulse radiator, and therefore have appropriate directivity, high efficiency and relatively low natural frequency (of hundreds of kHz or several MHz). Selected simulation results of the pulse-forming of a signal and its subsequent emission in the form of EMFP have been presented in this paper.

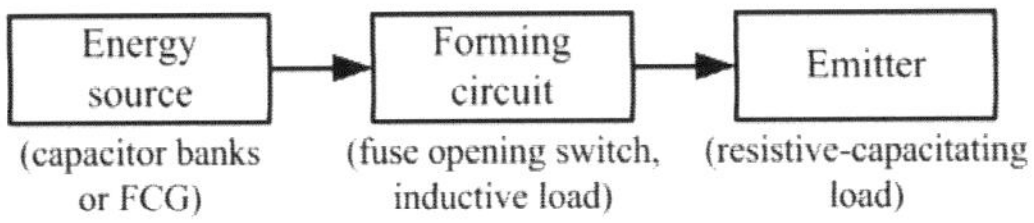

Fig. 1. The block diagram of forming system idea.

2 Model of the pulse-forming system

The substitute scheme of the examined circuit along with the adopted values of its parameters have been presented in Figure 2. Low-inductance capacitor C_0 charged to the voltage U_0 serves as an energy source. The fuse B modelled as non-linear resistance described by formulae (1) is located on the source node along with the elements L_C and R_C. The current i in the loop with the additional operating node containing the elements L_R and R_R is rapidly reduced to zero by the quickly increasing resistance of the fuse which leads to the voltage spike in the additional operating node, causing the ignition of the spark gap IS situated on the same node as the EMFP emitter. The emitter is modelled as elements R_L and C_L which parameters' values have been determined based on the results of numerical simulation regarding only the near field region of the emitter. Detailed studies of HVR (High Voltage Radiator) emitter solutions have been described in [5].

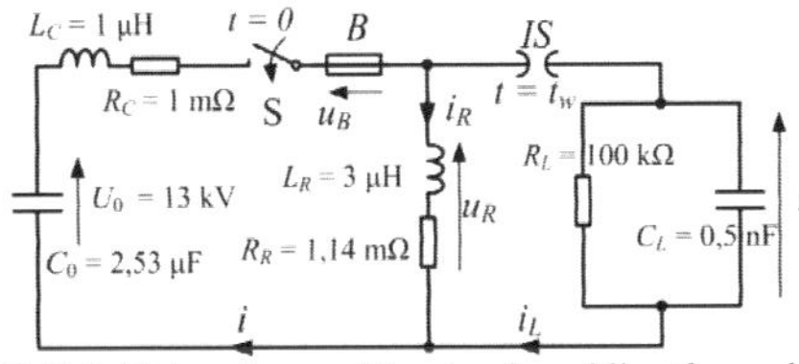

Fig. 2. Substitute scheme of the circuit enabling the analysis of the pulse-forming and emission of EMFP (the description of the elements in the text).

Calculations presented in detail in the papers [1, 2] have been performed in Matlab Simulink software. Fuse B is modelled as a non-linear resistor which resistivity depends on the integral of current action h described by formulae (1) [3, 4]:

$$\rho(h) = \begin{cases} \rho_0 \left(1 + A \left(\dfrac{h}{h_e} \right)^B \right) & \text{dla } h \le h_e \\ \rho_0 \left(A + e^{C\left(\frac{h-h_e}{h_e}\right)} \right) & \text{dla } h > h_e \end{cases} \qquad (1)$$

$$h = \frac{1}{S_f^{\ 2}} \int_0^t i(t')^2 \, dt'$$

where: ρ_0 - the resistivity of the material of the fuse element in the temperature of 0°C, S_f - surface area of fuse element, A, B, C, h_e - constants based on the experimental research [4].

The analysis of the effects of construction parameters of the fuse on the parameters of the pulse-forming circuit has been presented in the papers [1, 2].

* Corresponding author: kazimierz.jakubiuk@pg.edu.pl

3 Computational results

Exemplar computational results for the circuit with values of parameters proposed in Figure 2 and the fuse element of diameter d = 0,16 mm and length l_f = 20 mm have been presented on Figures 3 and 4.

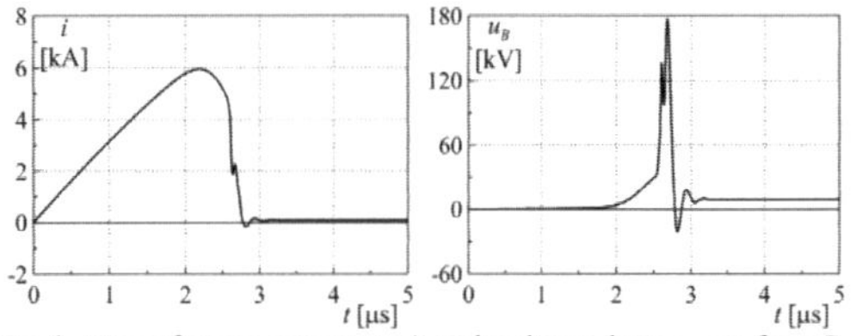

Fig. 3. Waveforms: current i a) and voltage drop u_B on fuse B b): i_{max} = 5.95 kA, $|u_B|_{max}$ = 268 kV.

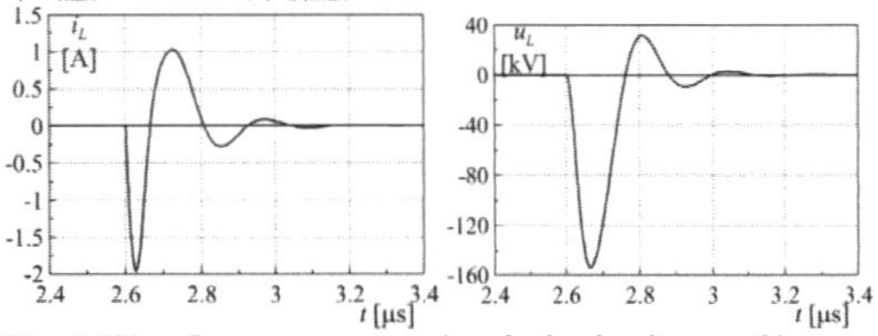

Fig. 4. Waveforms: current i_L a) and a load voltage u_L b), i_{Lmax} = 1.98 kA, $|u_L|_{max}$ = 154 kV, f_{eq} = 4.4 MHz.

4 Studies of an electric field emitter

Due to the criterion of the maximum value of the electric field, the withstanding voltage and the proper directivity of a beam, the topology of the HVR electric field emitter which consists of paraboloidal, conductive reflector and the armature in the form of a conductive tube has been chosen. The discrete emitter simulation model and a prototype at the test stand are shown in Figure 5.

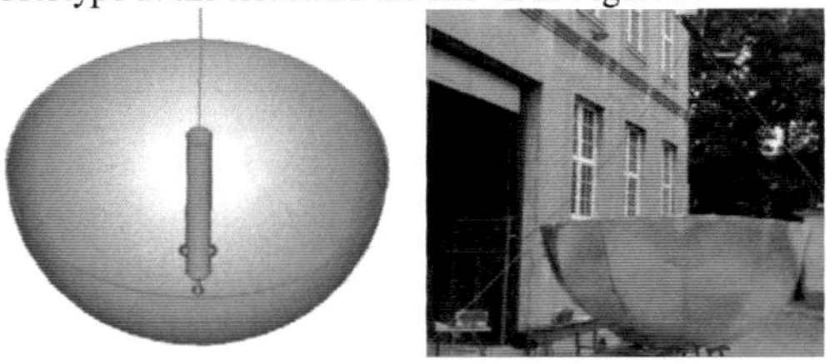

Fig. 5. Discrete emitter simulation model a) and a physical prototype b) at the test stand.

The load voltage pulse obtained from the Matlab Simulink simulation results has been used to supply the emitter simulation model implemented in the EMCOS AntennaVLab [6] software, which uses the Method of Moments in the frequency domain and inverse FFT to solve issues in the time domain.

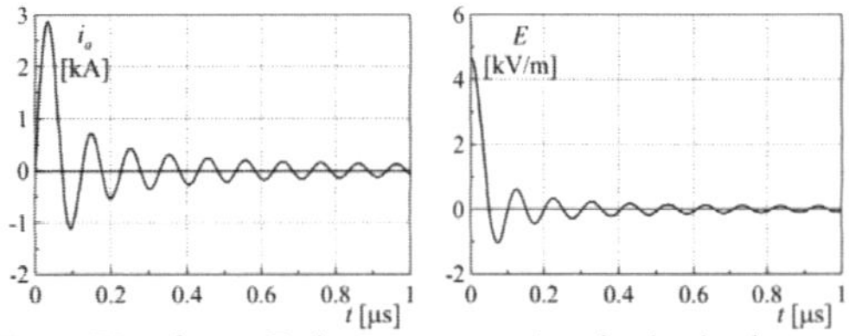

Fig. 6. Waveforms: Emitter current i_a a) and a the dominant component of the electric field E b), at a distance of 2 m; i_{amax} = 2.82 kA, E_{max} = 4.6 kV/m, f_{eq} = 3.7 MHz.

The simulation results in a form of current waveforms of the emitter and a dominant component of the electric field at a distance of 2 m from the emitter are shown in Figure 6. The results of the experimental tests performed with the use of the paraboloidal emitter prototype and a synthetic pulse-forming system are shown in Figure 7.

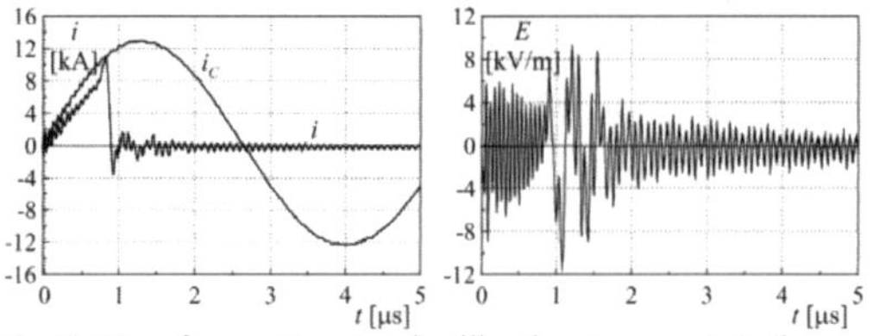

Fig. 7. Waveforms: Fuse i and calibration i_C current a), the dominant component of the electric field E b), at a distance of 2 m; i_{Cmax} = 13 kA, i_{max} = 9,2 kA, E_{max} = 10.6 kV/m, f_{eq} = 12.1 MHz.

5 Conclusions

1. Based on the presented simulation and experimental research following conclusions have been drawn:

- Application of a fuse opening switch is an effective high-power pulse-forming method allowing to achieve over tenfold reduction of pulse duration with concurrent over tenfold increase in its peak voltage.
- The considerable energy loss in the fuse is a major flaw of the examined system that reduces electrical efficiency of the pulse-forming process.
- A proposed solution of the emitter with a paraboloidal reflector was appropriate in terms of electrical strength, high value of emitted electric field, low natural frequency and directivity.

The research has been performed as a part of the project financed by the Polish National Centre for Research and Development – contract DOB-1-1/1/PS/2014.

References

1. K. Jakubiuk, D. Kowalak, *The forming of high power impulse using fuse opening switch*. Conf. on Fundamentals of Electrotechnics and Circuit Theory XLI SPETO 2018, 45-46 (2018)
2. D. Kowalak, K. Jakubiuk, M. Nowak, *Application of fuse opening switches for conditioning high power pulses*, Pozn. Univ. Technol. Acad. J. Electr. Eng. **93**, 291-298 (2018)
3. D. McCauley, D. Belt, J. Mankowski, J. Dickens, A. Neuber, M. Kristiansen, IEEE Trans. on Plasma Science, 1018-1021 (2007)
4. A. Neuber, *Explosively Driven Pulsed Power. Helical Magnetic Flux Compression Generators*, (Springer–Verlag. Berlin Heidelberg, 2005)
5. M. Nowak, K. Jakubiuk, D. Kowalak, Pozn. Univ. Technol. Acad. J. Electr. Eng. **93**, 9-20 (2018)
6. www.emcos.com, (date of access: 05.04.2018)

Comparison of active and passive EMI filters to reduction conducted noise

Marian Pasko[1], *Marek* Szymczak[1,*]

[1]Silesian University of Technology, Faculty of Electrical Engineering, 44-100 Gliwice, Poland

Abstract. The article presents the results of experimental studies of passive and active EMI filters for reduction of conducted noise. Firstly, the article presents selected structures of passive filters that have been tested in terms of insertion loss parameter describing their efficiency. Then, active filters were used to improve the efficiency of insertion loss of passive filters under the same conditions. Finally, the results and conclusions are drawn from the measurements of both types of filters for the reduction of conducted noise.

1 Introduction

Electric power systems used in electric cars use the power supply voltage (from 200 V to 550 V) keyed at high frequency (up to 200 kHz) which cause high level of EMI noise [1]. The limitation of the level of EMI is restricted by IEC/CISPR standards (EN 55025: 2008) which force the construction of larger and more complex filters what directly increases their cost [2]. Therefore, research is being conducted on the possibility of using active solutions to suppress EMI noise by replacing passive filters or significantly improving their properties [3].

2 EMI filters

Two passive filters and a combination of a passive and an active EMI filter were evaluated in this article. Attention was focused on measurements of common mode EMI noise, whose currents propagate in both supply lines + and − in the same direction and close through the PE grounding wire.

2.1 Passive EMI filters

CM inductors, in order to have high efficiency in suppressing CM EMI, must have high inductance. This can be achieved in two ways, by increasing the number of turns or by using high permeability ferromagnetic materials. In the case of using bus bars for power distribution in automotive, the problem is the winding of several turns on the core using copper flat bars, thus leading to using cores made of expensive ferromagnetic materials (e.g. nanocrystalline [4]) or increasing the number of cores.

In this chapter, an insertion losses study of two passive filters was carried out using cores of nanocrystalline material with different magnetic permeability. Figure 1 presents a schematic of the measurement stand proposed by the authors.

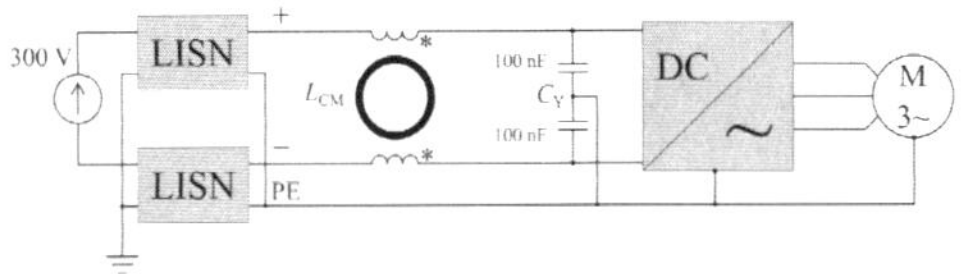

Fig. 1. Schematic diagram of the proposed measuring station for passive filters.

The first core tested was Hitachi FT-3K50T with one turn. The resulting L_{CM} choke had an inductance of about 2x 50 μH. The attenuation properties of the resulting filter (1 turn) depend only on the magnetic and geometric properties of the core. The second tested core was W424-04 from VAC. The choke is made of 4 nanocrystalline cores with a total inductance value of 2x 600 μH.

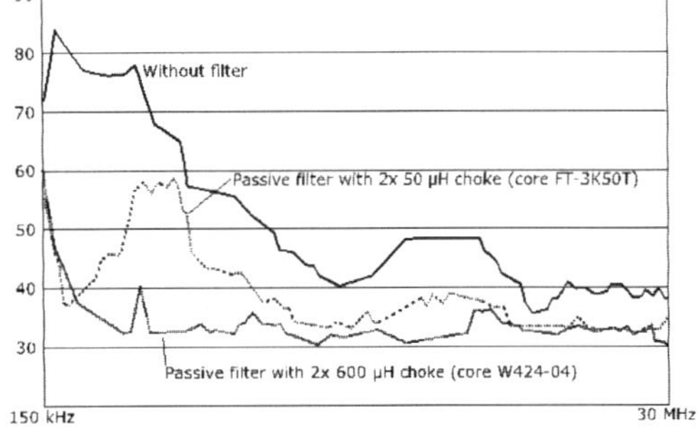

Fig. 2. Obtained spectra of CM EMI generated by inverter without filter, with passive filter with core FT-3K50T and W424-04.

Figure 2 presents a comparison of obtained spectra of CM EMI generated by the power inverter with a passive filter with core FT-3K50T and W424-04. When

* Corresponding author: Marek.Szymczak@polsl.pl

comparing both filters in terms of attenuation, one can notice a significant increase in attenuation for the W424-04 core, which is due to the fact that the choke built on it has a much higher inductance value.

2.2 Active EMI filters

The article focuses on the group of feedback filters whose operation consists in creating a compensating signal to suppress the ripples generated by the source (closed loop).

Figure 3 presents a diagram of a measurement stand proposed by the authors, in which a type III active filter (voltage detection and current cancelation) was applied.

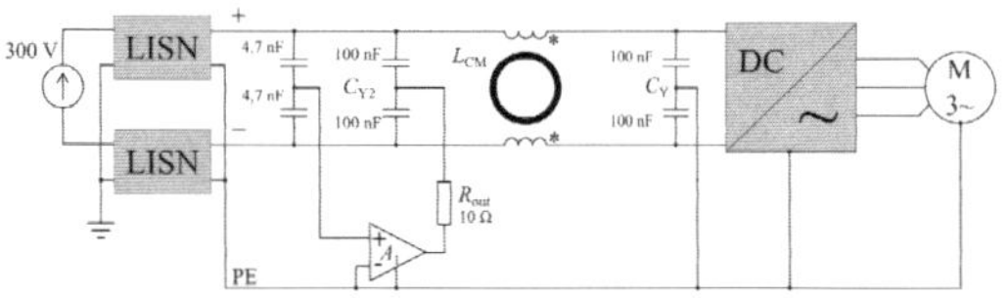

Fig. 3. Schematic diagram of the proposed measuring stand for active EMI filters.

This filter is a cascade connection of a passive filter (with a coil on the FT-3K50T core with a inductance of 2x 50 μH), and a current cancelation active filter. The core used is the same as in the previously constructed passive filter, and the amplifier has a gain of A_1 = 100 V/V. The spectrum of CM EMI that has been registered with the analyzer is shown in Figure 4.

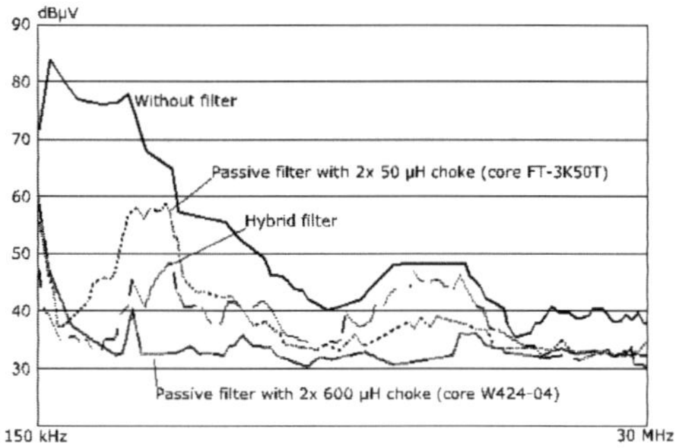

Fig. 4. Obtained spectra of CM EMI generated by inverter without filter, with passive filter with core FT-3K50T and W424-04, and cascade combination of active and passive filters.

When comparing the obtained spectrum with the spectrum after suppression with the passive filter itself with the FT-3K50T core (2x 50 μH), one can notice that the attenuation of the hybrid filter is 20 dB higher in the range of 150 kHz – 6 MHz.

3 Summary

The article investigates two passive filters and one cascade connection of a passive and an active filter. Passive filters were built using two different cores (nanocrystalline) with different permeabilities, obtaining extremely different inductance values of L_{CM}. This experiment was used to check what effect the inductance of inductors has on filter attenuation.

In the case if a filter with the inductor of 2x 50 μH, based on the FT-3K50T core, attenuation was obtained from 10 dB to 40 dB depending on the frequency. The filter with an inductor of 2x 600 μH inductance, in which the W424-04 core was used, had an insertion loss modulus of 30 dB to 50 dB. The difference in attenuation results mainly from different inductance values, and for a filter in which the inductor has a higher inductance, the insertion loss modulus is higher.

The next tested system was a cascade of a passive and an active filter, in which the L_{CM} inductor had the inductivity of 2x 50 μH, and a type III active filter (voltage detection and current cancelation). The obtained insertion loss modulus, depending on the frequency, reached even 60 dB, in the frequency range from 150 kHz to 6 MHz. For higher frequencies (from 15 MHz to 24 MHz) there was a slight amplification effect in relation to the passive filter itself. The insertion loss modulus of the passive filter itself in this band was about 10 dB, whereas the cascade connection showed a loss rate of only from 1 dB to 5 dB. This is caused by the phase shift in the active filter due to the limitation of the frequency response of the A_1 amplifier.

When comparing a passive filter (with an L_{CM} inductor of 2x 600 μH inductance) with a cascade combination of a passive and an active filters, it can be noticed that in the frequency band from 150 kHz to 4 MHz similar attenuation values were obtained. This allows us to state that by using a choke of lower inductivity, made of a material with lower magnetic permeability, but adding an active filter system, an insertion loss modulus can be obtained at a similar level to a filter with a higher inductance choke. Thanks to this, one can use a cheaper ferromagnetic material with worse parameters, thus reducing the cost of the filter, its weight and dimensions.

References

1. M. Böh, A. Lohner, N. El Amrani, *Efficiency increasing by a variable DC link voltage in combination with a bang-bang controlled inverter for an automotive application* PCIM Europe (2017)
2. S. Schefler, C. Keller, K. Spanos, S. Weber, *Systemsimulations with EMI-Filter in an Automotive HighVolt Environment* PCIM Europe (2017)
3. M. Heldwein, H. Ertl, J. Biela, J. Kolar, IEEE Trans. On Industrial Electron. **57**, 5 (2010)
4. P. Cantillon-Murphy, T. C. Neugebauer, C. Brasca, D. J. Perreault, IEEE Power Electron. Letters **2**, 2 (2004)

Optimisation of additional coils of a vibration energy harvester using interior point algorithm

Marcin Kulik[1,*], *Mariusz* Jagieła[1] and *Bernard* Baron[1]

[1]Opole University of Technology, Faculty of Electrical Engineering, Automatic Contr. and Informatics, Opole, Poland

Abstract. The paper aims at applying the interior point algorithm in optimisation of additional coils of a small resonant electromagnetic vibration energy harvester. The system, which consists of a coreless microgenerator is driven by external vibration through a cantilever-beam spring element. Originally, the system contains only one coil mounted centrally between the moving magnets. It was found that the very low induced voltage can be significantly increased by exploitation of leakage flux outside the magnets using additional coils, whose are optimised for maximum voltage.

1 Introduction

The system considered in this work, which belongs to the group of electromagnetic vibration energy harvesters [1-3] is shown in Fig. 1.

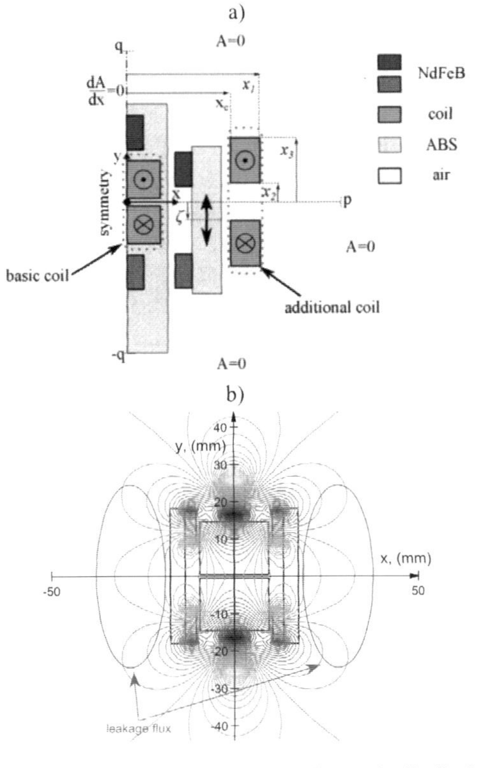

Fig. 1. Considered system: a) schematic diagram b) distribution of magnetic flux lines at displacement of magnets $\zeta = 0$.

The distribution of magnetic field in Fig. 1b was obtained by analytic solution of the Poisson equation

$$\nu_0 \nabla^2 A = J_M \tag{1}$$

with A being the magnetic vector potential, ν_0 the reluctivity of air, and J_M the equivalent current density due to permanent-magnets. The equation that describes the flux linkage of coil Ψ was derived in [2]. In this work we optimise the maximum value of induced voltage which appears at $\zeta = 0$, consequanty the objective function is

$$f(\boldsymbol{x}) = -\left.\frac{\partial \Psi(\boldsymbol{x},\zeta)}{\partial \zeta}\right|_{\zeta=0} \tag{2}$$

where (see Fig. 1a) $\mathbf{x} = [x_1, x_2, x_3]$ is a vector of decision variables. In order to provide feasibility of the design space the follwing constraints are acounted for

$$\boldsymbol{g}(\boldsymbol{x}) \geq \mathbf{0} \tag{3}$$

where :

$$\boldsymbol{g} = \Big[x_1 - x_c \quad x_2 - 1 \quad x_3 - x_2 - 1 \quad q - x_2 - x_3 - 1 \quad \ldots$$
$$\ldots\, p - x_2 - x_3 - 1 \quad \sqrt{\frac{4\mathrm{k}(x_1 - \mathrm{x_c})(x_3 - x_2)}{N\pi}} - 0.2mm \quad \ldots$$
$$0.4mm - \sqrt{\frac{4\mathrm{k}(x_1 - \mathrm{x_c})(x_3 - x_2)}{N\pi}}\Bigg]$$

with x_c = 18.39 mm, p = 75 mm, q = 75 mm (see Fig. 1a), k = 0.8 is a coil fill factor by wires, N = 1000 is the assumed number of turns. The constraints provide that the area of the optimised coils' cross-sections do not exceed the value equal to the $N{\cdot}d$/k, where d is the wire diameter. Since $f(x)$ is given analytically its variation could be explored before the optimisation. Fig. 2 presents such the variations with repsect to the two

* Corresponding author: marcin.kulik@doktorant.po.edu.pl

selected design variables, whilst the third one was set as constant.

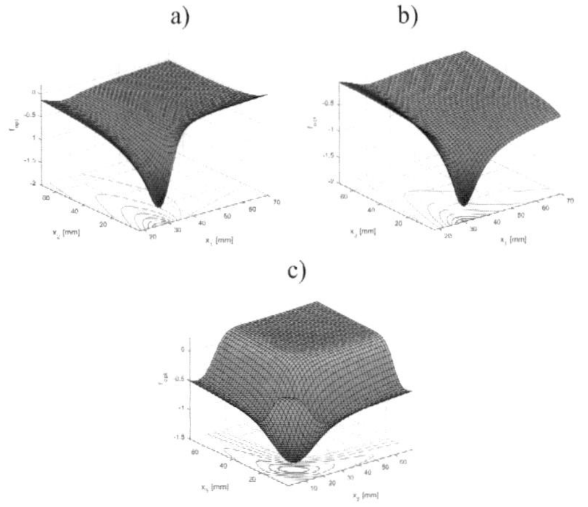

Fig. 2. Variations of objective function: a) vs. x_1 and x_2, b) vs. x_1 and x_3, c) vs. x_2 and x_3.

2 Optimisation

Minimisation of (2) subject to (3) using the interior point (IP) algorithm ensures that neither design variable can leave the feasible region [4].This is possible thanks to introduction of the logarithmic barrier function which modifies the orginal minimisation algorithm to [4]

$$\min_{\mathbf{x}}\left(f(\mathbf{x}) - \mu_k \sum_{i=1}^{n_g} \ln(z_i) \right) \tag{4}$$

$$\mathbf{g}(\mathbf{x}) - \mathbf{z} = 0, \ \ \mathbf{z} \geq 0 \tag{5}$$

where μ_k is a barrier parameter which is calculated using formula in [4]. In the IP algorithm the optimisation problem is to find the stationary point of the following Lagrange function

$$L_\mu(\mathbf{y}_k, \mu_k) = f(\mathbf{x}) - \mu_k \sum_{i=1}^{n_g} \ln(z_i) + \boldsymbol{\pi}^{\mathrm{T}}(\mathbf{g}(\mathbf{x}) - \mathbf{z}) \tag{6}$$

with $\boldsymbol{\pi}$ being the vector of Lagrange multipliers, which is carried out using the Newton-Rhapson method [4].

3 Results

The starting points for the algorithm were selected using the Latin Hypercube sampling. From the 50 random solutions the three best ones, which fall into the area restriced by (3), are selected. The results of optimisation for such starting points are given in Tab.1.

Table. 1. Results of optimisation.

Starting point $\mathbf{x}_0$	No. of iterations	Exec. time	Solution $\mathbf{x}_{\mathrm{opt}}$
$[20.97\ 4.03\ 0.05]^{\mathrm{T}}$	14	2.8 s	$[22.51\ 10.22\ 9.75]^{\mathrm{T}}$
$[22.39\ 7.82\ 3.40]^{\mathrm{T}}$	13	2.7 s	$[22.51\ 10.22\ 9.75]^{\mathrm{T}}$
$[28.43\ 11.04\ 15.86]^{\mathrm{T}}$	13	2.7 s	$[22.51\ 10.22\ 9.75]^{\mathrm{T}}$

Fig. 3 shows the variations of (2) for the optimal solution as well as for the three other randomly selected initial designs. The most favoured optimal solution (due to high voltage at small displacement) is plotted using solid line. As one can notice the induced voltage was increased by some 20 per cent with respect to the best initial solution.

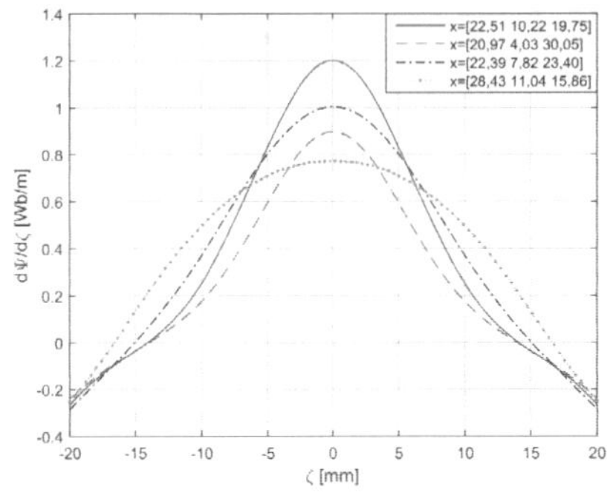

Fig. 3. Variations of flux linkage derivative for initial and optimal designs.

4 Conclusion

In this work the application of the interior point algorithm to maximisation of voltage induced in additional coils of a vibration energy harvester was presented. One important advantage of the method, beside a good numerical performance, is that in contrast to other tested local search algorithms, such as Powell, Jives-Hooke, Broyden-Fletcher-Goldfarb-Shanno, and conjugate gradient algorithms, it ensures that during evaluation of the objective function the design variables never leave the feasible region. This is very important advantage from the point of view of optimisation of physical structures, especially when the objective function is determiend from numerical models such as the finite element models.

The results obtained in this works are the basis for development of new system which is currently under construction.

This work was carried out under project 2016/23/N/ST7/03808 of the National Science Centre, Poland

References

1. P. D. Mitcheson, E. M. Yeatman, G. K. Rao, A. S. Holmes, T. C. Green, Proceedings of the IEEE **96**, 9 (2008)
2. M. Jagieła, M. Kulik, Int. Journ. of Applied Electromagn. and Mechanics **51**, S1 (2018)
3. H. Lee, M. D. Noh, Y. W. Park, IEEE Trans. Magn. **53**, 11 (2017)
4. M. Połomski, B. Baron, Acta Energ. **1**, 14 (2013)

Optimization of the eddy current transducer using COMSOL Multiphysics® and MATLAB® software

Konrad Dudziak[1*], *Krzysztof* Stawicki[2], and *Andrzej* Brykalski[2]
[1]West Pomeranian University of Technology, Faculty of Civil Engineering and Architecture, al. Piastów 50, 70-311 Szczecin, Poland
[2]West Pomeranian University of Technology, Faculty of Electrical Engineering, Sikorskiego 37, 70-313 Szczecin, Poland

Abstract. The article presents a method of optimizing the eddy current transducer. The transducer is made of three toroidal air cored coils: one excitation coil and two receiver coils. The transducer is used for eddy current nondestructive testing (NDT).

1 Introduction

The article presents the capabilities gained by interoperation of the COMSOL Multiphysics® and MATLAB® software. The COMSOL module allows, among other things, to use the Finite Element Method (FEM) for simulation of the electromagnetic phenomena occurring in the NDT [1] transducer model. The MATLAB software utilizes the genetic algorithm method (GA) found in the *Optimization Toolbox* for optimization and post-processing.

Interoperability of both software allows for effective optimization of transducer's dimensions.

2 Optimization solution

Interoperability of different types of calculation software requires an efficient data transfer. Automatic data transfer between COMSOL and MATLAB software is possible thanks to "LiveLink™ *for* MATLAB®" within the COMSOL software. The LiveLink module is based on the *Java* environment and works as a client-server model. The COMSOL server provide the computation tools (solvers) for the MATLAB software. The interoperation model is visible in Figure 1.

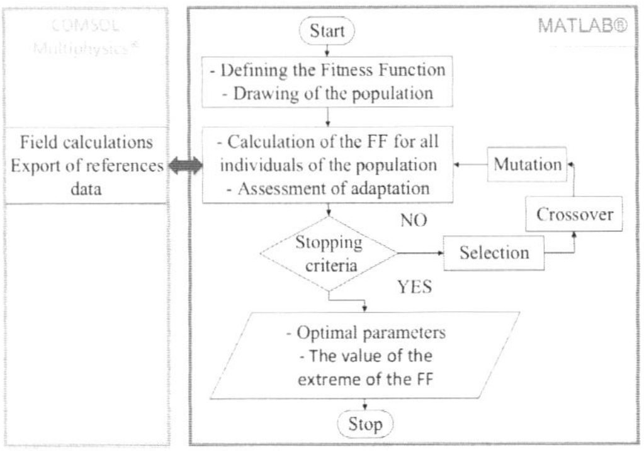

Fig. 1. Optimization with COMSOL and MATLAB software.

The genetic algorithm [2] used in this study is a stochastic method of optimization. It utilizes the mechanisms taken among other from environmental sciences, including natural selection and inheritance. Included genetic operators such as selection, crossover and mutation, allow to produce more successful offspring that will pass the data to further generations.

3 Transducer optimization

The simulations included the optimization of the dimensions of a transducer (Fig.2) used for determination of the material characteristics of given object [3]. The transducer designed as 2D axisymmetric is made of excitation coil (air cored coil) powered by alternating current with frequency of 200 Hz that generates magnetic field. Two differentially connected receiver coils are placed in a certain distance from the excitation coil [4-5]. The distance between the coils is determined by the maximum thickness of the object.

Following parameters were put to optimization:
a_2, h_2 – width and height of the receiver coil 1,
a_3, h_3 – width and height of the receiver coil 2.

Based on those parameters it is possible to determine remaining characteristics:
n_2 and n_3– number of turns in receiver coil 1 and coil 2:

$$n_2 = k \cdot a_2 \cdot h_2 / S \quad (1)$$

$$n_3 = k \cdot a_3 \cdot h_3 / S \quad (2)$$

where: k=0.86 is the fill factor of the coil, S- cross-section of a turn
r_3 – radius of the receiver coil 2:

$$r_3 = r_2 + \frac{a_2}{2} + \frac{a_3}{2} \quad (3)$$

z_3 – location on the z axis of the receiver coil 2:

$$z_3 = \frac{h_1}{2} + \frac{h_3}{2} + h_2 + h_0 + z_1 \quad (4)$$

* Corresponding author: konrad.dudziak@zut.edu.pl

https://doi.org/10.1051/itmconf/20181901004

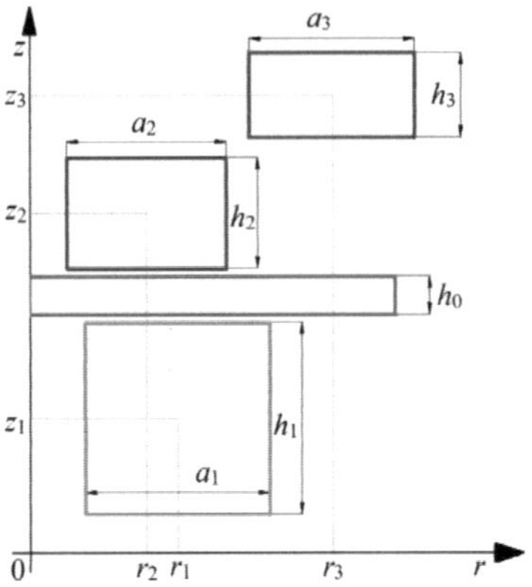

Fig. 2. Eddy current transducer model.

Objective function (fitness function) taken for the optimization assumes minimization of the differential voltage (V_diff) induced in the receiver coils (V_1, V_2) in the case when the object is not present.

Performed study was limited by the range of values assumed for optimized geometrical parameters.

3.1 Results of the optimization

Results of the optimization are shown in the Table 1. The numbers in the head show the optimization range. The table contains only partial results of conducted simulations. To find the minimum value of objective function and shorten the computation time, the process was performed with different genetic algorithm settings. Chosen variables were: population size (P) (from 200 to 5), number of generations (G) (from 100 to 5), selection method (Roulette) and other GA elements. Best results (in millimeters) and minimal fitness function (FF) values (in volts) shown in Table 1 were obtained for following combination: population size and number of generations equaled to 15 and 15.

Table 1. Optimization results.

P	G	a_2 10-35	h_2 10-40	a_3 35-120	h_3 35-120	FF value
10	10	16.4	10.5	85.1	83.1	0.248
15	5	10.7	16.3	73.1	108.2	0.196
5	15	11.9	12.7	56.3	94.1	0.188
15	15	11.1	11.4	52.0	108.8	0.158
25	5	11.9	14.8	50.9	90.9	0.202
5	25	11.4	13.2	56.3	95.1	0.185

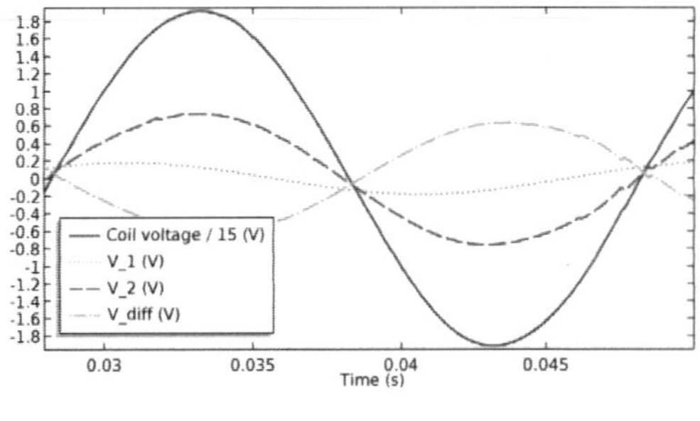

Fig. 3. Voltage values.

The values of the voltage for obtained combination (15 and 15) of optimized parameters are visible in Figure 3. The voltage in excitation coil have been scaled down (divided by 15). Figure 4 presents the magnetic flux density (T) of the excitation and receiver coils in the optimized model (15 and 15 combination).

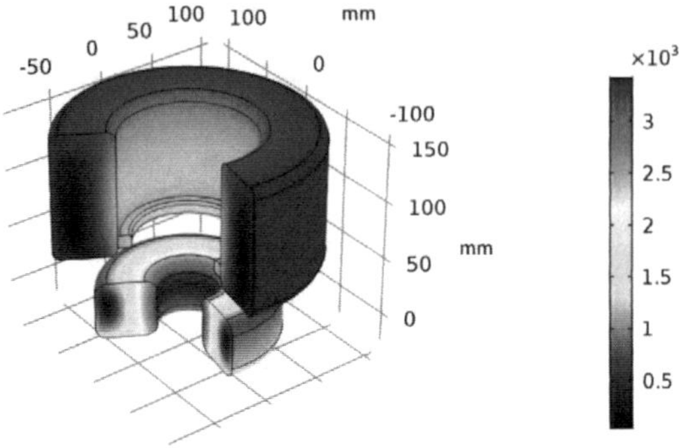

Fig. 4. Optimized model of the eddy current transducer.

4 Conclusions

Optimization of the four chosen dimensions allowed to reduce the output signal for the case when the object is not present. At the same time, it did not allow to nullify the differential voltage. Nullification of the differential voltage requires optimization of additional design characteristic. This includes coil radius, distance between coils and possible other elements of the transducer – ferromagnetic core and conducting screen, which were not taken into account in this work.

Performed study have shown that efficient optimization of the NDT transducer design can be performed with interoperable COMSOL and MATLAB software. The same procedure can be used for similar problems [5-6] by modifying the model.

References

1. S. Nagata, M. Numachi, IEEE Tran. Magn **53,** 1–4 (2017)
2. J. McCall, J Comput Appl Math. **184**, 205–222 (2005)
3. S. Wang, S. Huang, A. Velichko, P. Wilcox and W. Zhao, Ultrasonics **81**, 23–31 (2017)
4. K. Stawicki, S. Gratkowski, Choice of parameters of the excitation system in eddy current testing of tubes, *11th IGTE Symposium* (2004)
5. M. Wrzuszczak, J. Wrzuszczak, Zeszyty Naukowe WEiA P Gdańskiej, 89–91 (2014)
6. H.T. Zhou, K. Hou, H.L. Pan, J.J. Chen, Q.M. Wang, Procedia Engineering **130**, 1649-1657 (2015)

Selected issues of control voltage source inverter with self-excited synchronous generator as DC grid voltage source

Maciej Kozak[1,*]

[1]Maritime University of Szczecin, Institute of Marine Automation and Electrotechnics, 70-500 Szczecin, Poland

Abstract. Synchronous self-excited generators are the most popular AC voltage sources installed in power plants of seagoing vessels. Because of fuel savings varying revolutions Diesel drives can be found on selected types of ships (platform support vessels, cable layers, tug boats etc.). Very interesting issue is use of such type of alternator working with inverter acting as rectifier in direct current grid system. In direct current type of electrical grid the problems with synchronization and reactive power balance are absent. As the control method most suitable to use is modified version of field oriented control (FOC) known from induction machines. Aforementioned method involves decoupling of currents and control voltages to flux and torque components and keeping them in the most optimal condition. Theoretical background of inverter and synchronous generator adopted FOC control method along with numerical situations and experimental results obtained in laboratory test bench of such a system were included in following article.

1 Introduction to synchronous generator control method

The classical approach of the synchronous generators control with independent exciting winding is the active and reactive power control by means of the voltage and frequency adjustment [1]. In the most cases the two control loops are operating separately each to others with use of RPM's governor and voltage regulator. This kind of operation may be considered as a scalar control procedure, which disregards some phenomena, i.e. the coupling effect between electrical axis the synchronous generator [2]. The vector control is based on the field-orientation principle. It can be used as an AC induction motor drives control, but also for squirrel cage generator running. Because of its performance during transient operation modes, it comes quite close to direct current machines. The mathematical background of the dynamic model and vector control of AC machine is given by the space-phasor theory [2], [4]. The rotor flux oriented synchronous machine model is similar to a shunt excited direct current machine. It is suitable for the simulation of the synchronous generator operation, but the control will be realized with the field oriented model considering the resultant stator flux. This model leads to the analogy with the compensated DC machine, which allows the independent control of the two variables that produce the machine torque [2], [3], [4], [5]. In Fig. 1 there are shown the stator field oriented components of the stator current:

$$i_s = i_{sd\lambda} + \mathrm{j}\, i_{sq\lambda} \tag{1}$$

while the armature coil flux equals to:

$$\Psi_{ss} = \Psi_{ssd\lambda s} + \mathrm{j}\,\Psi_{ssq\lambda s} = L_{md} i_{sd\lambda} + \mathrm{j}\, L_{mq} i_{sq\lambda} \tag{2}$$

where λ_s is the angular position of the resultant stator flux Ψ_s.

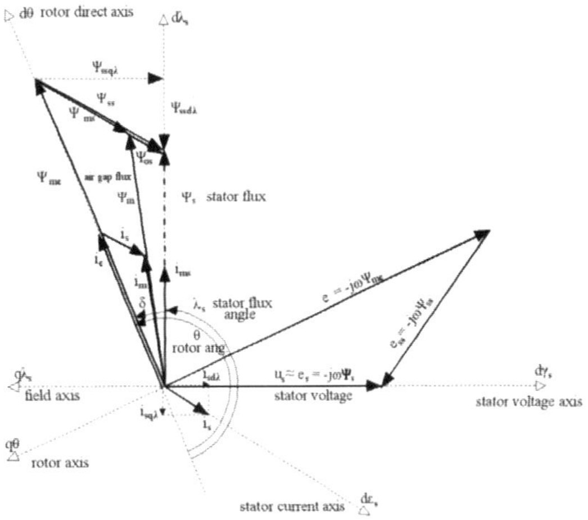

Fig. 1. Diagram of the synchronous generator with leading stator current, and the stator-field oriented space phasors of the stator current [2].

In the generating mode, the quadrature component of the armature flux $\Psi_{ssd\lambda}$, which determines the active power and DC intermediate circuit voltage will be negative due to the reversed active energy flow. Flux denoted as $\Psi_{ssq\lambda}$ is also negative, due to its demagnetizing character. This flux corresponds to the reactive power produced by alternator and covering the reactive load.

[*] Corresponding author: m.kozak@am.szczecin.pl

1.1 Self-excited synchronous generator FOC control properties

In order to have a full control for generator some simplification has been taken into consideration regarding the produced torque. The load torque coming from PI regulator in outer DC voltage control loop can be regulated by controlling the generators torque angle. In the constant torque angle control strategy, the d axis current is kept at zero value for all of the operation time, while the vector current is aligned with the q axis in order to maintain the torque angle equal close to 90°. The torque equation for a synchronous alternator, taking into account both i_{sd} and i_{sq} currents is the one derived in:

$$T_e = \frac{3}{2} p \left[\Psi_m i_{sq} + (L_d - L_q) i_{sq} i_{sd} \right] \quad (3)$$

where: p is a number of pole pairs and ψ_m is field winding flux. After substituting the d-q currents in equation (3) and after a few simplifications the torque value is the one presented in equation (4).

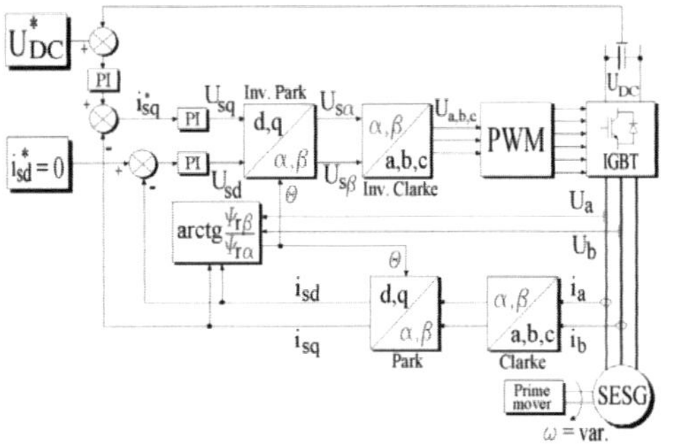

Fig. 2. Vector control structure of the self-excited synchronous generator with stator-field orientation.

$$T_e = \frac{3}{2} p \Psi_m i_{sq} \quad (4)$$

From above equation it can be easily observed that the control property is very simple to implement, just by representing the linearization between the torque and machine active current.

2 Test bench and experimental results

To fully test presented system laboratory setup was prepared. The test bench consists of synchronous generator driven by electric motor. Terminals of generator are connected to the 3-phase inverter controlled by real time operating DSP-FPGA board. Control method used was sensorless technique which omits encoder and rotor angle was calculated from measured currents and Clarke transformation. As the load the resistor connected to the DC intermediate circuit was used. System was equipped also with another generator powered inverter that produced DC voltage and was used to prove robustness of power sharing algorithm.

While in so called island operation synchronous generator worked in the principle of maintaining constant DC voltage on inverter's intermediate circuit capacitors for wide range of rotational speeds.

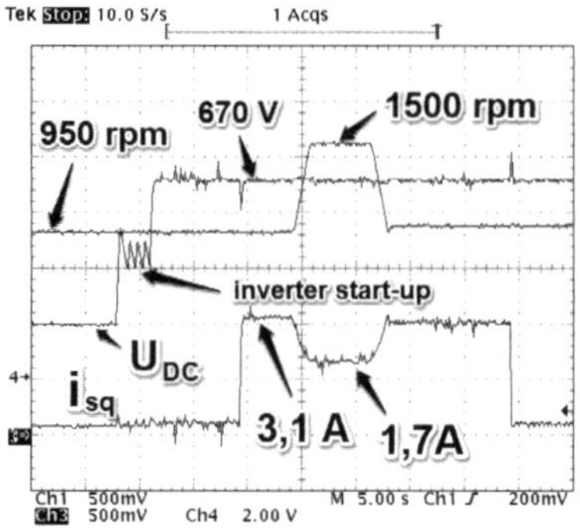

Fig. 3. Experimental results of start-up, load apply and speed change under load of synchronous generator-inverter set.

While inverter startup procedure different set of PI regulators coefficients was used to proper compensation of changing with speed electromotive force what can be clearly seen in some U_{DC} oscillations. Presented system has also possibility to work in parallel power sharing mode along with other DC current controlled sources with use of auctioneering diodes.

3 Conclusions and further work

As it was proven in laboratory test bench proposed system is very stable and DC voltage variations does not exceed 5% in steady state and 10% in transient operation in both island and power sharing mode. Further work will focus on integrating ultracapacitors with controlled DC-DC converter to presented system. Thanks to its properties, the system will be further developed towards further optimization and easy integration with existing solutions.

References

[1] Z. Qing-Chang, Z. Yu, *Parallel Operation of Inverters with Different Types of Output Impedance*, Industrial Electronics Society, IECON 2013 - 39th Annual Conference of the IEEE
[2] M. Imecs, I. Iov Incze, C. Szabo, *Stator-Field Oriented Control of the Synchronous Generator: Numerical Simulation,* 2008 International Conference on Intelligent Engineering Systems, ISSN 1543-9259, 2008
[3] M. Kozak , A. Bejger, R. Gordon, Zeszyty Naukowe Akademii Morskiej w Szczecinie **45**, 17-22, 2016
[4] S. A. Baktyono, *Study of Field-Oriented Control of a Permanent Magnet Synchronous Generator and Hysteresis Current Control for Wind Turbine Application*, The Ohio State University, 2006
[5] R. Balog,, P.T. Krein, IEEE Transactions on Power Electronics **26**/3, 860–867 (2011)

The effects of LED light sources on the parameters defining the quality of electricity

Andrzej Lange[1,*], *Marian* Pasko[2]

[1]University of Warmia and Mazury in Olsztyn, Department of Electrical and Power Engineering, Electronics and Automation, EDP Sciences, Editorial Department, 10-736 Olsztyn, ul. Oczapowskiego 11, Poland
[2]Silesian University of Technology, Institute of Electrical Engineering and Computer Science, 44-100 Gliwice, Akademicka 2A, Poland

Abstract. The article presents the regulations and standards relating to the quality of electricity, with special emphasis on higher current and voltage harmonics in high-voltage, medium-voltage and low-voltage power grids and the power factor (PF). The parameters defining the quality of electricity consumed by modern LED bulbs for lighting homes, industrial premises such as offices and production halls, as well as roads and yards were measured and analyzed. The current waveforms for LED lights were presented upon connection to the power grid.

1 Preface

Light sources based on the LED technology are increasingly used to light homes, industrial premises and outdoor sites such as roads. LED bulbs are gradually replacing less economical incandescent bulbs and energy-saving gas-discharge lights. Gas-discharge bulbs are more energy efficient, but they exert a negative effect on the power grid by causing overvoltage on ignition, generating higher current harmonics to the power grid, and absorbing passive inductive power from the grid (when inductive ignition systems are used). LED bulbs are characterized by high luminous efficacy and long life.

2 Standards and regulations on electricity quality

Selected provisions of the European Union directives, Polish regulations and standards are presented in the References section in points [1] to [12]. These regulations define the minimum requirements for electricity quality and supply voltage (higher harmonic frequencies) and the power factor cosφ.

3 Structure of LED light sources

LED bulbs have the following components: a rectifier circuit, a capacitor for smoothing the voltage supplied by the rectifier, a current-voltage regulator, and light-emitting diodes connected in series and in parallel. The complexity of the rectifier and power supply system varies in different types of LED bulbs (for home or industrial use), which significantly influences current waveforms.

4 Measurements and analysis of results

The quality of electricity drawn by LED lights was analyzed by testing more than ten randomly selected LED bulbs for lighting homes, industrial premises and roads with the use of the HIOKI 3196 power quality analyzer. The analyses involved measurements of current, voltage and power as well as higher current and voltage harmonics at the place of supply. Transient states during connection and disconnection from the power grid were evaluated. The registered higher current harmonics generated to the grid are presented in Figure 1 for home lights, in Figure 2 for industrial lights, and in Figure 3 for road lights. The phase angle between current and voltage for the first harmonic is presented in Figure 4. The current waveform for a household light is presented in Figure 5a, and for a road light – in Figure 5b.

5 Conclusions

Modern LED lights have high luminous efficacy and long life, as well as the following characteristics:

- LED lights draw deformed current by generating higher current harmonics to the power grid (Fig. 1, 2 and 3),
- LED lights decrease the power factor to PF=0.53 for household lights (Fig. 4) and PF=0.93 for road lights, and they draw passive inductive power from the grid,

* Corresponding author: andrzej.lange@uwm.edu.pl

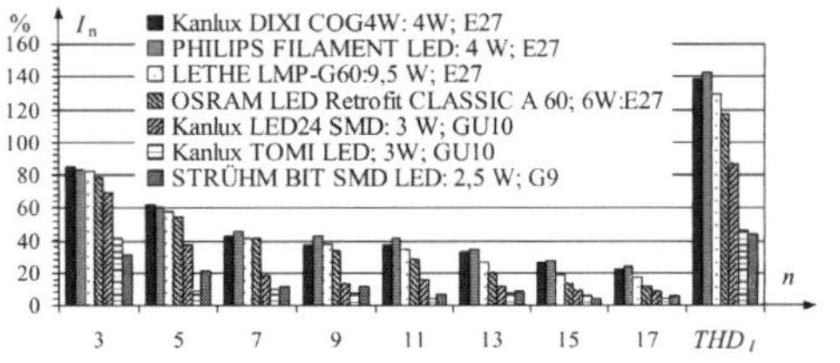

Fig.1. Percentage of higher current harmonics and THD_I drawn from a low-voltage power grid by household LED bulbs.

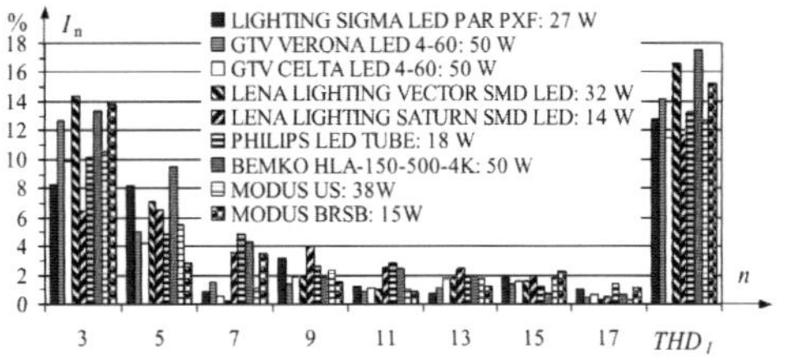

Fig.2. Percentage of higher current harmonics and THD_I drawn from a low-voltage power grid by industrial LED bulbs.

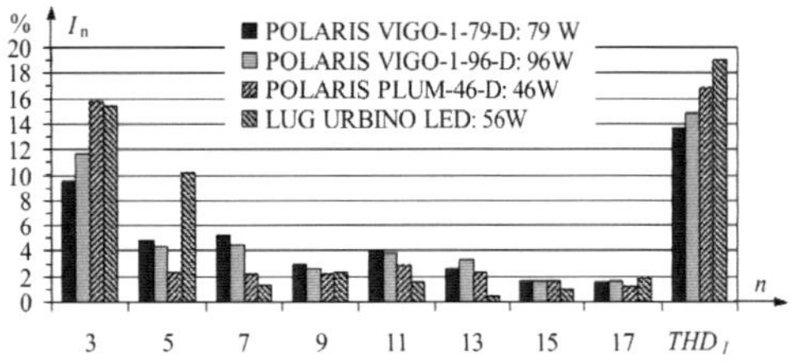

Fig.3. Percentage of higher current harmonics and THD_I drawn from a low-voltage power grid by road LED lights.

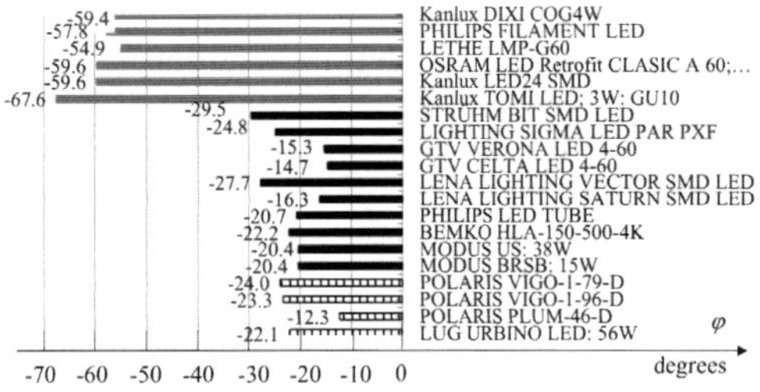

Fig.4. Phase angle between voltage and current for the first harmonic in the tested LED bulbs.

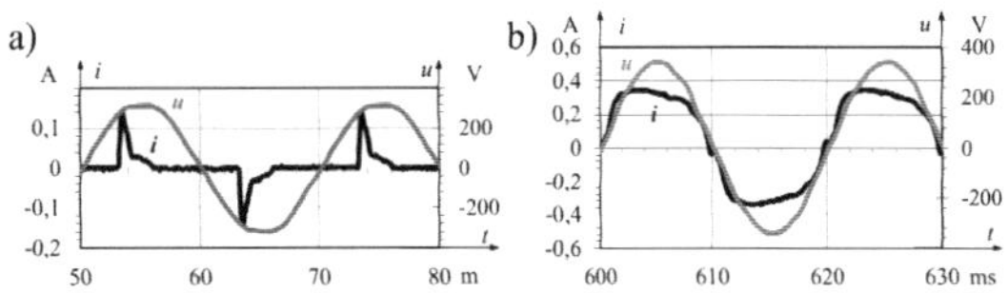

Fig.5. Steady-state current waveform for: a) PHILIPS FILAMENT LED bulb for household use: 4 W; E27; b) POLARIS PLUM-46-D road light.

- most household bulbs have a simple rectifier system with a capacitor for smoothing the voltage transmitted to LED diodes (Fig. 5); therefore, they also generate higher values of higher harmonics reaching THD_I = 140% (Fig. 1) than industrial and road lights which generate higher harmonics that do not exceed THD_I = 20% (Fig. 2 and 3),
- lighting fixtures for home use should be equipped with passive [12] or active [13] filters, whereas industrial and road lighting fixtures should be fitted with active filters [13] to minimize their negative effects on the power grid;
- higher harmonics in supply voltage increase with the absorption of higher current harmonics, which can lead to electrical current resonance,
- all of the tested LED lights meet the limits for higher harmonics generated to the power grid, as stipulated by the referenced standards and regulations in [1] to [12],
- industrial and road lights first charge the capacitor, and LED diodes are gently activated after more than ten voltage waveforms.

References

1. Polish Power Law of 25 September 2012. Journal of Laws, item 1059, volume 1
2. Directive 2014/30/EU of the European Parliament and of the Council of 26 February 2014 on the harmonisation of the laws of the Member States relating to electromagnetic compatibility
3. Regulation of the Minister of the Economy of 4 May 2007 on the detailed operating requirements for the electric power system.
4. EN 50160: 1998. Voltage characteristics of electricity supplied by public distribution systems
5. IEEE Std 1459-2010 Standard Definitions for the Measurement of Electric Power Quantities Under Sinusoidal, Nonsinusoidal, Balanced, or Unbalanced Conditions; IEEE, New York, 2010
6. EN 61000-3-2:2014-10: Electromagnetic compatibility (EMC) - Part 3-2: Limits for harmonic current emissions (equipment input current ≤ 16A per phase)
7. EN 61000-3-12:2012: Electromagnetic compatibility (EMC) –Part 3-12: Limits – Limits for harmonic current produced by equipment connected to public low-voltage systems with input current > 16 A and ≤ 75A per phase
8. EN 61000-4-30:2015 Electromagnetic compatibility (EMC) – Part 4-30: Testing and measurement techniques – Power quality measurement methods
9. EN 61000-4-7:2007/A1:2011: Electromagnetic compatibility (EMC) - Part 4-7: Testing and measurement techniques - General guide on harmonics and interharmonics measurements and instrumentation, for power supply systems
10. Commission Regulation (EU) No 1194/2012 of 12 December 2012 implementing Directive 2009/125/EC of the European Parliament and of the Council with regard to ecodesign requirements for directional lamps, light emitting diode lamps
11. Commission Regulation (EC) No 244/2009 of 18 March 2009 implementing Directive 2005/32/EC of the European Parliament and of the Council with regard to ecodesign requirements for non-directional household lamps
12. T. Białoń, M. Pasko, J. Mirowski, M. Kurkowski, Elektryka **238**, 49-68 (2016)
13. T. Adrikowski, Elektryka, **228**, 77-88 (2013)

Artificial neural network inspired by quantum computing solutions using the movement model of the PR-02 robot

Jerzy Tchórzewski[1,*], *Dariusz* Ruciński[1], and *Przemysław* Domański[1]

[1]Institute of Computer Sciences, University of Natural Sciences and Humanities, 3-Maja 54, 08-110 Siedlce, Poland

Abstract. The paper proposes a new method of quantum computing using control and systems theory as well as matrix-quantum computing. The algorithm developed on the basis of the PR-02 robot's arm's movement was implemented in using the Neural Network Toolbox. The application of the neural model instead of the analytic model allowed for obtaining the improvement of the trajectory of the PR-02 robot's arm movement, while the application of the quantum artificial neural network for the assumed number of quasi-parallel computations equal 1000 did not result in the improvement of the model.

1 Introduction

Currently, more and more accurate modeling methods are being sought, especially smart grid systems. High accuracy is achieved using neural and evolutionary modeling methods. Obtained, among others detailed neural models of the Polish Electric Power Exchange [1-2] and models of the PR-02 robot movement [3]. It is possible to increase the accuracy of models when inspiring artificial intelligence methods with quantum computing solutions, which is associated with the slowing down of computations due to quasi parallel processing [2-3]. In this spirit, the example of the movement of the end of the robot's arm PR-02 shows that the quantum-inspired artificial neural network (ANN) increases the accuracy of the end position of the robot arm at the starting point and at the end point and raises hope for a more precise trajectory.

2 Quantum computing

Fundamentals of the control and systems theory were used to describe the quantum-inspired artificial neural network [4], in particular, the definition of the state of the system, which was used as the basis for determination of mixed states of a quantum number. Using numerical data related to the changes of the four above mentioned parameters, described in detail in works, i.a. [2-3] the artificial neural network was designed and taught the movement of the PR-02 movement, followed by the development of the method of quantization, dequantization and quantum computing, thus making an attempt to improve the accuracy of the neural model. Quantum computing was interpreted based on the example of a single neuron, described by, e.g. the activation function of the sigmoidal tangent type of the i-th neuron of k-th weights layer of the perceptron artificial neural network [2-3], as follows:

$$y(net_i^k(t)) = \frac{1 - e^{-2\begin{bmatrix} net_{i,lm}^k & net_{i,lm}^k \\ net_{i,lm}^k & net_{i,lm}^k \end{bmatrix}}}{1 + e^{-2\begin{bmatrix} net_{i,lm}^k & net_{i,lm}^k \\ net_{i,lm}^k & net_{i,lm}^k \end{bmatrix}}}, \quad (1)$$

where net_i^k – quantum summator of the i-th neuron in the k-th weights layer defined as the sum of weighted quantum values of input signals to the k-th neuron layer, $net_{i,lm}^k$ - the element of the summator net^k_i with the index $_{lm}$ as quantum weighted input signal to the k-th neuron layer of ANN with the clean state nature resulting from two mixed states.

3 Analytical model of the PR-02 robot

Robots of this type feature uncomplicated trajectory programming and a simple power-supply system [6]. Simple equation of the PR-02 robot's grab kinematics movement is presented using a transformation graph using the following form of matrix X:

$$\mathbf{X} = \begin{bmatrix} C_1S_4 & C_1C_4 & -S_1 & l_2C_1 - S_1\lambda_3 \\ S_1S_4 & S_1C_4 & C_1 & l_2C_1 + S_1\lambda_3 \\ C_4 & -S_4 & 0 & l_3 + \lambda_5 \\ 0 & 0 & 0 & 1 \end{bmatrix}, \quad (2)$$

with values of cosines and sines of respective angles at the joint being denoted as the values of parameters C_i and S_i, and described in detail in table 1 [2-3,5]. Change of H-D parameters directly controls the movement of the PR-02 robot's arm's endpoint; as a result of which, the robot's arm's end draws in the Cartesian space XYZ the trajectory shown in Table 2 [2-3, 5].

Table 1. Values of Hartenberg-Denevit (H-D) parameters used to describe the PR-02 manipulator [5].

No	α_i [°]	l_i [m]	λ_i [m]	θ_i [°]
1	0	0	0	-300÷0
2	-90	-0.11	0÷0.200	0
3	0	0	0.367÷0.676	-90
4	0	0	0	0÷360

* Corresponding author: jerzy.tchorzewski@uph.edu.pl

4 Neural and quantum PR-02 models

In order to obtain the neural model of the PR-02 robot's arm's end movement, a perceptron artificial neural network was designed-described in detail in works e.g. [1-3,6-7]. Values of parameters presented in table 1 were used for the purpose of training the Artificial Neural Network (ANN), with the number of epochs equal 1 164. As a result of training ANN, MSE error of the order of magnitude 10^{-3} – 10^{-4} was obtained after approx. 80 epochs (train) [3]. A model of quantum artificial neural network is presented in fig. 1, and its subsystems in works [5-7].

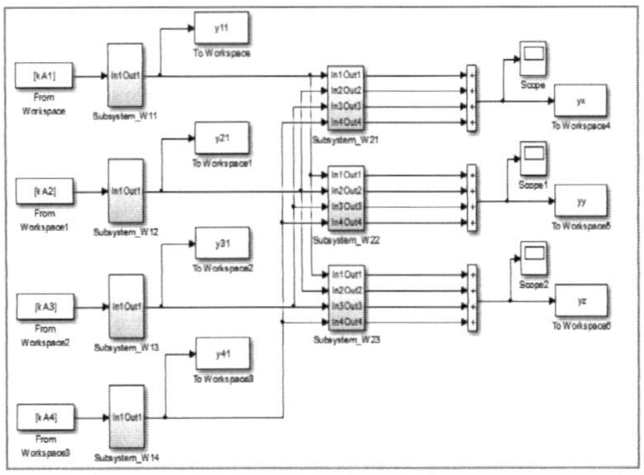

Fig. 1. A model of the Quantum ANN [3].

5 The behavior of the PR-02 models

The comparison of functioning of the three models of the PR-02 robot's arm's end movement, i.e. the analytic model, the neural model and the quantum model (neural, quantum computer science-inspired model – table 2), showed that the neural model obtained as a result of training the ANN the movement of the robot's arm's end was very similar to the analytic model. As a result of the calculations, the corresponding coordinates of the end point of the robot arm's trajectory for calculations were obtained: analytical - Pr (0,20001,0,7,074,20001), neural - Pn (0,277556, 0,92218, 0,189762) and quantum - pq (0.112611, 0.867, 0.200009).

Noteworthy are the better results regarding the position of the end point trajectory of the PR-02 robot arm received for quantum calculations than for the neuronal calculations. The Euclidean distance determined in relation to the real point is smaller for the Quantum Artificial Neural Network and amounts to 0.087398624, while for the Artificial Neuron Network - 0.090151236.

Unfortunately, it turned out that for 1 000 quasi parallel calculations, the course of the trajectory of the neural model inspired by quantum computation was similar but not continuous. It was caused by a small number of quasi-parallel calculations considering the quantum computer science requirements (occurrences of mixed states with infinite number), hence, it would be necessary to increase the number of mixed states both in quantization and in quantum computing in further research, at least by one order of magnitude, e.g. to 10 or even 100 thousand of mixed quantum states and quantum calculations. The research is being continued.

References

1. D. Ruciński, Studia Informatica. Systems and Information Technology **1-2 (21)**, UPH, 63-83 (2017)
2. J. Tchórzewski, D. Ruciński, Pozn. Univ. Technol. Acad. J. Electr. Eng **96**, 21-32 (2018)
3. J. Tchórzewski, P. Domański, Pozn. Univ. Technol. Acad. J. Electr. Eng **96**, 33-46 (2018)
4. T. Kaczorek, Basics of Control Theory, (WNT, Warszawa, 2005)
5. T. Szkodny, Kinematics of industrial robots, (Publisher of the SUT, Gliwice, 2013)
6. S. Osowski, Neural networks for information processing, (OW PW, Warszawa, 2013)
7. R. Tadeusiewicz, M. Szaleniec, Lexicon of neural networks, Publisher of Foundation "Project Science Leksykon", (Wrocław, 2015)

Table 2. Trajectories of the PR-02 robot's arm: analytic (a), neural (b), quantum-neural (c) models. Source: [3,5-7].

In the analytic model (a)	In the neural model (b)	In the quantum-neural model (c)
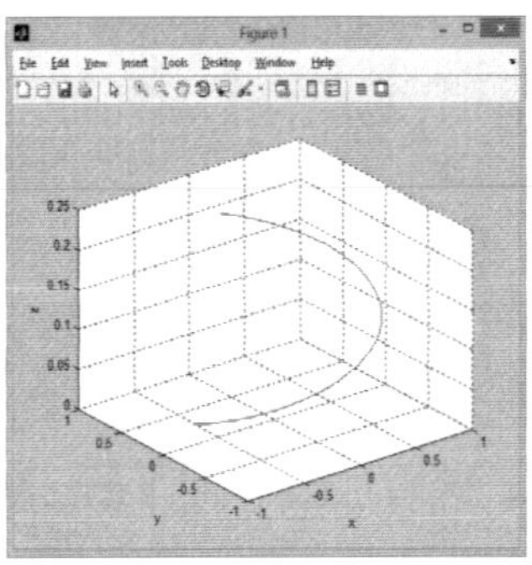	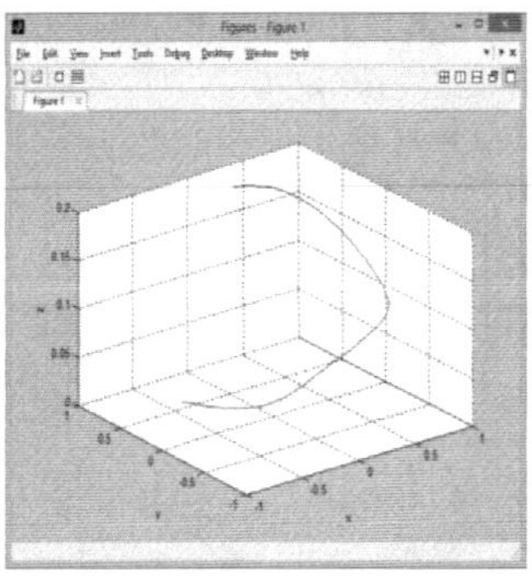	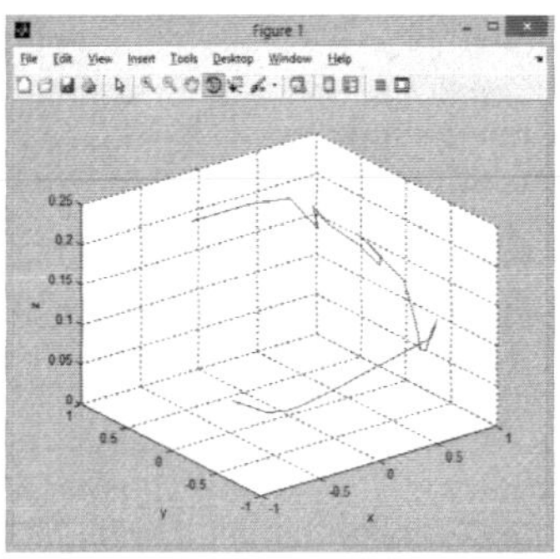

Solving fractional circuits with sinusoidal sources by using the gcdAlpha method

Marcin Sowa[1,*]

[1]Silesian University of Technology, Faculty of Electrical Engineering, Akademicka 2A, 44-100 Gliwice, Poland

Abstract. This paper concerns a study being part of a larger project aiming at solutions of problems with fractional time derivatives. The presented study concerns gcdAlpha – a semi-analytical method for solving fractional differential equations. The basis of the method is recalled along with the general form of problems it was designed to solve. Sources represented by sinusoidal time functions are considered and the general formulae for gcdAlpha are presented for this case. An exemplary circuit problem (containing fractional elements and a sinusoidal source) has been brought forward and solved. The results are compared with ones obtained through a solver basing on the numerical method called SubIval.

1 Introduction

Fractional calculus [1] is a quite popular field of late, where the concepts of fractional derivatives (and fractional integrals) are tested through their applications in various fields, e.g. circuit analyses [2] and control theory [3].

The introduction of fractional coils and fractional capacitors as elements in a circuit problem is associated with complications when it comes to solutions. The possibilities for obtaining solutions are: evaluations of analytical solutions [4], the use of semi-analytical methods [5] and numerical methods [6]. Numerical methods allow to solve the widest variety of problems. The author's main research revolves around SubIval – a numerical method. The acronym comes from how it has been named when it first appeared in [7], i.e. "the subinterval-based method".

The paper concerns a secondary project aiming at the design of methods, by which referential solutions can be obtained, which can be later applied when designing SubIval and its improvements.

The analysis is limited to problems with the Caputo definition of the fractional derivative [8] (of order $\alpha \in (0, 1]$):

$$ {}_0\mathrm{D}_t^{\alpha} x(t) = \frac{1}{\Gamma(1-\alpha)} \int_0^t \frac{x^{(1)}(\tau)}{(t-\tau)^{\alpha}} \mathrm{d}\tau. \quad (1)$$

2 The method details

The gcdAlpha method, appearing in the title of this paper, is a semi-analytical method able to solve fractional differential equations (FDE) of the form:

$$ \mathbf{d}^{\alpha} \boldsymbol{x}(t) = \boldsymbol{A}\boldsymbol{x}(t) + \boldsymbol{B}\boldsymbol{v}(t), \quad (2)$$

with $\boldsymbol{x}(t)$ being the vector of N state variables, $\boldsymbol{v}(t)$ being the vector of M source time functions and $\mathbf{d}^{\alpha}\boldsymbol{x}(t)$ being the vector of the fractional derivatives (i.e. the i-th entry is the fractional derivative of $x_i(t)$ of order α_i).

For a more detailed description of the basics of the method the reader is referred to the previous paper, where the method was first introduced [9].

The name of the method was inspired by its first characteristic feature, where the greatest common divisor is found:

$$ \gcd(\alpha_1, \alpha_2, \alpha_3, \ldots \alpha_N) = \alpha. \quad (3)$$

This allows the problem in the form of (2) to be expressed in a form:

$$ \mathbf{d}^{\alpha} \boldsymbol{w}(t) = \boldsymbol{C}\boldsymbol{w}(t) + \boldsymbol{D}\boldsymbol{v}(t), \quad (4)$$

with only one derivative order α. There is a well-described procedure [9] on how to obtain $\boldsymbol{C}$ and $\boldsymbol{D}$ from $\boldsymbol{A}$ and $\boldsymbol{B}$. The first entries of $\boldsymbol{w}(t)$ contain the actual solution vector $\boldsymbol{x}(t)$.

The solution for $\boldsymbol{w}(t)$ can be given as:

$$ \boldsymbol{w}(t) = \sum_{k=0}^{\infty} \frac{\boldsymbol{C}^k t^{k\alpha}}{\Gamma(k\alpha+1)} \boldsymbol{w}(t_0) + \sum_{k=0}^{\infty} \frac{\boldsymbol{C}^k}{\Gamma((k+1)\alpha)} \begin{bmatrix} \mathbf{0}_{\sigma-N} \\ \boldsymbol{S}_{(k)}(t) \end{bmatrix}, \quad (5)$$

where the notation $\mathbf{0}_n$ is applied for vectors of n zeros ; $\boldsymbol{S}_{(k)}(t)$ is a special notation for the integral:

$$ \boldsymbol{S}_{(k)}(t) = \int_0^t (t-\tau)^{(k+1)\alpha-1} \boldsymbol{B}\boldsymbol{v}(t) \mathrm{d}\tau. \quad (6)$$

The entries for the vector are given by:

$$ S_{(k),i}(t) = \sum_{j=1}^{M} B_{i,j} a_{(k),j}(t). \quad i = 1,2,\ldots N, \quad (7)$$

where:

$$ a_{(k),j}(t) = \int_0^t (t-\tau)^{(k+1)\alpha-1} v_j(\tau) \mathrm{d}\tau. \quad (8)$$

has been introduced in order to separately take into account the integrals appearing in the solution.

This is the second characteristic feature of gcdAlpha – for general forms of the source time functions $v_j(t)$ one can determine the forms of $a_{(k),j}(t)$ so that the integration

* Corresponding author: marcin.sowa@polsl.pl

can be handled analytically. In [9] the forms of $a_{(k),j}(t)$ have been determined and tested for step functions; this paper concerns their form for $v_j(t)$ being sinusoidal functions of the form:

$$v_j(t) = v_{j\mathrm{A}} \sin(\omega_j t + \varphi_j). \tag{9}$$

One can compute:

$$\underline{a}_{(k),j}(t) = (\mathrm{j}\omega_j)^{-\alpha(k+1)} v_{j\mathrm{A}} \mathrm{e}^{\mathrm{j}(\omega_j t + \varphi_j)} \gamma(\alpha(k+1), \mathrm{j}\omega_j t), \tag{10}$$

whose imaginary part is $a_{(k),j}(t)$; in (10) one can notice the lower incomplete gamma function:

$$\gamma(s,z) = \int_0^z t^{s-1} \exp(-t)\, \mathrm{d}t. \tag{11}$$

For the computation of this function one can apply the formula in [10] applying Gauss's continued fraction.

3 Computational example

The simple example depicted in Fig. 1 has been considered.

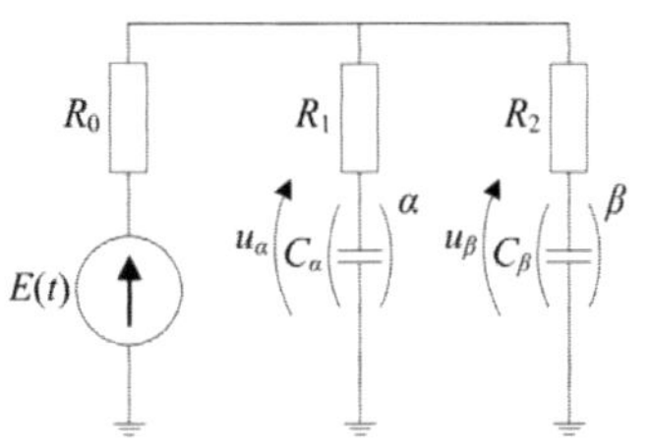

$E(t) = E_{\max} \sin(\omega t)$
$R_0 = 0.9\,\Omega$
$R_1 = 0.5\,\Omega$
$R_2 = 0.7\,\Omega$
$E_{\max} = 20\,\mathrm{V}$
$\omega = 2\pi f$
$f = 50\,\mathrm{Hz}$
$\alpha = 0.9$
$C_\alpha = 1\,\mathrm{F{\cdot}s}^{1-\alpha}$
$\beta = 0.6$
$C_\beta = 2\,\mathrm{F{\cdot}s}^{1-\beta}$

Fig. 1. Exemplary circuit example with a sinusoidal source and fractional elements.

The state variables for the problem are the fractional capacitor voltages. The obtained time functions for $t \in [0, 4/f]$ are depicted in Fig. 2.

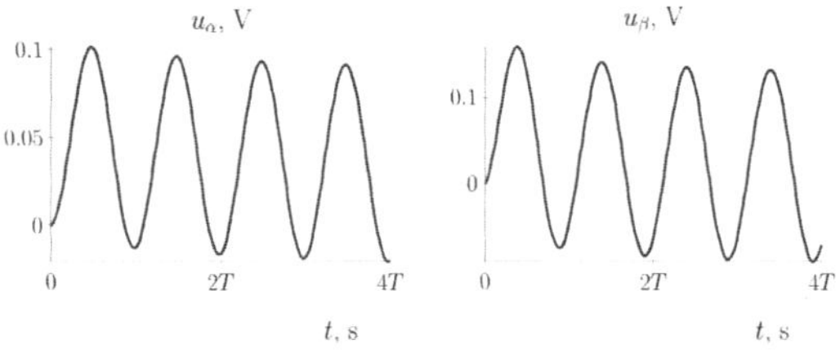

Fig. 2. Fractional capacitor voltage time functions obtained through the gcdAlpha method.

The result has been compared with one obtained through a numerical solver basing on SubIval [11]. There are no visible differences between the results when plotting them in the same figure. The error is computed through the formula:

$$e_j = 100 \cdot \frac{|x(t_j) - x_j|}{\max\limits_{j=1,2,\ldots n_t} |x(t_j)|} \%, \tag{12}$$

with x being the considered variable, t_1, t_2, … t_{n_t} being the time instances selected by the numerical solver, $x(t_j)$ are the values obtained through gcdAlpha and x_j is the numerical solution for x at t_j. The averages of these error values are $1.62 \cdot 10^{-3}$ % for u_α and $4.31 \cdot 10^{-4}$ % for u_β.

The most important parameters selected for the SubIval solver are: $p = 4$ (the maximum applied approximating polynomial order) and $e_{\mathrm{ctrl}} = 0.01$ % (the desired error for the computations of the fractional derivative).

4 Conclusions

The semi-analytical method gcdAlpha has been recalled. The basis of the method has been briefly described. In the previous work the method has been tested for unit step sources. With the study presented in this research the method now allows to solve problems where sinusoidal sources appear.

Other forms of the source time functions can also be supported – it all comes down to computing a general, analytical formula for the integral (8), e.g. as was given in (10) for sources in the form of (9).

References

1. KB. Oldham, J. Spanier, *The Fractional Calculus*, Academic Press, New York (1974)
2. W. Mitkowski, P. Skruch, Bull. Pol. Ac.: Tech. **61**, 3 (2013)
3. A. Dabiri, B.P. Moghaddam, J.A. Tenreiro Machado, J. Comput. Appl. Math. **339** (2018)
4. T. Kaczorek, *Fractional linear systems and electrical circuits*, Springer (2015)
5. N.S. Khodabakhshi, S.M. Vaezpour, D. Baleanu, Fract. Calc. Appl. Anal. **17**, 2 (2014)
6. R. Garrappa, J. Comput. Appl. Math. **276** (2016)
7. M. Sowa, Bull. Pol. Acad. Sci.: Tech. **62**, 3 (2014)
8. M. Caputo, Geophys. J. Int. **13**, 5 (1967)
9. M. Sowa, Computer Applications in Electrical Engineering **96** (2018)
10. M. Duckett, *Fourier Series and Gamma Function*, (Learning Press, New York, 2016)
11. M. Sowa, Springer, (2019)

Learning algorithm analysis for deep neural network with ReLu activation functions

Stanisław Płaczek[1,*], *Aleksander* Płaczek[2]

[1]University of Business, Wroclaw Poland
[2]Faculty of Automatic Control, Electronic and Computer Science, Silesian University of Technology, WASKO, Poland

Abstract. In the article, emphasis is put on the modern artificial neural network structure, which in the literature is known as a deep neural network. Network includes more than one hidden layer and comprises many standard modules with ReLu nonlinear activation function. A learning algorithm includes two standard steps, forward and backward, and its effectiveness depends on the way the learning error is transported back through all the layers to the first layer. Taking into account all the dimensionalities of matrixes and the nonlinear characteristics of ReLu activation function, the problem is very difficult from a theoretic point of view. To implement simple assumptions in the analysis, formal formulas are used to describe relations between the structure of every layer and the internal input vector. In practice tasks, neural networks' internal layer matrixes with ReLu activations function, include a lot of null value of weight coefficients. This phenomenon has a negatives impact on the effectiveness of the learning algorithm convergences. A theoretical analysis could help to build more effective algorithms.

1 Module structure

A deep neural network is built with topologically and logically uniform modules known as layers. A network's structure includes input layer, a lot of hidden layers, and finally an output layer. Usually, a network is built with "$1 \div L$" different or identical structure layers. From a mathematical point of view, a layer could be described by a matrix of weight coefficients $\boldsymbol{W}^l$, an input vector $\boldsymbol{X}^{l-1}$, a hidden vector $\boldsymbol{U}^l$, an activation function $ReLu(\boldsymbol{U}) = \max(\boldsymbol{0}, \boldsymbol{U})$, and an output vector $\boldsymbol{X}^l$ (Fig. 1).

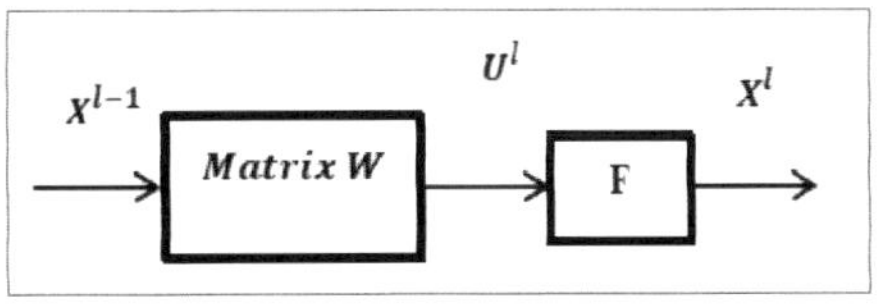

Fig. 1. The architecture of a neural network layer.

A deep neural network includes "L-1" hidden layers and one output layer which contains a different activation function. An output layer needs to aggregate a set of partial features from previous layers and achieve the final result, that is an output signal. Using Fig.1, one can define the target function:

$$\Phi = \frac{1}{2} \cdot (\boldsymbol{X}^L - \boldsymbol{Y})^T \cdot (\boldsymbol{X}^L - \boldsymbol{Y}) \quad (1)$$

where:
$\boldsymbol{X}^L[1 : \boldsymbol{N}^L]$- the output vector,
$\boldsymbol{N}^L$ - the dimensionality of the output vector,
$Y[1 : \boldsymbol{N}^L]$- the vector of teaching data,

For all hidden layers, one can write:

$$\boldsymbol{U}^l = W^l \cdot \boldsymbol{X}^{l-1} \quad (2)$$

$$\boldsymbol{X}^l = \boldsymbol{F}(\boldsymbol{U}^l) \quad (3)$$

where:
$l = 1 \div L$ –number of layers,
$\boldsymbol{U}^l$- the internal vector,
$\boldsymbol{F}$ – the vector of activation functions,
$\boldsymbol{W}^l$- the matrix of weight coefficients for layer "l",
$\boldsymbol{X}^{l-1}, \boldsymbol{X}^l$ – the input and output vector of layer "l", accordingly.

The process of selecting an activation function is a very important and difficult task. When building standard networks, usually sigmoid and tanh activation functions are used. A sigmoid function has two areas of value in which the function, in an asymptotic way, achieves the value of zero or one. This characteristic has a negative impact on the derivative value and, at the same time, on the algorithm convergence. At the moment, a new activation function is used in a deep neural network – a Rectified Linear Unit –ReLu, which is defined as follows:

$$f = ReLu(u) = \max(0, u) \quad (4)$$

From a mathematical point of view, this function is discontinuous for $u = 0$. In a computers application, this problem is solved by the accepted value $f = 0 \; for \; u = 0$.

* Stanisław Płaczek: stanislaw.placzek@wp.pl

2 Learning algorithm

In computer applications, a back propagation learning algorithm is the most popular one. A learning error is calculated from an output layer, through all the hidden layers to the input data. From (1), one can calculate the first derivatives for the output layer:

$$\frac{\partial\Phi}{\partial X^L} = \boldsymbol{E}^L = X^L - \boldsymbol{Y} \tag{5}$$

$$\frac{\partial\Phi}{\partial \boldsymbol{W}^L} = \boldsymbol{E}^L \cdot \frac{\partial \boldsymbol{X}^L}{\partial \boldsymbol{U}^L} \cdot \frac{\partial \boldsymbol{X}^L}{\partial \boldsymbol{W}^L} \tag{6}$$

where:
$\boldsymbol{E}^L = [\varepsilon_1^L, \varepsilon_2^L, \dots \varepsilon_{N^L}^L]$- the vector of an output layer error.

The derivative of the ReLu function could be written as follows:

$$\frac{\partial \boldsymbol{X}^L}{\partial \boldsymbol{U}^L} = \max(\boldsymbol{0}, \boldsymbol{U}^L)' = \boldsymbol{1}(\boldsymbol{U}^L) \tag{7}$$

Finally, formula (6) can be written:

$$\frac{\partial \boldsymbol{X}^L}{\partial \boldsymbol{W}^L} = \boldsymbol{E}^L \cdot \boldsymbol{1}(\boldsymbol{U}^L) \cdot \boldsymbol{X}^{L-1} \tag{8}$$

For the last hidden layer, the output error can be calculated:

$$\frac{\partial\Phi}{\partial \boldsymbol{X}^{L-1}} = \boldsymbol{E}^{L-1} = \boldsymbol{E}^L \cdot \frac{\partial \boldsymbol{X}^L}{\partial \boldsymbol{U}^L} \cdot \frac{\partial \boldsymbol{X}^L}{\partial \boldsymbol{X}^{L-1}} \tag{9}$$

In the matrix form

$$\boldsymbol{E}^{L-1} = (\boldsymbol{W}^L)^T \cdot (\boldsymbol{1}^L \odot \boldsymbol{E}^L) \tag{10}$$

where:
$\odot$- the Hadamard product of two vectors,
$\boldsymbol{E}^{L-1}$-the output error vector of the layer "L-1".

Formula (10) describes the algorithm how the output error vector $\boldsymbol{E}^l$ of the layer "l" is back propagated to the output error vector $\boldsymbol{E}^{l-1}$ of the layer "l-1" (Fig.2).

2.1 Upper error valuation

Formulas (3) and (10) are nonlinear. Many assumptions are made to achieve an analytical form of the upper error valuation back propagated through the neural network.

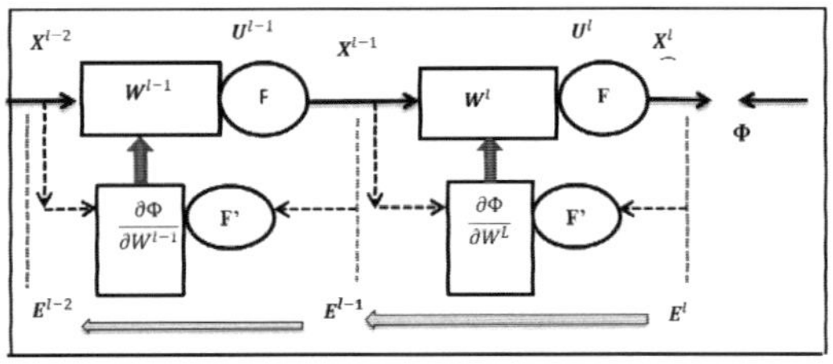

Fig. 2. A scheme of an error back propagated through the layers.

For all hidden and output layers $\boldsymbol{U}^l \geq \boldsymbol{0}$, l=1,2...L, and a ReLu activation function is positive for all $\boldsymbol{U}^l$, therefore:

$$\boldsymbol{X}^L = \boldsymbol{F}(\boldsymbol{U}^L) = \boldsymbol{U}^L \tag{11}$$

$$\boldsymbol{F}'(\boldsymbol{U}^L) = (\boldsymbol{U}^L) = \boldsymbol{1} \tag{12}$$

Equation (5) could be written as:

$$\boldsymbol{E}^L \approx \boldsymbol{X}^L \tag{13}$$

Using the same assumptions, formulas (10) and (3) can be rewritten as:

$$\boldsymbol{E}^{L-1} \approx (\boldsymbol{W}^L)^T \cdot \boldsymbol{E}^L \tag{14}$$

$$\boldsymbol{X}^L \approx \boldsymbol{W}^L \cdot \boldsymbol{X}^{L-1} \tag{15}$$

Finally, connecting formulas (13), (14) and (15):

$$\boldsymbol{E}^{L-1} \approx [(\boldsymbol{W}^L)^T \cdot \boldsymbol{W}^l] \cdot \boldsymbol{X}^{L-1} \tag{16}$$

The output error of "L-1" layer $\boldsymbol{E}^{L-1}$, depends on the matrix of weight coefficients layers $\boldsymbol{W}^L$, and the output vector $\boldsymbol{X}^{L-1}$. By repeating the calculation process above for "L-2" layer, a more complicated formula can be achieved:

$$\boldsymbol{E}^{L-2} \approx \{(\boldsymbol{W}^{L-1})^T \cdot [(\boldsymbol{W}^L)^T \cdot \boldsymbol{W}^L] \cdot \boldsymbol{W}^{L-1}\} \cdot \boldsymbol{X}^{L-2} \tag{17}$$

According to formulas (16) and (17), the dimensionalities of the input layer vector **X** and the output error vectors **E**, are the same. A more general form of the aforementioned formulas could be written as:

$$\boldsymbol{D} = \boldsymbol{A}^T \cdot \boldsymbol{B} \cdot \boldsymbol{A} \tag{18}$$

This general form could help in finding simpler relations between the forward and back calculation of the neural network learning. Repeating above calculation process and coming back to the first layer, the error vector $\boldsymbol{E}^1$ depends directly on the input vector of data $\boldsymbol{X}^0$. Internal error vectors depend on both the structure of a neural network, which is described by the set of **W** matrixes, and the input data. Data vectors are organized in an epoch that contains hundreds or thousands of vectors. Therefore, formula (18) describes the relation only for one iteration and will be changed from iteration to iteration.

References

1. S. Placzek, IJARAI **3** (12), (2004)
2. V.Vapnik, *Statistical Learning Theory*, Wiley, New York, (1998)
3. I. Goodfellow, Y. Bengio, A. Courville, *Deep Learning*, (MIT Press, 2016)
4. S.K. Zhou, H. Greenspan, D. Shen, *Deep Learning for Medical Image Analysis*, (Academic Press, 2017)
5. M. Nielson, *Neural Network and Deep Learning*, (Determination Press, 2015)

Magnetic field of a ribbon busbar of finite length

Dariusz Kusiak[1,*], *Tomasz* Szczegielniak[2], and *Zygmunt* Piątek[3]

[1]Department of Electrotechnics, Czestochowa University of Technology, Częstochowa, Poland
[2]Institute of Environmental Engineering, Czestochowa University of Technology, Częstochowa, Poland
[3]Professor emeritus, Czestochowa University of Technology, Częstochowa, Poland

Abstract. Using the analytic method based on the Biot-Savart law for the electromagnetic field, the distribution of the magnetic field of a ribbon busbar of finite length has been determined. The *Mathematica* program was used to visualize the solutions obtained. This allowed quick field analysis after changes of geometrical or electrical parameters of systems under examination.

1 Introduction

In case of a ribbon busbar of length l (Fig. 1), i.e. the conductor of rectangular section for which $b>>a$, the magnetic field generated by the direct current or slow alternating sinusoidal current $\underline{I}$ at any point $X(x,y,z)$ is determined much easier than in case of rectangular bus [1,2], because the result is obtained after single integration [1].

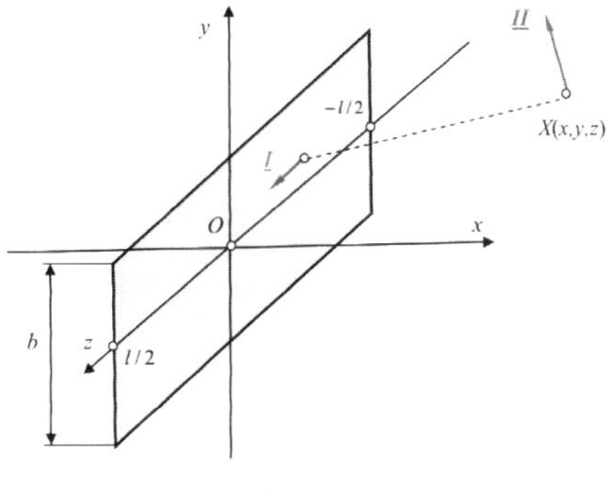

Fig. 1. Ribbon busbar of finite length.

However, if we already have solutions of studies [1,3] at our disposal, then we can determine the magnetic field components through determination of limits of these functions when the crosswise dimension of the busduct is $a\to 0$. Then, the magnetic field component along the axis Ox is as follows

$$\underline{H}_x^{(t)}(x,y,z) = \underset{a\to 0}{\text{Limit}}\,\underline{H}_x(x,y,z) = \frac{\underline{I}}{8\pi b}\left\{\begin{array}{l} 2\ln\dfrac{2z-l+F_1(x,y,z)}{2z-l+F_2(x,y,z)} + \\ \ln\dfrac{F_2(x,y,z)(l-2z)+8lz+(l+2z)F_3(x,y,z)}{F_1(x,y,z)(l-2z)+8lz+(l+2z)F_4(x,y,z)} + \\ \ln\dfrac{-F_2(x,y,z)(l-2z)+8lz+(l+2z)F_3(x,y,z)}{-F_1(x,y,z)(l-2z)+8lz+(l+2z)F_4(x,y,z)} \end{array}\right\} \quad (1)$$

and the magnetic field component along the axis Oy is as follows

$$\underline{H}_y^{(t)}(x,y,z) = \underset{a\to 0}{\text{Limit}}\,\underline{H}_y(x,y,z) = \frac{\underline{I}}{4\pi b}\left\{\begin{array}{l} \text{arctg}\dfrac{(b-2y)(l-2z)}{2xF_1(x,y,z)} + \text{arctg}\dfrac{(b+2y)(l-2z)}{2xF_2(x,y,z)} + \\ \text{arctg}\dfrac{(b-2y)(l+2z)}{2xF_4(x,y,z)} + \text{arctg}\dfrac{(b+2y)(l+2z)}{2xF_3(x,y,z)} \end{array}\right\} \quad (2)$$

where:

$$F_1(x,y,z) = \sqrt{4x^2 + (b-2y)^2 + (l-2z)^2}\,,$$

$$F_2(x,y,z) = \sqrt{4x^2 + (b+2y)^2 + (l-2z)^2}\,,$$

$$F_3(x,y,z) = \sqrt{4x^2 + (b+2y)^2 + (l+2z)^2}\,,$$

$$F_4(x,y,z) = \sqrt{4x^2 + (b-2y)^2 + (l+2z)^2}\,.$$

1.1 Magnetic field of the ribbon busbar - visualization

Distribution of the magnetic field modulus for the ribbon busduct of finite length on the plane xOy is shown in the Figure 2, whereat this field is expressed in relative values as the function shown with the formula

$$h^{(t)}(x,y,z) = \frac{H^{(t)}(x,y,z)}{H_0^{(t)}} \quad (3)$$

where the magnetic field modulus [4]

$$H^{(t)}(x,y,z) = \sqrt{\left[\underline{H}_x^{(t)}(x,y,z)\right]^2 + \left[\underline{H}_x^{(t)}(x,y,z)\right]^2} \quad (4)$$

and the reference magnetic field

$$H_0^{(t)} = \frac{I}{2b} \quad (5)$$

Effect of the conductor length on the magnetic field distribution is shown [5] in the Figure 3.

* Corresponding author: dariuszkusiak@wp.pl, d.kusiak@el.pcz.czest.pl

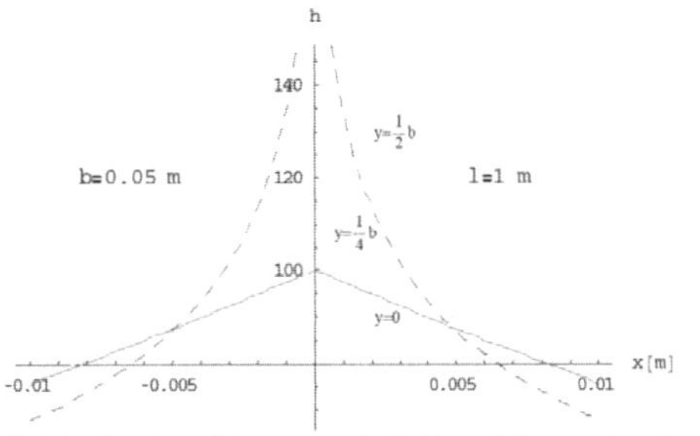

Fig. 2. Distribution of the magnetic field modulus on the plane *xOy* of the ribbon busduct of finite length.

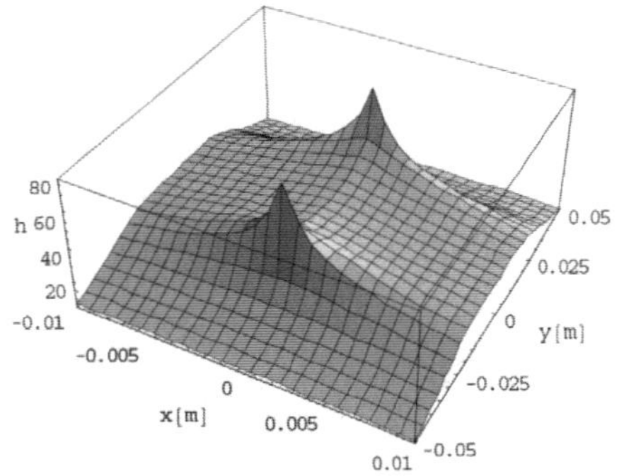

Fig. 3. Spatial distribution of the magnetic field modulus on the plane $z = l/2$ of the ribbon busduct of finite length; $l = 1$ m, $b = 0.05$ m.

2 Magnetic field line of the three ribbon busbar of finite length

Our assumption is as follows: in the three-phase line of three ribbon busbars of dimensions $b \times l$ (Fig. 4) and the distance d between them, there is the direct current or slow alternating sinusoidal current of complex rms values $\underline{I}_1$, $\underline{I}_2$ and $\underline{I}_3$.

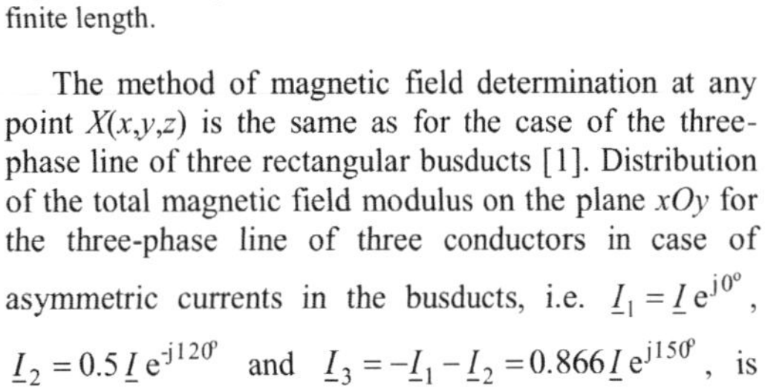

Fig. 4. The three-phase line of three ribbon conductors of finite length.

The method of magnetic field determination at any point $X(x,y,z)$ is the same as for the case of the three-phase line of three rectangular busducts [1]. Distribution of the total magnetic field modulus on the plane *xOy* for the three-phase line of three conductors in case of asymmetric currents in the busducts, i.e. $\underline{I}_1 = \underline{I}\,e^{j0^o}$, $\underline{I}_2 = 0.5\,\underline{I}\,e^{-j120^o}$ and $\underline{I}_3 = -\underline{I}_1 - \underline{I}_2 = 0.866\,\underline{I}\,e^{j150^o}$, is shown in the Figure 5, whereat this field is expressed in relative values as the function shown with the formula (3), where the reference magnetic field are expressed with the formula (5). Conductor length effect on distribution of the total magnetic field in such a line is shown in Figures 6.

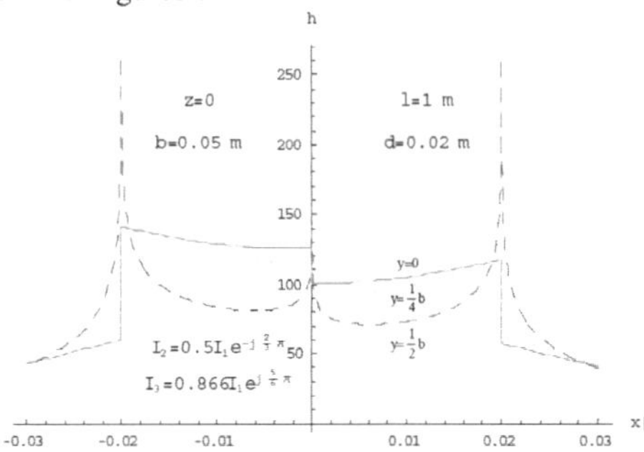

Fig. 5. Distribution of the magnetic field modulus of the three-phase line of three ribbon busbars of finite length on the plane *xOy* for asymmetric currents.

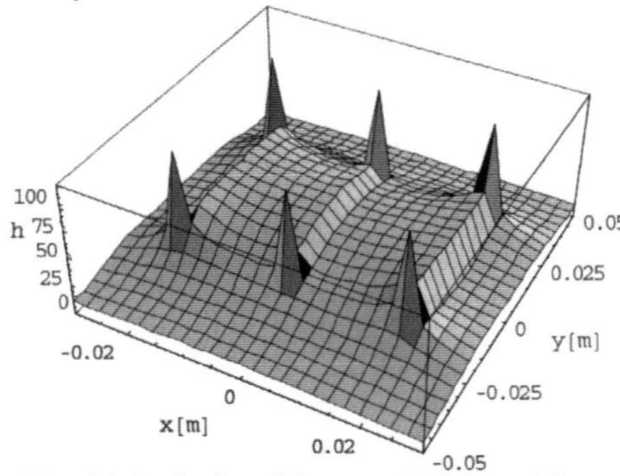

Fig. 6. Spatial distribution of the magnetic field modulus on the plane $z = l/2$ for the three-phase line of three ribbon busbars of finite length for asymmetric currents; $l = 1$ m, $d = 0.02$ m, $b = 0.05$ m.

3 Findings

The derived formulas that describe the magnetic field have the complex structure even in the ribbon conductor and, based on them, it is difficult to foresee a change of the magnetic field distribution after change of, eg., this conductor length. However, using any program with a graphic module, eg. *Mathematica*, we have the ready to use, very good tool to visualize the obtained solutions quickly. As you can see in Figures 3 and 6, this allows quick field analysis after changes of geometrical or electrical parameters of systems under examination.

References

1. D. Kusiak, T. Szczegielniak, *Electromagnetic calculations of busbars (in Polish)*, (Wyd. PCz, Czestochowa, 2017)
2. P. Sarajcev, R. Goic, Electr. Pow. Compo. Sys. **38**, (2010)
3. Z. Piątek, B. Baron et. al., Prz. Elektrotech. **89**/8, (2013)
4. Z. Piątek, *Impedances of high-current busducts*, (Wyd. PCz., Czestochowa, 2008)
5. H. Gliński, R. Grzymkowski et. al., *Mathematica 8 (in Polish)*, (Wyd. Skalmierskiego, Gliwice, 2012)

Immunity test of the lighting installation for electromagnetic surge disturbances

Dorota Typańska[1,*], *Wojciech* Machczyński[1]

[1]Poznan University of Technology, Poznan, Poland

Abstract. The paper presents the results of computer simulation of the operation of a lighting installation disturbed by a voltage surge of 1.2 / 50 μs. The components included in the model of the system were: voltage surge generator (accordance with the PN-EN 61000-4-5 Standard), coupling - decoupling system, over-current circuit breaker, iluminance level controller and incandescent lamp. The results of simulation tests with the results of tests carried out in an accredited electromagnetic compatibility laboratory were compared.

1 Introduction

All electrical and electronic devices placed on the European market should be tested and certified by accredited electromagnetic compatibility laboratories. Certification of individual devices does not guarantee that a fully completed, fixed installation will be electromagnetically compatible [1, 2, 3]. Performing specialized tests of electromagnetic compatibility increases the functional safety of the devices used and improves the quality of energy in the supply networks. [4].

Due to the complexity and possible harmfulness of the installation's immunity tests to electromagnetic disturbances, it is reasonable to simulate of the system operation when the specific interfering signals are introduced. The article presents the results of computer simulation of the operation of the power regulator disturbed by lightning impulse, made in the MATLAB/Simulink software [5]. The simulation results and results of tests carried out in an accredited electromagnetic compatibility laboratory were compared.

2 Computer simulation

The model tests included simulation of the operation of a part of a lighting installation equipped with an over-current switch, a lighting power controller and an incandescent lamp with a rated power of 200 W supplied from a 230 V power grid. A 1.2 / 50 μs voltage signal disturbing the system through a coupling and decoupling system (CDN) according to PN EN 61000-4-5 Standard was supplied. Figure 1 presents a modelled circuit.

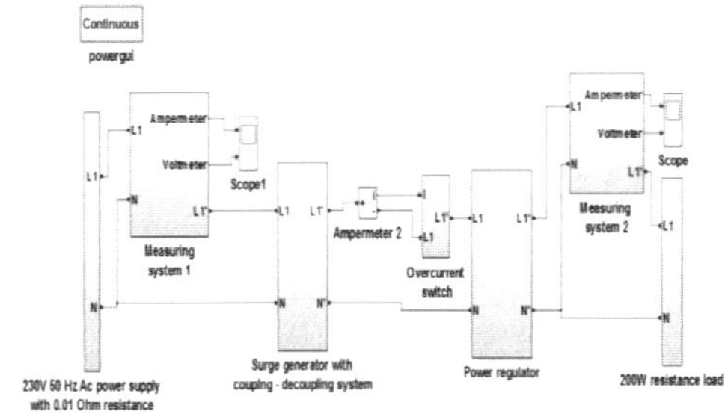

Fig. 1. Scheme of the simulated system.

On the voltage characteristic considered on the load side (measuring system 2) during the pulse disturbance, a pulse with an magnitude of 1280 V is visible (Fig. 2). The shape of the current waveform is coincides with the shape of the voltage. The magnitude of the current pulse resulting from the introduced disturbance is about 7.8 A (fig. 3).

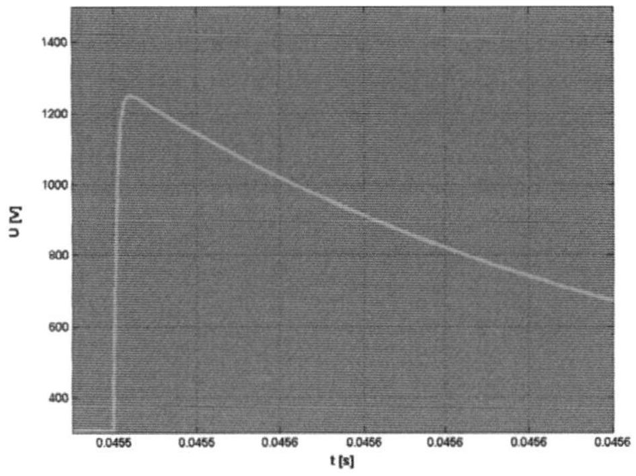

Fig. 2. The course of the voltage signal on the receiver.

corresponding author: dorota.typanska@put.poznan.pl

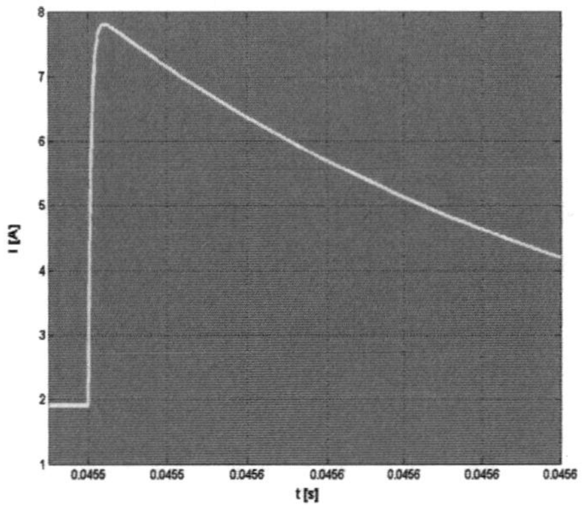

Fig. 3. The course of the current signal on the receiver.

3 Laboratory tests

In order to confirm the simulation tests in Matlab/Simulink software, a laboratory test stand (according to Standard [6] consisting of a power regulator limiting the intensity of light emitted by the incandescent lamp, over-current protection, surge generator 1,2 / 50 us with CDN, and measuring system in the form of voltage and current differential probes with digital oscilloscope were prepared.

The research were carried out in an accredited electromagnetic compatibility laboratory located in the Office of Technical Inspection in Poznań. The tested system is presented in Fig. 4. The voltage accross and the current through the load were observed using an oscilloscope.

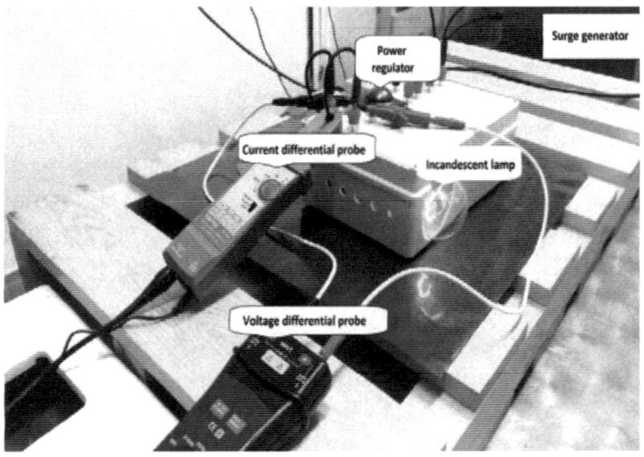

Fig. 4. Tested system.

On the voltage characteristic (Fig. 5, blue line) during the pulse disturbance, a pulse with an magnitude of 1325 V is visible. The shape of the current waveform (Fig. 5, yellow line) is coincides with the shape of the voltage. The magnitude of the current pulse resulting from the surge disturbance is 7.76 A.

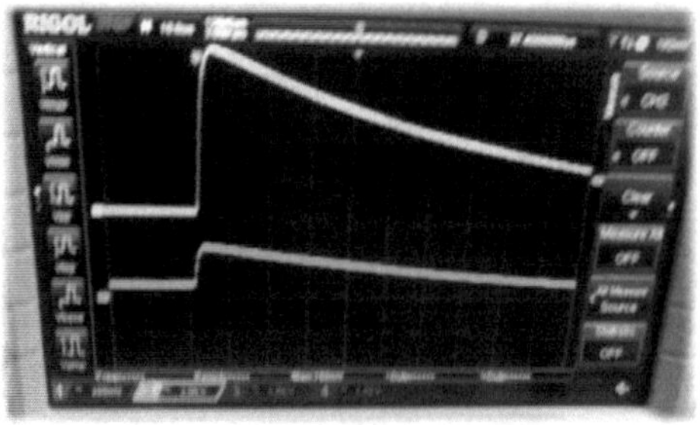

Fig. 5. The current and voltage waveform seen on the oscilloscope.

The simulated magnitude of the voltage at input of the receiver circuit due to disturbance of its operation with voltage pulse 1,2 / 50 μs, is 4% lower than voltage magnitude obtained in laboratory tests. The magnitudes of the currents in the simulated and the tested system are the same.

4 Summary

The current state of knowledge about disturbances occurring in electrical circuits and the causes and sources of the formation of these disturbances allows the execution of test signal model, described in the relevant general standard relating the electromagnetic compatibility testing [7, 8].

Preliminary results of own simulation analyzes for a selected receiver and a disturbance generator indicate the convergence of simulation results of the model of the system under consideration and laboratory tests.

References

1. D. Typańska, A. Maćkowiak, K. Sieczkarek, Prz. Elektrotech. **92/4**, 38-42 (2016)
2. K. Bednarek, D. Typańska, J. Misiorny, Pozn. Univ. Technol. Acad. J. Electr. Eng. **93**, 241-252 (2018)
3. D. Typańska, A. Maćkowiak, K. Sieczkarek, Prz. Elektrotech. **92/9**, 243-245 (2016)
4. K. Bednarek, D. Typańska, Prz. Elektrotech. **93/12**, 63-66 (2017)
5. W. Machczyński, D. Typańska, *International Conference on Electromagnetic Disturbances*, 63-66 (2017)
6. PN-EN 61000-4-5:2014-10 Electromagnetic compatibility (EMC) - Part 4-5: Testing and measurement techniques - Surge immunity test
7. K. Bednarek, R. Nawrowski, A. Tomczewski, *Studies in Applied Electromagnetics and Mechanics* **22**, 363-368, (IOS Press, Amsterdam, Berlin, 2002)
8. L. Kasprzyk, A. Tomczewski, K. Bednarek, Prz. Elektrotech. **87/12b**, 82-85 (2011)

Calculation of energy loss due to macroscopic eddy currents in ferromagnetic materials considering hysteresis loop

Michał Bereźnicki[1,*], *Paweł* Jabłoński[2]

[1]Czestochowa University of Technology, Department of Electrical Engineering, Ph.D. student
[2]Czestochowa University of Technology, Department of Electrical Engineering, Czestochowa, Poland

Abstract. The paper presents an algorithm for calculating the energy loss due to macroscopic eddy currents considering the non-linearity of magnetization characteristics and magnetic hysteresis. It was found that for non-oriented steel sheet with a silicon content of 6.5% and thickness 0.1 mm the consideration of non-linearity and magnetization characteristics has a little effect on the energy loss, at least up to 400 Hz. In the application of the algorithm, there are some limitations resulting from the assumption of the average value of the induction flux in the sample cross-section, numerical problems and hysteresis loop shapes.

1 Introduction

Energy loss is one of the fundamental parameters of magnetic materials. It is described via empirical and theoretical formulas [1-5]. According to the classical approach, energy loss in magnetic materials is related to eddy currents and change in magnetization (hysteresis loss). The classic equation determining the energy loss due to macroscopic eddy currents was derived by adopting a series of simplifications, i.e. neglecting not only magnetic hysteresis, but also the non-linearity of magnetic material. The authors of the study decided to check how the non-linearity and hysteresis loop affect the classical energy loss due to eddy currents. The algorithm is an original extension of that given in [7].

2 Algorithm of energy loss calculation

The theoretical description of macroscopic eddy current loss is presented in several works, e.g. [3, 8]. For a cuboidal sample of thickness g, height $a \gg g$ and length $l \gg g$, as in Fig. 1, after several simplifications the formula for the energy loss per unit time and volume of the sample becomes as follows:

$$P_{\mathrm{cl}} = \frac{\pi f B_{\mathrm{m}}^2 \gamma}{2\mu}\left(\frac{\sinh\gamma - \sin\gamma}{\cosh\gamma - \cos\gamma}\right). \tag{1}$$

where f - frequency, B_{m} - magnetic flux density, μ - magnetic permeability, $\gamma = g/, \delta$ – skin depth.

The Maxwell equations for the sample are as follows:

$$\frac{\partial J_x(y,t)}{\partial y} = \sigma \frac{\partial B_z(y,t)}{\partial t}, \tag{2}$$

$$\frac{\partial H_z(y,t)}{\partial y} = J_x(y,t), \tag{3}$$

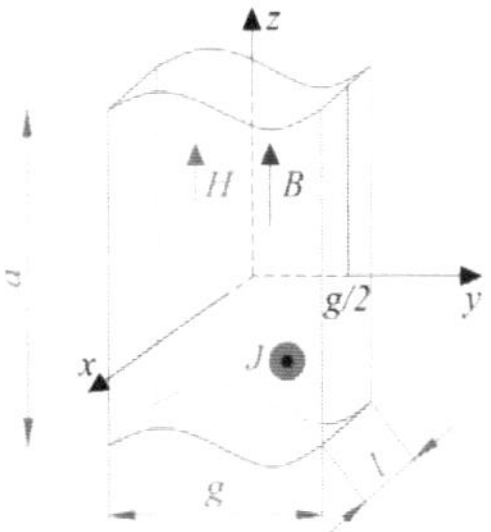

Fig. 1. The geometry of the analyzed sample.

where: J_x – x component of current density vector, B_z – z component of magnetic flux density vector, σ – sample conductivity, H_z – z component of magnetic field intensity vector. Magnetic properties of the sample are detected via measurement and are denoted as follows:

$$B_z = f_{\mathrm{HB}}(H_z), \quad H_z = f_{\mathrm{BH}}(B_z), \tag{4}$$

where f_{HB} and f_{BH} are mutually inverse relationships between B_z and H_z (they can be vertex characteristics or hysteresis loop family). Equations (2)-(4) are solved iteratively, maintaining sinusoidal the total magnetic flux. Then the energy loss is calculated as follows:

$$P_{\mathrm{eddy}} = \frac{4f}{\sigma g}\int_{t=0}^{1/2f}\int_{y=0}^{1/2g} J_x^2(y,t)\,\mathrm{d}y\,\mathrm{d}t. \tag{5}$$

The algorithm for solving field equations is presented in Fig. 2. In the first step, a certain spatial and temporal distribution of magnetic flux density is assumed. Based on the distribution of the flux density, the density of eddy currents and the magnetic field intensity are determined – Eqs. (2) and (3). Then B field is found via

* Corresponding author: michal.bereznicki@interia.pl

Eq. (4). This field is adjusted so that the total magnetic flux remains sinusoidal. If the difference between the induction of the current step obtained and the previous step is larger than a presumed value, the iterations are repeated, otherwise the procedure is finished and energy loss is calculated using Eq. (5). Other condition for finishing the iterative process is reaching a maximum number of iterations.

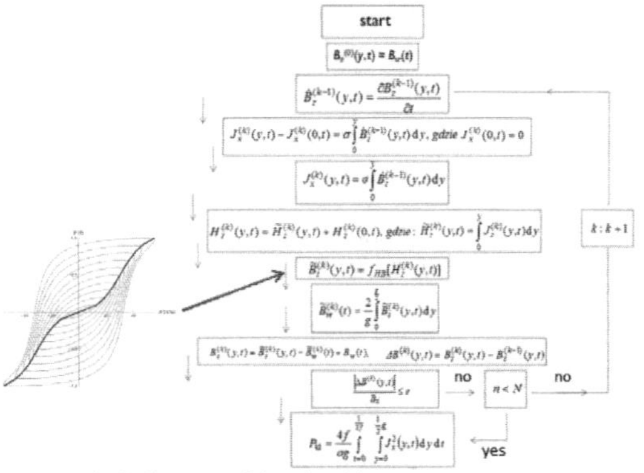

Fig. 2. Block diagram of the algorithm.

3 Results and discussion

The algorithm was used for non-oriented 6.5% Si-Fe steel in the form of a sheet of dimensions 500 mm × 500 mm, with thickness g = 0.1 mm and conductivity σ = 1.22 × 10^6 S/m, for frequencies in the range 10-400 Hz, and magnetic flux density B_m within 0.1-1.2 T. The measurements were carried out using an MAG-RJJ-2.0 computerized measurement system. The resulting energy loss was compared with that determined via Eq. (1) by calculating the percentage relative difference:

$$\delta_P = \frac{P_{\text{eddy}} - P_{\text{cl}}}{P_{\text{cl}}} \times 100\%. \tag{6}$$

The results of calculations are presented in Figures 3-5. They indicate the nonlinearity as well as the hysteresis have a relatively small effect on the macroscopic eddy current loss for the considered material.

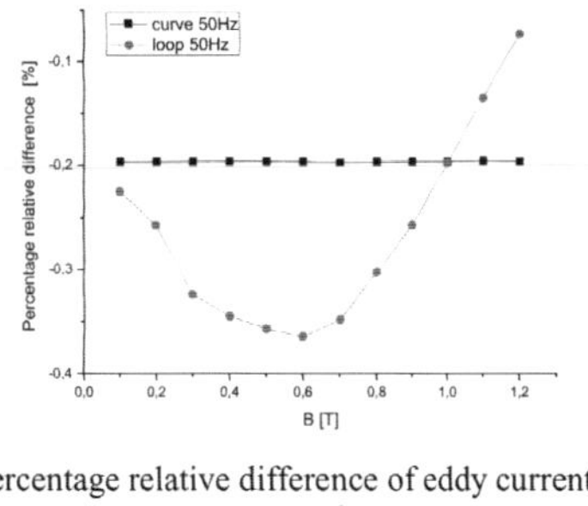

Fig. 3. Percentage relative difference of eddy current energy loss for 6.5% Si-Fe, g = 0.1 mm, f = 50 Hz.

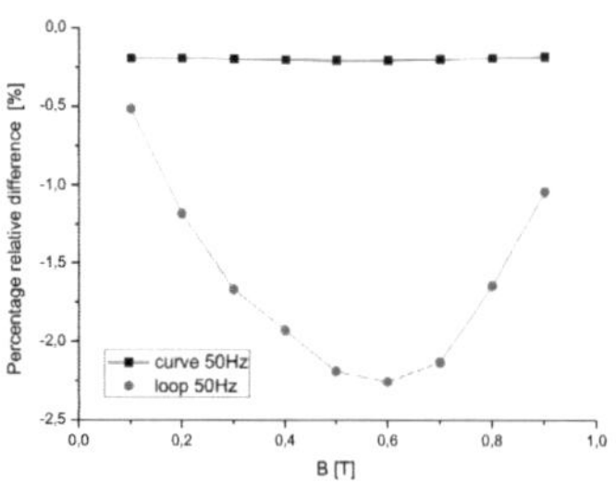

Fig. 4. Percentage relative difference of eddy current energy loss for 6.5% Si-Fe, g = 0.1 mm, f = 400 Hz.

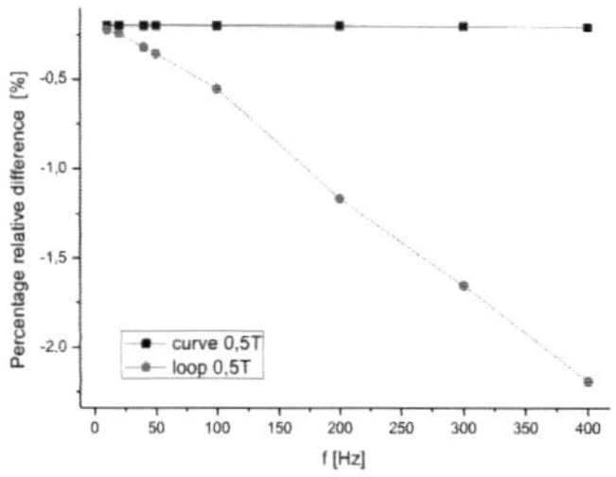

Fig. 5. Percentage relative difference of eddy current energy loss for 6.5% Si-Fe, g = 0.1 mm, B_m = 0.5 T.

The relative difference between losses calculated according to the algorithm and those calculated in accordance with the classical formula did not exceed 0.2% and 2.4% when taking into account the nonlinearity and the hysteresis, respectively. This a rather small influence can be attributed probably to a very weak skin effect (small thickness, small frequencies). It can be expected that stronger skin effect affects the results much more. To check this, it is required to improve the algorithm, because the it is not free of restrictions; in particular the conversion between B and H field should be improved. This is the subject of further considerations.

References

1. A. Krings, J. Soulard, *Electrical Engineering* (ISSN 1582-4594) Vol. 10/2010 No. 3, paper 10.3.22
2. C. Steinmetz, *Proceeding of the IEE* **72/2010**, 197-221 (1984)
3. J. Barranger, *NASA Technical Note*, D-3114, 1965
4. G. Bertotti G, *J. Magn. Mater.* **54-57**, 1556-1560 (1986)
5. S.E. Zirka, Y.I. Moroz, P. Marketos, *IEE Trans. Magn.* **46**, 286-289 (2010)
6. M. Bereźnicki, Selected Problems of Electrical Engineering and Electronics, 17-19 Sept. 2015
7. J. Górecki, L. Nowak, J. Poltz, Electrical hearings in 1976 **22**, z. 3, 677-685
8. G. Bertotti, *Academic Press*, San Diego (1998)

Calculation of magnetic field intensity under power line with taking into account conductor sag

Krzysztof Król[1,*], *Krzysztof* Budnik[1], and *Piotr* Jarek[1]

[1]Poznań University of Technology, Institute of Electrical Engineering and Electronics, Piotrowo 3A, 60-965 Poznań, Poland

Abstract. The paper presents a calculation method of the magnetic field under an overhead power line taking into account conductor sag, which is described by the catenary curve. The calculations take into account the variability of the charge distribution along the conductor and wire sag for the eclectic field, while the calculation of intensity of the magnetic field take into account the impact of induced currents in the wires of lightning. The simulation results were compared with results measurements.

1 Introduction

Transmission lines are used to transfer the electric energy for a long distance transmission between substations. Power lines, generate magnetic fields that adversely affect living organisms. The intensity of the magnetic field depends on the current flowing in the phase conductors, currents induced in the earth wires, and wires deployment, wire suspension height, conductor lengths.

Several publications calculated the magnetic fields created by power transmission lines assume that lines are parallel to a flat ground and the sag is neglected or introduced by taking an effective or average height in between the maximum and the minimum height of the line [2, 3].

The paper presents method of calculation the magnetic field intensity with taking into account sag conductors and comparison of calculation results with measurement results [2, 3].

2 Intensity of the magnetic fields of a power line including the sag of wires

To take into account the sag in the calculations, divide a conductor of a span which are between the spans into n equal segments (s_1, s_2, ...s_{i-1}, s_i, s_{i+1}, s_n) as Figure 1 shows. H is the maximum height of the conductors suspension, h is the minimum height of the conductors suspension in the middle of the span, S is the conductor sag, $S = H\text{-}h$. The calculation should assume the principle that the number of simulated charges must correspond to the number of defined segments.

Each of the segments (s_1, …, s_n) can be described by the curve equation [3, 4]:

$$z'(x') = h + 2\alpha sinh^2(\frac{x'}{2\alpha}) \tag{1}$$

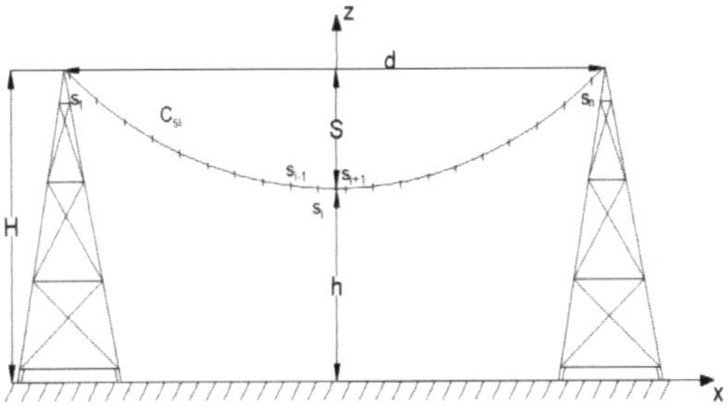

Fig. 1. The power line conductor division of into n segments.

where α is related to the mechanical parameters of the line: $\alpha=T_h/w$. T_h is the mechanical stresses in the middle of the line, w is the weight per unit of the length of the line.

Magnetic field of a power line is produced by currents flowing in phase coductors as well as in earth wires. Method for calculating induced currents in earth wires was taken from [1], which uses the complex ground return plane approach. The current induced in earth wires in case of two earth wires μ and v can be calculated from the relation:

$$\begin{bmatrix} I_\mu \\ I_v \end{bmatrix} = -\begin{bmatrix} Z_\mu & Z_{\mu v} \\ Z_{v\mu} & Z_v \end{bmatrix}^{-1} \begin{bmatrix} Z_{1\mu} & Z_{2\mu} & Z_{3\mu} \\ Z_{1v} & Z_{2v} & Z_{3v} \end{bmatrix} \begin{bmatrix} I_1 \\ I_2 \\ I_3 \end{bmatrix} \tag{2}$$

where I_μ, I_v – currents (phasors) induced in earth wires μ and v, I_1, I_2, I_3 - phasors of the phase currents of the power line, (Z_k, Z_l) - Z_s self-complex impedance of the earth wire calculated from equations:

$$Z_s = j\omega\frac{\mu_0}{2\pi} ln\frac{2(h + p)}{r} \tag{3}$$

where h- height of earth wire, r- wire radius,

$$p = \frac{1}{\sqrt{j\omega\mu_0\gamma}} = \frac{\delta_S}{2}(1 - j) \tag{4}$$

* Corresponding author: krzykrol6@wp.pl

$$\delta_S = \frac{1}{\sqrt{\pi f \mu_0 \gamma}} \tag{5}$$

and γ - ground conductivity, f - frequency.

Mutual complex impedances between earth wires k and l, (Z_m) can be obtained from the equation:

$$Z_m = j\omega \frac{\mu_0}{2\pi} ln \frac{g}{a} \tag{6}$$

$$g = \sqrt{(h_k + h_l + 2p)^2 + d_{kl}^2} \tag{7}$$

$$a = \sqrt{(h_k - h_l)^2 + d_{kl}^2} \tag{8}$$

where d_{kl} - distance between the earth wires k and l, h_k, h_l - height of earth wire k and l. The magnetic flux density produced by current in a single sagging coductor can be calculated using the Biot-Savart's law [3, 5]:

$$\boldsymbol{B}(r') = \mu_0 \left(\int_{C_{si}} \frac{I(l'_{si})\left[dl'_{si} \times \boldsymbol{R}(l'_{si}) \right]}{4\pi \left| \boldsymbol{R}_{si}(l'_{si}) \right|^2} \right) \tag{9}$$

where μ_0=4π·10-7 H/m is the magnetic permeability of the vacuum $I(l'_{si})$, - current, $\boldsymbol{R}_{si}(l'_{si})$ is a vector from the source point, $\boldsymbol{R}(l'_{si})$ is a unit vector in the direction of $\boldsymbol{R}_{si}(l'_{si})$ as shown in Fig. 2.

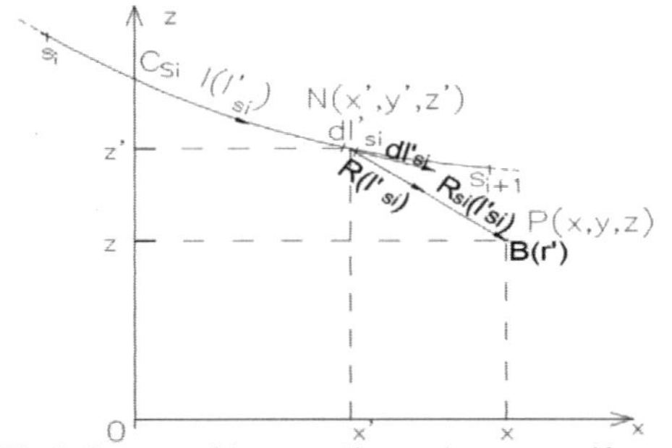

Fig. 2. Segment of the power line conductor – consider system.

The intensity of the magnetic field at any point above the earth's surface is determined from relation [3]:

$$\boldsymbol{H}\,(x,y,z) = \frac{I}{4\pi}\left[\int_{-d/2}^{d/2} \frac{\left[(x-x')\boldsymbol{a}_x + (y-y')\boldsymbol{a}_y + (z-z')\boldsymbol{a}_z \right] cosh\left(\frac{x'}{\alpha}\right)}{\left(\sqrt{(x-x')^2 + (y-y')^2 + (z-z')^2}\right)^3} dx' \right] \tag{10}$$

The total magnetic field is calculated from the vector summation of the fields from currents in all the transmission-line conductors [3, 5]:

$$H_T = \sqrt{\sum_{m=1}^{M} H_x^2 + \sum_{m=1}^{M} H_y^2 + \sum_{m=1}^{M} H_z^2} \tag{11}$$

3 Example

Measurements of magnetic field intensity were made with 3D E / H meter type of ESM-100. The device measures the field of the electric and magnetic intensities in real time and regardless of its direction. ESM-100 has six-channel measurements (Bx, By, Bz and Ex, Ey, Ez), while the resolution of the meter is determined at 1 nT and 100 mV.

The research object was a 110 kV line in the city Poznań on Nadwarciańska street, about half a kilometre from the GPZ station in the Czerwonak. The towers are type of the B2, voltage configuration $\underline{U_1}$ = 110 $e^{-j120°}$ kV, $\underline{U_2}$ = 110 kV, $\underline{U_3}$ = 110$e^{j120°}$ kV. The length between towers is 300 meters. The current during the measurements was 235 A.

Table 1 presents calculated earth wire currents and the maximum magnetic field intensity calculated for conductors on different heights (h_{L1}, h_{L2}, h_{L3}, h_e) in the middle of the span. Fig. 3 present comparison of calculated results magnetic intensity using of method CSM with result measurements made under the line.

Table 1. Calculation results.

$h_{L1, L2}$ [m]	h_{L3} [m]	h_e [m]	I_e [A]	$H_{T\,max}$ [A/m]	$H_{measure\,max}$ [A/m]
5,85	9,15	12,15		8,52	
7	9	11	-16,04-j0,04	6,16	3,05
8	10	12		4,73	
9	11	13		3,68	

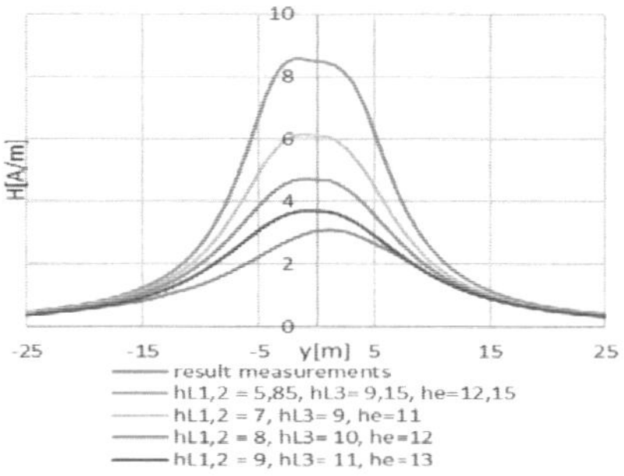

Fig. 3. Magnetic field strength charts - comparison of measurements with calculation method.

4 Conclusions

It is difficult to measure the height of the conductors - in the middle of the span, and this height influences magnetic field intensity under the power line.

The current measurement was obtained from the power industry in Poznań.

The presented method allows calculation fields magnetic intensity consistent with the results measured for the power line. The observation point in the calculations is at a height of 2 m above the ground in according to with the standard PN-EN 50341.

References

1. A. Deri, G. Tevan, A. Semlyen, A. Castanheira, IEEE Transactions on Power Apparatus and Systems, 100 (1981)
2. Z. Nadolny, A. Rakowska, Prz. Elektrotech. **86**, 5 (2010)
3. K. Król, K. Budnik, P. Jarek, Electrical Engineering **93**, (2018)
4. J. C. Fernandez, H. L. Soibelzon, EMC Europe 2002
5. M. Krakowski, *Elektrotechnika Teoretyczna*, t. 2. PWN (1995)

Influence of defect in an excited steel plate on the results of time-frequency analysis

Arkadiusz Dobrzycki[1,*], *Anna* Knitter-Piątkowska[2],

[1]Poznan University of Technology, Faculty of Electrical Engineering, Piotrowo 3A, 60-965 Poznan, Poland
[2]Poznan University of Technology, Faculty of Civil Engineering, Piotrowo 5, 60-965 Poznan, Poland

Abstract. The paper pertains the use of non-invasive diagnostic methods to assess the condition of metal elements of machinery and equipment or metal components of building structures. The conducted research concerns the analysis of acoustic signals generated during the excitation of a steel plate and the influence of discontinuities such as grooves and apertures in its structure on spectrogram of recorded acoustic emission signals. Since the presence of the opening causes a significant increase in the initial phase of the acoustic event, higher frequencies (20-55 kHz) and faster decay of the signal, so it should be noted that the frequency analysis of recorded signals, in the initial phase of the acoustic event, can be considered as an indicator of the damage presence.

1 Introduction

Awareness of the need to monitor the structure (SHM – structural health monitoring) and detection of damages at the earliest stage is an issue present in the society of engineers of various specialties. Damage identification methods have been developed for many years. Recently, the role of non-destructive methods (NDT) has significantly increased. The essence of NDT is to locate the damage in a structural element without changing its properties and functionality. Defect detection is the first level of a more general problem namely damage identification. There is a vast variety of methods evaluating the condition of the structure starting from the most basic visual inspection, through radiographic tests, magnetic fields, thermography, modal analysis, which is based on natural frequencies, modal shapes or damping changes and many others. In order to examine the state of technical objects, their models are often used [1,2] and the characteristic values are analyzed [3,4]. Another advanced, non-invasive diagnostic methods used in this research work, is the acoustic emission method AE [5-8]. However, the global structural response may be insensitive to local small changes caused by defects, so if one doesn't want to use or doesn't have an information about an intact structure it is advisable to use e.g. wavelet transform, also in its discreet form [9-12].

2 Results of analysis

2.1. Test setup and analysis method

In order to carry out the experiment, a test stand consisting of an examined (mechanically excited) steel plate (E = 210 GPa), a measurement (electroacoustic transducer with amplifying system) and recording signals (measuring card and computer) system was constructed. The exact schematic diagram of measuring unit with the detailed description was presented in [13]. In the very same paper one can find the conclusions from the influence of the substrate different types (on which the plate was placed during tests) and the type of excitation on registered signals frequency spectrum. The performed tests proved that the influence of the substrate, and indirectly its elasticity, does not change the spectrum of diagnostic signals, provided that the plate is induced by an inelastic element. However, the impact of damage on the average spectrum was relatively small, this was the reason for the time-frequency analysis. It is assumed that the frequency distribution may change during the impulse due to e.g. reflections of acoustic waves from the edge of the sample or damage.

The sample was excited at various distances from the transducer from 5 to 25 cm in increments of 5 cm, five times for each distance. A slight influence of the excitation-transducer distance on the spectrogram was observed.

Registered signals were analyzed while using numerical procedures developed in the Matlab environment. All tests were a real experiment.

2.2 Sample results

The individual spectrograms were plotted in relative units, the reference being the largest amplitude among the registered components for each excitation. The obtained spectrograms were compared and it was noted that for a given type of damage, in the analyzed distance

* Corresponding author: arkadiusz.dobrzycki@put.poznan.pl

interval, the distance from damage has little effect on the spectrogram.

Fig. 1 shows a spectrogram for the case of excitation of the undamaged plate, while Fig. 2 shows a spectrogram for a plate with damage in a form of a hole with a 9.5 mm diameter through the entire thickness, whereas the dimensions of the plate were: 200x300x10 mm

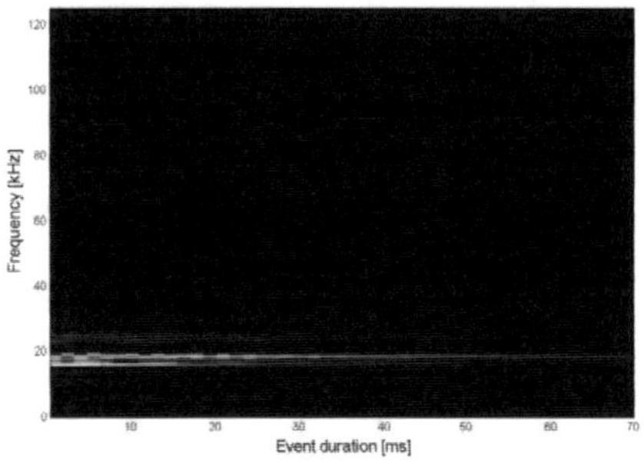

Fig. 1. Spectrogram for the case of excitation of the undamaged plate.

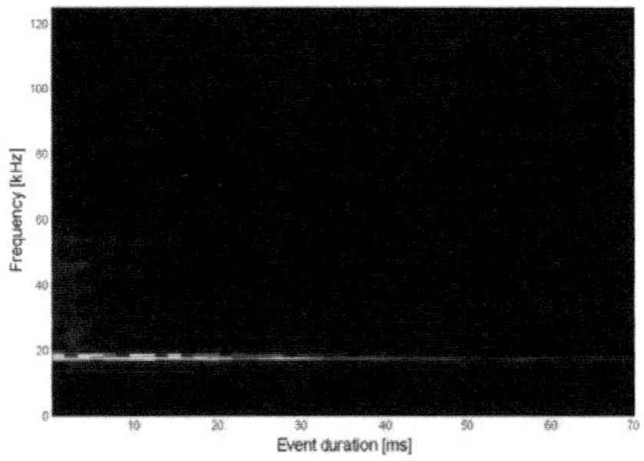

Fig. 2. Spectrogram for a plate with damage in a form of a hole with a 9.5 mm diameter through the entire thickness.

Analyzing the results presented above, it can be noticed that in both cases: the undamaged and defective element dominates the frequencies in the range of 15-20 kHz. One can, however, notice the clear difference in the initial phase of the analyzed acoustic event. In the case of the presence of damage it results in a much larger, the share of signals with frequencies from the 20-55 kHz, range.

It is a confirmation of preliminary frequency analysis of signals carried out for various types of damage [13].

3 Conclusions

Precise and quick diagnostics of structural elements is an important practical issue. The use of non-invasive methods reduces the time needed to perform the examinations.

Tests, which were carried out concerned the time-frequency analysis of AE signals generated during mechanical excitation of the sample, which was a plate made of steel. In the obtained results, it is important to notice that the severity of the damages, meaning superficial groove or apertures through the whole thickness of the element, affects spectra of signal spectrograms [13]. This influence is evident in the distinct frequency band designation from 20-50 kHz. However, it should be borne in mind that, while in laboratory tests it is relatively easy to notice this correlation, in real conditions, with an increased level of ambient noise, it may be more difficult. Therefore, it seems reasonable to use other signal parameters or develop the new one, clearly identifying the presence and type of damage as indicators, which is the goal of further work on this topic.

References

1. L. Kasprzyk, Eksploat. Niezawodn. **19** (2), 229–236 (2017), http://dx.doi.org/10.17531/ein.2017.2.10
2. G. Trzmiel, Eksploat. Niezawodn. **19** (4), 516–521 (2017), http://dx.doi.org/10.17531/ein.2017.4.4
3. J. Jajczyk, A. Dobrzycki, M. Filipiak, D. Kurz, *E3S Web Conf.* **19** 01027 (2017), doi: 10.1051/e3sconf/20171901027
4. K. Bednarek, R. Nawrowski, A. Tomczewski, *Electromagnetic Fields in Electrical Engineering, Studies in Applied Electromagnetics and Mechanics*, **22**, 363-368 (IOS Press, 2002)
5. W. Opydo, A. Dobrzycki, *Electr. Eng.* **94**, 37 (2012) https://doi.org/10.1007/s00202-011-0219-1
6. A. Dobrzycki, S. Mikulski, W. Opydo, *2014 ICHVE International Conference on High Voltage Engineering and Application*, 1-4. (2014) doi: 10.1109/ICHVE.2014.7035500
7. A. Dobrzycki, S. Mikulski, Prz. Elektrotech. **92** (4), 221-223 (2016), doi:10.15199/48.2016.04.44
8. A. Dobrzycki, S. Mikulski, Prz. Elektrotech. **92** (4), 26-29 (2016), doi:10.15199/48.2016.04.07
9. S. Mallat, *IEEE Trans. Pattern Anal. And Machine Intell.*, **11**, 674-693 (1989)
10. A. Knitter-Piątkowska, M. Guminiak, *Advances in Mechanics: Theoretical, Computational and Interdisciplinary Issues, proceedings of the 21st International Conference on Computer Mechanics*, red. M. Kleiber, 297-300, (CRC Press, 2016)
11. A. Knitter-Piątkowska, M. Guminiak, G. Hloupis, J. Theor. App. Mech. **55** (2), 481-496 (2017)
12. Z. Pawlak, A. Knitter-Piątkowska, *Proceedings of the 22nd International Conference on Computer Mechanics*, red. J. Podgórski, 130006-1-130006-9, (AIP Publishing, 2018)
13. A. Dobrzycki, A. Knitter-Piątkowska, Pozn. Univ. Technol. Acad. J. Electr. Eng. **93**, 323-334 (2018), doi: 10.21008/j.1897-0737.2018.93.0027 (in polish)

Field – Circuit Model of Wireless Transmission Power System using Ω-*T*-*T*0 Formulation

Milena Kurzawa[1,*], *Rafał M.* Wojciechowski[1]

[1]Institute of Electrical Engineering and Electronics, Poznan University of Technology, ul. Piotrowo 3a, 60—965 Poznan, Poland

Abstract. The paper discusses the field-circuit model of the wireless power transmission system (WPTS) with the air-core high-frequency transformer. While working on the field model, a formulation which uses scalar magnetic potential Ω and electric vector potentials $\boldsymbol{T}$ and $\boldsymbol{T}_0$ was implemented. Model equations were provided. The system which consists of magnetically coupled coils connected with the elements of external circuits was taken into consideration. The selected results of simulation calculations were presented. The obtained results of simulation calculations were compared with the results of measurements obtained at a laboratory post.

1 Introduction

Wireless power transmission systems (WTPS), in which energy is transferred by means of the high-frequency electromagnetic field (HF) are more and more frequently used in contactless charging systems for mobile devices [1], portable computers [2]; or electronic devices. The WPTS are also more and more willingly used in the systems of contactless power supply of electric vehicle batteries [3], or systems which constitute the power supply for industrial manipulators [4]. The WPTS are also used in systems of wireless power transmission through a human tissue, thus enabling the battery charge of devices which support the functioning of human organs [5], as well as in medical examinations and diagnostics [6]. Various aspects of the wireless power transmission were and still are undertaken in numerous publications. These papers refer to analysis, modelling and design of WPTS components as well as the possibility of using the same systems in different fields of science and technology.

In this article, the authors wish to present the results of their research on the development and implementation of the field-circuit model of phenomena for the wireless power transmission system by means of the high-frequency electromagnetic field. While developing the model, the popular finite element method and the formulation that uses the scalar magnetic potential and electric vector potentials $\boldsymbol{T}$ and $\boldsymbol{T}_0$ were implemented. The model was designed for analysis of the system which consisted of magnetically coupled coils, which were connected with external passive elements, thus developing the external circuits. Selected results of calculations were presented and the said results were subjected to comparative analysis with the measurement results.

2 Field – circuit model

For the purposes of the paper, a field-circuit model of phenomena was developed for modelling and analysis of the operating conditions of the wireless power transmission system consisting of the wireless high-frequency transformer and external circuits (Fig.1). The model implements a three-dimensional (3D) approach which involves the finite element method (FEM) and the formulation which uses $\boldsymbol{\Omega}$-$\boldsymbol{T}$-$\boldsymbol{T}_0$ potentials. In the used approach, the distribution of the magnetic field is described by means of nodal values of scalar potential Ω, whereas the distribution of eddy currents in massive wires of air transformer windings and the external circuit currents is described by means of edge values of electric potentials $\boldsymbol{T}$ and $\boldsymbol{T}_0$ respectively. The application of the $\boldsymbol{\Omega}$-$\boldsymbol{T}$-$\boldsymbol{T}_0$ formulation under consideration leads to the system of equations (1), which, as has been demonstrated in [7], are equivalent to the equations of the coupled permeance - resistance network method, i.e.:

$$\begin{bmatrix} \boldsymbol{\Lambda}_w & \boldsymbol{k}_w^T\boldsymbol{\Lambda}_g & \boldsymbol{k}_w^T\boldsymbol{\Lambda}_g\boldsymbol{z}_0 \\ \frac{\partial}{\partial t}\boldsymbol{\Lambda}_g\boldsymbol{k}_w & \boldsymbol{Z}_0+\frac{\partial}{\partial t}\boldsymbol{\Lambda}_g & \boldsymbol{R}_{co}^T \\ \frac{\partial}{\partial t}\boldsymbol{z}_0^T\boldsymbol{\Lambda}_g\boldsymbol{k}_w & \boldsymbol{R}_{co} & \boldsymbol{Z}_c+\boldsymbol{R}_c+\frac{\partial}{\partial t}\boldsymbol{z}_0^T\boldsymbol{\Lambda}_g\boldsymbol{z}_0 \end{bmatrix} \begin{bmatrix} \boldsymbol{\Omega} \\ \boldsymbol{i}_0 \\ \boldsymbol{i}_c \end{bmatrix} = \begin{bmatrix} \boldsymbol{0} \\ \boldsymbol{0} \\ \boldsymbol{u}_c \end{bmatrix} \tag{1}$$

where: $\boldsymbol{\Lambda}_w$ is the nodal permeance matrix of the edge network (SK), $\boldsymbol{\Lambda}_g$ is the branch permeance matrix of the edge network (SK), $\boldsymbol{Z}_0$ is loop impedance matrix of the facet network (SS) and $\boldsymbol{k}_w$ is the nodal incidence matrix. Symbols $\boldsymbol{\Omega}$, $\boldsymbol{i}_0$ and $\boldsymbol{i}_c$ represent the relevant vector of nodal values of potential Ω of the edge network and the vectors of edge values of potential $\boldsymbol{T}$ and $\boldsymbol{T}_0$, i.e. loop

* Corresponding author: milena.kurzawa@put.poznan.pl

currents of the facet network and external circuits. Furthermore, matrix z_0 describes the winding in the edge element space [8], $\boldsymbol{R}_c$ is the loop resistance matrix for the external circuit, $\boldsymbol{R}_{c0}$ describes the mutual resistances between the facet network loops and external circuit loops [9], while $\boldsymbol{Z}_c$ is the external impedance matrix, i.e. resistance and reactance contained in external circuits of the system under consideration (see, Fig. 1). The developed model equations allowed for the development of the software which can analyse the working conditions and the distributions of the electromagnetic field in the studied WPTS.

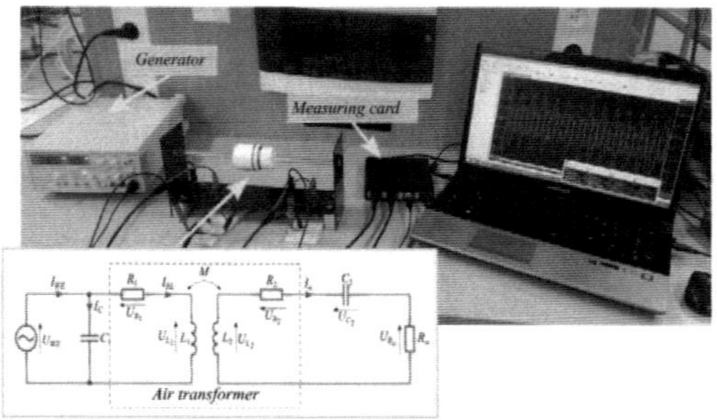

Fig. 1. View of the considered system of WTPS and its scheme diagram.

3 Results and Conclusions

The field-circuit model proposed in the paper has been tested based on the example of the existing WPTS from Figure 1, based on the parallel-series resonance circuit. A number of numerical calculations were performed for the system under consideration. Among other things, dependencies of self-inductances and mutual inductances between the air-core transformer coils were determined. On top of this, a number of static and dynamic calculations of operating conditions were performed, plotting numerous current and voltage waveforms. For instance, Figure 2 shows the voltage waveforms obtained from the calculations and measurements at the system input U_{in} and output (load) U_o for different distance values between coils. The calculations were performed for frequency of the power supply source equal to 840 kHz and the RMS value of supply voltage equal to 5 V.

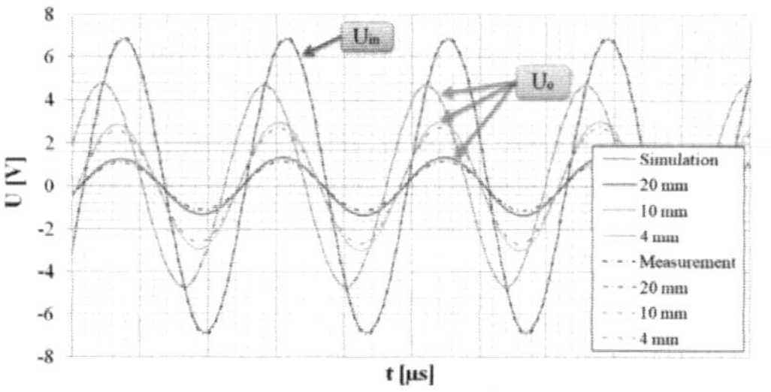

Fig. 2. Comparison of waveforms of input and output voltages obtained from the simulations and the measurements.

Figure 3, on the other hand, shows the comparisons of values of effective voltages $\boldsymbol{U}_o$ and currents $\boldsymbol{I}_o$ on the system load resistance $\boldsymbol{R}_o$ as a function of distance between the coils. In the studies, the value of resistance $\boldsymbol{R}_o$ was equal 50 Ω.

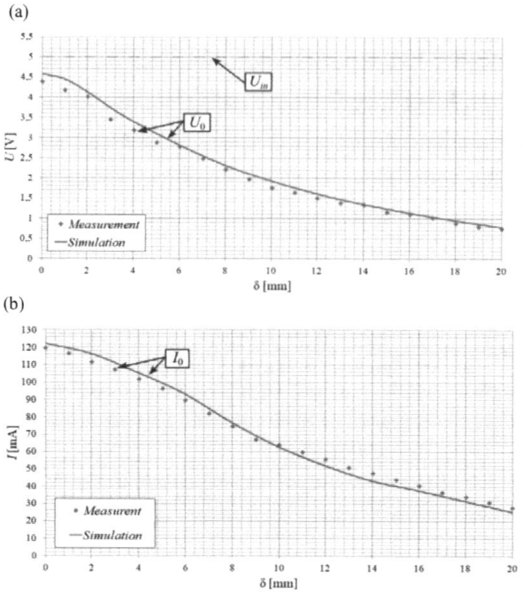

Fig. 3. Comparison of the values of output voltages (a) and currents (b) as a function of distance δ between coils of WTPS.

The presented comparisons show that the maximum values of differences between the results obtained from the measurements, and the results of calculations did not exceed 5.5% for the values of obtained voltages and 3.8% for the values of output currents in the system respectively. In the opinion of the authors, the developed model allows the results of calculations to be obtained with broad convergence in reference to the results.

References

1. Y. Jang, M. Javanović, IEEE Trans. Ind. Electron. **50**, 3, 520-527 (2003)
2. A. Moradewicz, R. Miśkiewicz, Prace Instytutu Elektrotechniki **236**, 47- 62 (2008)
3. H. Sakamoto, K. Harada, S. Washimiya, K. Tekehara, Y. Matsuo, IEEE Trans, Magn. **35**, 5, 3526-3528 (1999)
4. A. Maradewicz, M. Kaźmierkowski, JAMRIS **2**, 3, 20-25 (2008)
5. X. Li, H. Zhang, F. Peng, T. Yang, B. Wang, D. Fang, A Sensors **12**, 10292 – 10308 (2012)
6. G. Blakiewicz, Prz. Elektrotech. **9**, 12-14 (2014)
7. A. Demenko, J.K. Sykulski, ICS Newsletter **13**, 3, 3-13 (2006)
8. A. Demenko, J.K. Sykulski, R. Wojciechowski, IET Sci. Meas. Technol. **2**, 6, 434–439 (2008)
9. R. Wojciechowski, *Numerical analysis of the induced currents in simply and multiply connected regions*, *Ph.D* Thesis, Poznań University of Technology, Poznan (2010)

Heat transfer coefficient *α* of insulation liquid used in power transformers, based on measurements

Przemyslaw Goscinski[1], *Zbigniew* Nadolny[1,*]

[1]Poznan University of Technology, The Faculty of Electrical Engineering, 3A Piotrowo Str., 60-965 Poznan, Poland

Abstract. Proper work of the power transformer is determined by many factors. One of them is relatively low operating temperature of the transformer. Too high temperature has many negative consequences, such as fast aging process of the insulation system. The temperature depends on the load of transmission line, losses and heat exchange in transformer. Heat exchange depends on heat transfer factor α of insulation liquid, which is a component of insulation system of transformer. This factor depends on many factors: the type of insulation liquid, the length of the heating element (windings), temperature, winding surface heat load, the winding position (vertical, horizontal), place on the winding (upper, middle or bottom part). The article presents the results of the measurement of heat transfer factor α as a function of type of insulation liquid, winding surface heat load, and place on the windings. The results will be used by designers and operators of power transformers.

1 Introduction

Power transformer is one of the more crucial and sensitive part of electric power system. Its proper work depends on many factors, such as relatively low temperature [1-3].

Too high temperature has many negative consequences. It means first of all very fast ageing process of insulation system [4]. In accordance with the law of Montsinger, the increase in temperature by 5°C causes double reduction of lifetime of insulation system (cellulose paper impregnated by mineral oil). There are many reasons of the reduction, caused by high temperature, such as the decrease of breakdown voltage, the decrease of electrical resistance, the increase of dielectric losses, the cracking the polymer chains of cellulose, and the increase of acid number of oil [5-8]. In addition, the temperature rise may also contribute to the ignition of oil [9].

The temperature of power transformer depends on many factors. These include the load of electric power system, the losses in the transformer, and the effectiveness of transformer cooling system. The load of electric power system (current) decides on the losses in the windings of transformer. Losses in the transformer occur first of all in the windings (80%) and core (20%). The effectiveness of the cooling system depends on many factors, such as thermal conductivity coefficient λ of insulation paper (paper impregnated with liquid) and heat transfer coefficient α of insulation liquid. If the values of these coefficients are larger, the cooling system has a higher efficacy [10].

There is usually one value of coefficient α in literature, and catalogs of the liquid producers (for mineral oil – the more popular insulation liquid used in transformers). Meanwhile, the authors study suggests that this coefficient may be very different, because it depends on many factors, like the type of insulation liquid, the length of the heating element (the length of the windings), the position of the heating element (vertical, horizontal), the place on the element, and the heat load of the heat element surface.

2 Motivation and range of investigations

Measurements of heat transfer coefficient α of insulation liquid as a function of the type of the liquid, the place on the heat element, and the heat load of the heat element surface were a purpose of investigations.

Four types of the liquid were investigated: mineral oil, natural ester, synthetic ester and natural ester with reduced viscosity. Three places on the heat element were analyzed: upper, middle, bottom. Three values of the heat load of the heat element surface p were considered: 1000, 2000, and 3000 W·m^{-2}. The length of the heat element was 1600 mm, and its position was vertical.

3 Results of measurements

Table 1 presents the results of measurement of heat transfer coefficient α of insulation liquid. The coefficient was defined on the basis of following formula:

$$\alpha = p / (T_1 - T_2) \quad (1)$$

* Corresponding author: zbigniew.nadolny@put.poznan.pl

where α – heat transfer coefficient of insulation liquid, $W \cdot m^{-2} \cdot K^{-1}$, T_1 – temperature on heat element surface, °C, T_2 – temperature on the cooling surface, °C.

Table 1. Heat transfer coefficient α as a function of type of insulation liquid, heat load on the heat element surface p, and place on the heat element (upper, middle, bottom part).

Heat load p [$W \cdot m^{-2}$]	1000	2000	3000
Type of liquid	**mineral oil**		
Upper	61.48	74.22	103.95
Middle	72.08	112.71	128.21
Bottom	155.96	217.82	235.42
Average	**96.51**	**134.92**	**155.86**
Type of liquid	**natural ester**		
Upper	52.51	69.09	99.36
Middle	70.32	108.04	123.59
Bottom	130.66	191.14	219.91
Average	**84.50**	**122.76**	**147.62**
Type of liquid	**synthetic ester**		
Upper	54.70	70.92	89.78
Middle	69.60	107.25	121.12
Bottom	135.57	186.28	204.66
Average	**86.62**	**121.48**	**138.52**
Type of liquid	**natural ester with reduced viscosity**		
Upper	60.81	73.45	103.79
Middle	71.13	110.17	125.25
Bottom	140.24	194.49	223.92
Average	**90.73**	**126.04**	**150.99**

Type of insulation liquid has influence on heat transfer coefficient α of the liquid. Mineral oil has the biggest value of the coefficient, then natural ester with reduced viscosity, natural ester and synthetic ester. The difference between the best and the worst liquid exceeds 10%, independently on heat load on the heat element surface and place on the heat element. The reason of different values of coefficient α is viscosity, which plays important role in heat transfer. The biggest value of heat transfer coefficient α of mineral oil is caused by very small viscosity of the oil (about three times), comparing to viscosity of any analysed esters.

Heat load on the heat element surface p has significant influence on heat transfer coefficient α of insulation liquid. The increase of the heat load (from 1000 to 3000 $W \cdot m^{-2}$) causes the increase of the coefficient α about 60÷80%, independently on type of the liquid and place on the heat element. The reason of increase of the coefficient α with the increase of the heat load is temperature. The increase of the heat load causes the increase of temperature, which reduces the viscosity and increases the specific heat of the liquid.

Place on the heat element has very significant influence on heat transfer coefficient α of insulation liquid. Bottom place has the biggest value of the coefficient α (up to three times), comparing to middle and upper place. It means that bottom place has the more effectiveness transfer of heat. Theory of heat transfer of fluid says, that heated particles of a fluid move up. It is a reason, why upper and middle place of the element has more difficult conditions to cool, comparing to bottom.

4 Conclusions

All analyzed factors have some influence on heat transfer coefficient α. In case of type of insulating liquid, mineral oil has the biggest value of the coefficient α, comparing to all analyzed esters. The increase of heat load on the heat element surface causes the increase of the coefficient α. In case of place on the heat element, bottom place has the biggest value of the coefficient α.

The values of the coefficient α, presented in Table 1, are very different. The smallest α is for natural ester, for heat load 1000 $W \cdot m^{-2}$, and for upper place on the heat element, 52.51 $W \cdot m^{-2} \cdot K^{-1}$ (underlined in Table 1). The biggest is for mineral oil, for heat load 3000 $W \cdot m^{-2}$, and for bottom place on the heat element, 235.42 $W \cdot m^{-2} \cdot K^{-1}$.

On the basis on formula (1), it is possible to create a formula, which describes the temperature decrease in power transformer $T_1 - T_2$:

$$(T_1 - T_2) = p / \alpha \tag{2}$$

If we use extreme different values of coefficient α to calculate the temperature decrease, we can obtain very different results, shown in Table 2. How it can be seen, the values of temperature decrease are very different (44.39 °C of difference). It means that if we ignore the influence of mentioned factors on the heat transfer coefficient α, we can make serious mistake in calculation of temperature decrease in power transformer.

Table 2. Comparison between calculated temperature decreases using different values of heat transfer coefficient α.

Heat transfer coefficient α of insulating liquid [$W \cdot m^{-2} \cdot K^{-1}$]	52.51	235.42
Heat load p [$W \cdot m^{-2}$]	3000	3000
Temperature decrease $T_1 - T_2$ [°C]	57.13	12.74
Difference of temperature decrease [°C]	44.39	

References

1. T. Rouse, IEEE Electr. Insul. Mag. **14**, 6-16 (1998)
2. R. Lopatkiewicz, Z. Nadolny, Prz. Elektrotech. **84**, 50-52 (2008)
3. R. Lopatkiewicz, Z. Nadolny, P. Przybylek, Prz. Elektrotech. **86**, 55-58 (2010)
4. R. Lopatkiewicz, Z. Nadolny, P. Przybylek, W. Sikorski, Prz. Elektrotech. **88**, 126-129 (2012)
5. H. Ran, J. Li, J. Zhang, X. Li, J. Chen, IEEE ICHVE, 1-4 (2016)
6. M. H. Hamid, M. T. Ishak, M. F. Din, N. S. Suhaimi, N. I. Katim, IEEE PECon, 54-57 (2016).
7. M. S. Mohamad, H. Zainuddin, S. A. Ghani, I.S. Chairul, IEEE PECon, 1-4 (2017)
8. J. Xie, M. Dong, L. Wang, A. Ma, IEEE ICEMPE, 414-418 (2017)
9. G. Dombek, J. Gielniak, R. Wroblewski, IEEE ISEIM, 227-230 (2017)
10. Z. Nadolny, G. Dombek, P. Przybylek, D. Przadka, IEEE CEIDP, 538-541 (2016)

Applying of hygroscopic materials to dry transformer insulation

Mateusz Cybulski[1], *Piotr* Przybylek[1,*]

[1]Poznan University of Technology, Institute of Electric Power Engineering , Piotrowo 3A, 60-965 Poznan, Poland

Abstract. The problems related to the effects of high moisture content in the transformer insulation system and the risk resulting from the need for its immediate drying can be avoided by using a non-invasive method of continuous drying of solid insulation by means of high hygroscopic sorbents. The article compared the hygroscopicity of selected sorbents: molecular sieves 3A, 5A and 13X, aluminum oxide and silica gel. It was found that the highest hygroscopicity, for a low value of relative air humidity, is characterized by a 13X molecular sieve. For this reason, this material was selected for further testing by checking its ability to dry mineral oil.

1 Introduction

Power transformers are one of the most important elements of the power system. Their reliable operation affects on the stability of the electricity transmission and distribution systems. The lifetime of transformer is closely related to the lifetime of its insulation system, which largely depends on the moisture content in transformer's insulation [1,2].
Three basic reasons for the presence of water in the transformer insulation system can be distinguished:

- residual moisture, which has not been removed at the stage of manufacturing a transformer,
- penetration of moisture from the atmosphere,
- material aging – especially cellulose oxidation [3].

Currently, there are several methods of drying cellulose transformer insulation at the place of its installation. The first group of methods use vacuum drying supported by various techniques of insulation heating, and the second group are based on drying transformer's insulation system by means of electro-insulating liquid. Drying of the insulation system by the electro-insulating liquid is based on the phenomenon of water migration from cellulose material with higher relative humidity to the insulating liquid with lower relative saturation. The continuity of the process can be ensured by drying the oil using a high hygroscopic sorbent.

The method of drying cellulose insulation by means of electro-insulating liquid is much less efficient than the vacuum method [4], nevertheless it is much less invasive for the insulation system, and therefore more secure.

Drying the electro-insulating liquid by means of a sorbent can be used to maintain a low level of water content in oil-paper insulation throughout entire lifetime of transformer.

2 Hygroscopicity of sorbents in the aspect of their use to dry electro-insulating liquid

2.1 Comparison of hygroscopicity of selected sorbents

The aim of the study was to compare the water content in sorbents conditioned in the air under strictly defined relative humidity and temperature and select the material characterized by the highest hygroscopicity. Several sorbents were selected for the study, which according to the literature, show high hygroscopicity and could be used as a material for drying electro-insulating liquids, and indirectly also for drying the transformer's cellulose insulation. The following materials were chosen: 3A, 5A and 13X molecular sieves, aluminum oxide and silica gel.

The ability of the above mentioned materials to water sorption was checked using a saturated salt solution of cesium fluoride (RH=2.69%, T=35°C) [5]. The water content in the investigated sorbents was determined by the gravimetric method. The research results are presented in Figure 1.

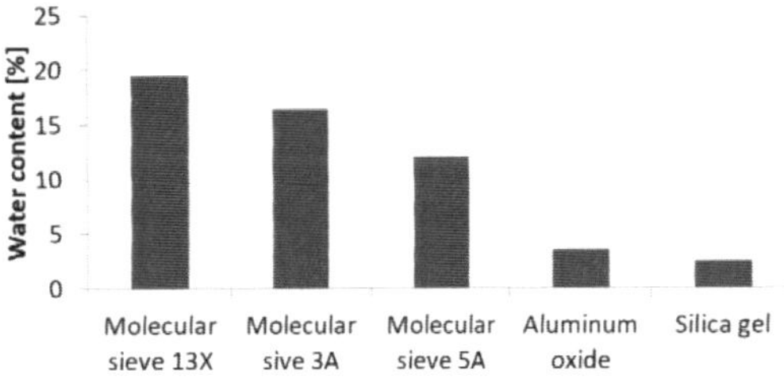

Fig. 1. Comparison of water content in selected materials conditioned in the air of RH=2,69% and T=35°C.

* Corresponding author: piotr.przybylek@put.poznan.pl

The conducted experiment allowed for the selection of a sorbent characterized by the highest hygroscopicity for the assumed experimental conditions. Among the analyzed materials, the highest water absorption capacity was found in the 13X molecular sieve, where the final water content was equal to 19.45%. For this reason, this material was selected for further research.

2.2 Application of 13X molecular sieve to dry mineral oil

The scheme of measurement system used to evaluation of the possibility of drying mineral oil by means of 13X molecular sieve is shown in Figure 2.

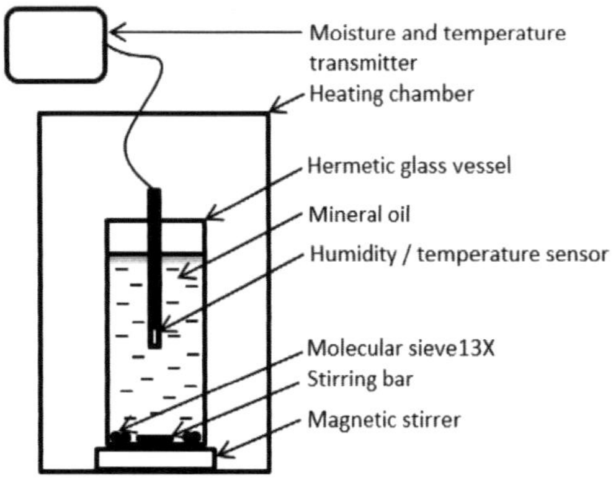

Fig. 2. Scheme of the measurement system for testing the water content in mineral oil during its drying by means of the molecular sieve 13X.

The drying of mineral oil was carried out in a sealed glass vessel with a volume of one liter. 850 ml of oil were poured into the vessel. The measurements of the relative saturation of water in oil *(RS)*, water content in oil (*WCO*) and oil temperature (T_o) were carried out using a probe equipped with a capacitive and temperature sensors. To eliminate the influence of temperature on the results of relative saturation, the measuring system was placed in a heating chamber. The oil temperature was maintained at 35°C. First the system was conditioned for 24 h to achieve thermodynamic equilibrium (RS=26.5%, T_o=35°C). Subsequently, dried 13X molecular sieve with a mass of 0.1077 g was added to the oil. The sieve mass, needed to completely dry the oil, was calculated on the basis of the results shown in Figure 1 and the weight of water in oil before drying (0.0174 g). Figure 3 shows the results recorded by means of measuring probe during oil drying.

Analyzing the results presented in Figure 3, it can be noticed that the obtained drying effect was differ from the expected result calculated from the determined ability of the 13X molecular sieve to adsorb water from the air. After the drying process the relative saturation of the oil was stabilized at 9.6%, and thus it was not possible to completely dry the oil. A weighted amount of sorbent was enough to adsorb 0.011 g of water from the oil.

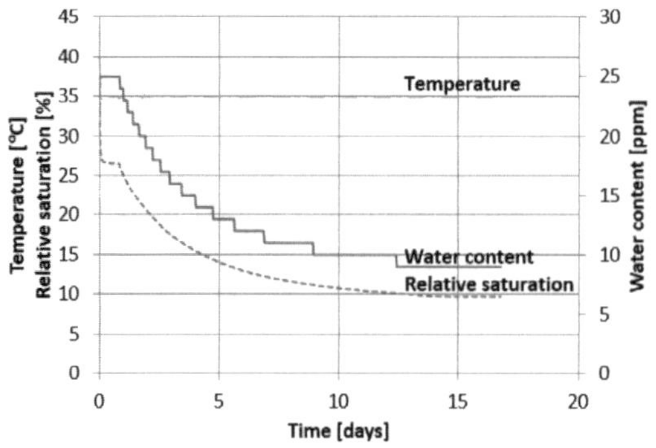

Fig. 3. The relative saturation of water in oil, water content in oil and oil temperature during drying of oil by means of molecular sieve.

The discrepancy between the expected drying result and the obtained effects may be related to the presence of dissolved gases in the oil. If the diameter of the gas molecule is smaller than the pore diameter of the molecular sieve, which in the case of the 13X molecular sieve is 9Å, then these particles will also be able to penetrate its crystalline structure, which may cause the decrease of their hygroscopicity. Therefore, further research of sorption selectivity of various sieves are necessary. Nevertheless, it should be noted, that the ability of the 13X molecular sieve to dry the oil is very high.

3 Conclusions

The article indicates sorbents that show high hygroscopicity and could be used as a material for drying electro-insulating liquids, and indirectly also for drying cellulose insulation. Using the saturated salt solution of cesium fluoride, the hygroscopicity of 3A, 5A and 13X molecular sieves, alumina and silica gel was compared. On the basis of the conducted research, the material with the highest water sorption capacity was indicated. This material is the 13X molecular sieve. The measurements confirmed the high potential of the molecular sieves for their application to dry insulation systems of power transformers. It should be noted that further research are necessary, especially in the context of drying efficiency by means of molecular sieve and operational safety of such dried transformers.

References

1. J.S. N'cho, I. Fofana, Y. Hadjadj, A. Beroual, Energies **9(5)**, 367 (2016)
2. P. Przybylek, IEEE Trans. Dielectr. Electr. Insul. **23**, 1886-1893 (2016)
3. Brochure, Cigre, **349** (2008)
4. P. Koestinger, E. Aronsen, P. Boss, G. Rindlisbacher, Cigre, **A2-205** (2004)
5. L. Greenspan, J. Res. Natl. Bur. Stand. **81A** (1977)

Adaptive functions in G0> and YY0 earth fault protection

Józef Lorenc[1,*], *Krzysztof Łowczowski*[1], and *Bogdan* Staszak[1]

[1]Poznan University of Technology, Institute of Electric Power Engineering, Piotrowo 3A, 60-965 Poznań, Poland

Abstract. In this paper, the benefits resulting from the application of YY0 and G0> earth fault protection with adaptive functions – limiting the risk of outsiders being shocked and reducing the likelihood of two-phase short-circuiting with the ground, are presented. The possibilities of improving the effectiveness of admittance protection by introducing special adaptive functions in control algorithms of station automation and decision algorithms of YY0 and G0> criteria are shown. The rules for using such functions have been described and it has been shown that they have a very significant impact on improvement the effectiveness of protection system. It can be stated that in typical medium voltage networks and solutions of active adaptive functions, good conditions are obtained for the operation of admittance protections even at several times higher resistances in the place of earth fault than when these functions are deactivated or not implemented.

1 Introduction

Currently, the admittance criteria are commonly used in earth fault protections [1,2,3], in which the decision parameter is the admittance described as quotient of the zero sequence components of current and network voltage or active components (conductivity) and passive components (susceptance) of the specified admittance. Such protection devices are sensitive to resistance short circuits whose values in the fault location do not exceed 3000 Ω. Practice in recent years shows that there are short circuits with resistances significantly greater than 3000 ohms. It is estimated that in Polish medium voltage networks, the number of such disturbances can account for about 5% of all ground faults, and these constitute about 80% of all disturbances in MV grids. These short-circuits can remain on the network for several hours or more, generating a very strong shock hazard for people and animals around the damaged area.

The limits of the admittance protection sensitivity result inter alia from the setting conditions of the voltage criterion

$$U_{0p} >= U_{0n} \tag{1}$$

where:

$$\underline{U}_{0p} = \frac{E_{ph}}{1 + R_F \omega C_{0S}(d_0 + js)} \tag{2}$$

$$d_0 = \frac{G_{0S}}{\omega C_{0S}} \tag{3}$$

$$s = \frac{1}{\omega^2 L_d C_{0S}} - 1 \tag{4}$$

where:

U_{0p} - zero sequence voltage component of the measurement voltage,

E_{ph} -phase power source voltage,

R_F - resistance in the fault location,

C_{0s} - ground capacity of the network,

ω - network pulsation,

d_0 - damping coefficient of network suppression, defined by the quotient of the earth conductance of the G_{0S} network to its susceptance in C_{0S},

s - coefficient of earth fault compensation,

L_d - inductance of the compensating choke (Petersen coil).

By analyzing formulas (1) and (2), it is easy to show that the voltage sensitivity of the protection can be improved by affecting the values of coefficients d_0 and s or by lowering the setting value U_{0n} under certain short-circuit conditions. However, the decision to use such options should be made only during the earth fault and after the analysis of the ground fault parameters. For this purpose the control algorithms of the devices for enforcing the additional ground fault current and the decision-making algorithms of the protection should be supplemented with adaptive functions. Paragraph below present a solution that meets the features of such functions for two criteria: conductive G0> and comparative-admittance YY0.

2 Adaptive functions in G0> protection

The essence of the adaptive function in the G0> protection is the connection of the U_{0n} and G_{0n} setting values with the logical information on the effective operation of the active zero sequence current forcing arrangement (ACF) [4]. The adaptive function is active only when following the operation of the ACF device:

$$G_{0p} > G_{0n} \tag{5}$$

$$U_{0n} > U_{0p} > U_{0min} \tag{6}$$

* Corresponding author: bogdan.staszak@put.poznan.pl

and consists in changing both setting values. It manages this algorithm, which determines new G_{0nad} and U_{0nad} values based on the zero-sequence value of G_{0p} conductance and U_{0p} voltage measured during fault time. U_{0min} in formula (6) means the smallest value of the zero voltage component for the faultless condition.

The effect of the adaptive function is a significant increase in the detected fault resistances, what is shown in Fig. 1.

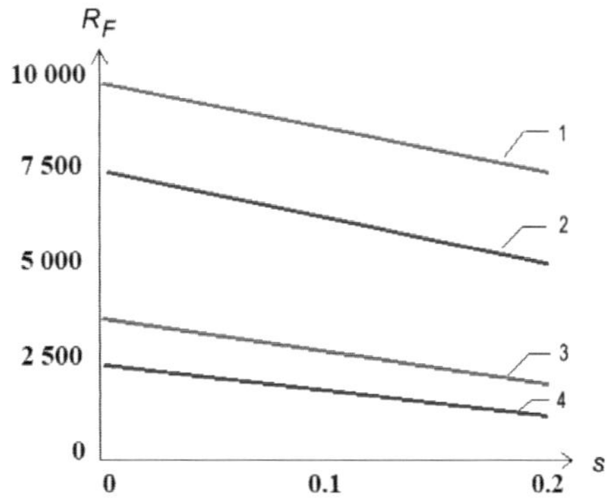

Fig. 1. Effects of protection G0> with adaptive function.

Range of detected fault resistance for various values of the earth fault compensation factor s is presented, assuming that U_{0min} is equal to 0.05 phase voltage (U_{ph}). In Fig.1 R_F is shown in ohms, curves 1 and 2 relate to protection with adaptive functions, 3 and 4 without. Curves 1 and 3 apply when the d_0 coefficient equal to 0.2, curves 2 and 4 when d_0 is equal to 0.4.

3 Adaptive functions for YY0 protection

The adaptive functions can be implemented in a similar way as in the case of G0> protection. Additionally, functionality is extended by selecting the system for enforcing additional active zero sequence current (ACF) or passive current (PCF). During the operation of ACF devices, the coefficient d_0 is increased, but after replacing the resistor by the reactance the value of the coefficient s changes. In practice, the changes in the coefficient s refer to a value or sign and can be implemented by switching on or off the reactance realizing the automatic operation of the reactive component of the ground fault current (PCF device). The use of the effects of the PCF operation requires the use of a criterion in the YY0 protection system to investigate the increase in susceptance in the zero-sequence components of the line. Past experience indicates that PCF systems can in many cases be more effective for the needs of earth fault protection than ACF. This applies first of all to earth faults, which are accompanied by significant resistances of the transition at the fault location.

The analysis of the effectiveness of the YY0 protection in 15 kV compensated network with total earth fault capacitive current equals to 120 A after operation of ACF/PSF forcing devices are given below. Share coefficient of capacitive earth fault of protected line in current of the total network is equal to 20% and it was assumed that the control value U_{0n} voltage criterion is 15% network phase voltage. It was also assumed that the network is symmetrical in the range of phase earth capacities, and the natural attenuation of the earth circuit d_0 does not exceed 0.04.

The maximum efficiency (4000 Ω) is obtained after the PCF devices operate to the compensating conditions level of 0.1. However, this effect can only occur if an undercompensated network (detuning s not greater than − 0.1) after operation of PCF goes into a compensating state (coefficient s not greater than 0.1) or if overcompensated network (coefficient s not greater than 0.1) after operation of PCF goes into a state of undercompensation (detuning not bigger than − 0.1).

In other states of compensation, the effectiveness will be reduced and in the case of relatively large detuning factor caused by the operation of PCF devices, the range of detected resistances will be below 2000 Ω, which is worse than in the case of ACF devices in a well compensated network.

The adaptive function of the forcing device controller can therefore decide on the type of automation (ACF or PCF) and the method of implementing enforcement in the PCF system. The rule should be followed that in the situation of the state of undercompensation the reactance of the coil should be reduced, in case of overcompensation, is increased. An important role in this solution is fulfilled by the control system, in which the voltage level U_0 is measured and the condition of earth fault compensation is controlled. There are two modes of the PCF system operation. In the first mode the induction current is increased by switching on additional reactance (ALN), whereas in second mode increasing the capacitive current is increased by switching off this reactance (reducing the induction current). In the latter case, the ALN reactance is a permanent element of the compensation system and is included in the undisturbed network operation mode. The system requires continuous information on the current compensation status. The widespread application of follow-up compensation solutions [1] and stationary network-level control systems [5] fully allow access to such information.

In addition, as in the case of G0>, the effectiveness of the YY0 protection can be increased by lowering the setting value of zero sequence voltage.

References

1. J. Lorenc, A. Rakowska, B. Staszak, Prz. Elektrotech. **4** (2007)
2. A. Wahlroos, J. Altonen, *ABB library* (2011)
3. A. Wahlroos, J. Altonen, *12th IET International Conference on Developments in Power System Protection* (2014)
4. J. Lorenc, B. Staszak, A. Wiśniewski, Patent PL No 226282 (2017)
5. J. Lorenc, M. Torbus, B. Staszak, Wiad. Elektrotech. **12**, (2013)

Grid conected inverter for alternative sources of energy

Ryszard Porada[1,*], *Adam* Gulczyński[1]

[1]Poznan University of Technology, 60-965 Poznań, Poland

Abstract. The general characteristic of power electronic couplers for alternative energy sources with electrical power grid was presented. The power electronic current source, working as a closed loop system, generating sine wave shaped current transfering the energy to the grid was discussed. The chosen results of simulation model of such system for sinusoidal reference signals were presented. The test results of the laboratory prototype were also presented.

1 Introduction

The energy obtained from alternative sources of energy may be used for supplying local, individual AC voltage receivers or transferred directly to the electrical power grid. For this purpose, the power electronic voltage inverters with voltage output or working as controllable current sources, are used. Controlling of such devices is a difficult task because of presence of nonlinearity effects [1,2].

In this paper the studies of power electronic coupler for low voltage alternative energy source (i.e. low voltage solar panel) with electrical power grid, which requires the matching transformer, were presented. The structure of the system and the method of generated current synchronization with grid voltage were shown. Selected results of simulation tests with a discrete corrector, as well as test results of a laboratory system test are included.

2 Structure of the system

The block diagram of the 1-phase power electronic current source cooperating with electrical power grid is presented on figure 1.

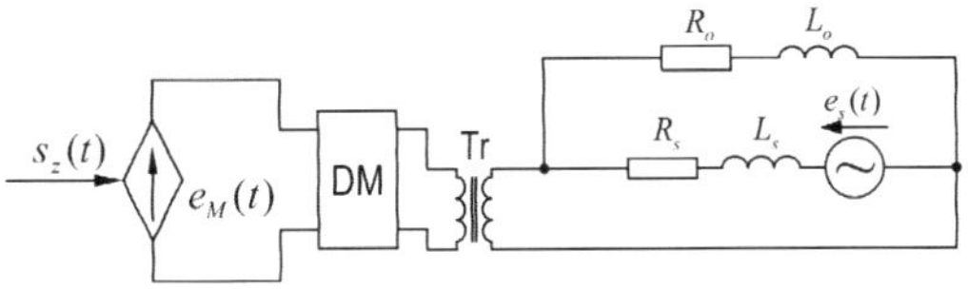

Fig. 1. The structure of the current source conected to grid.

The system consists of controllable modulated voltage source $e_M(t)$ as the voltage inverter with current output, supplied from the DC voltage source. The control signal $s_z(t)$ is generated by the corrector of the main track in closed current feedback loop system, defined according to the rules presented in the works [3,4]. On the output of modulated voltage source is passive demodulator (DM block), which acts like lowpass filter. Two structures were adopted- inductie in series or *LCL* filter type T. Becuase of voltage match the transfomer with properly chosen voltage ratio was used. The output of the transformer is connected to the electrical power grid, represented on the schematic by serial $e_s(t)R_sL_s$ branch. The other receivers are represented by serial R_oL_o branch.

3 Simulation tests

The simulation test were conducted to initially select parameters of the corector due to laboratory model of one phase inveter, with two types of modulation- unipolar and bipolar.

The following parameters of the system were adopted: supply voltage of the inverter 50 [V], carrier frequency of PWM modulation f_{PWM} = 12,5 kHz. Parameters of the coupling choke: R_{sp} =0,09 [Ω], L_{sp} = 1,1 [mH], LC filter: R_L = 0,05 [Ω], L_L = 440 [μH], C= 44 [μF]. The power grid is modeled by a serial branch with parameters R_s = 0,005 [Ω], L_s = 55 [μH]. The other receivers are represented by the serial branch with parameters R_o =19,55 [Ω], L_o = 385 [μH] (cosφ = 0,85).

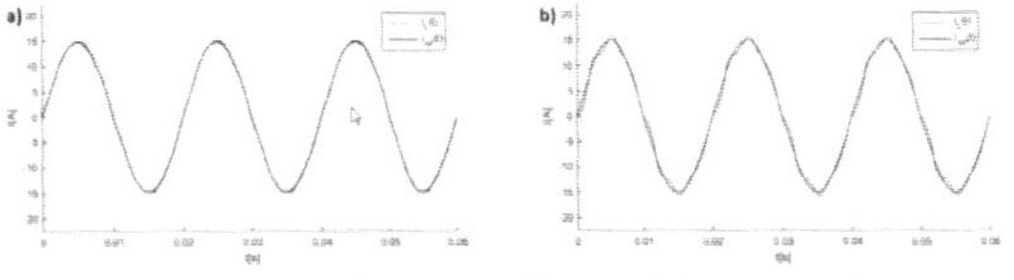

Fig. 2. Current and voltage waveforms of the system for current source: a) without LC filter; b) with LC filter.

Simulation studies for the discrete version of the corrector were performed in the Matlab / Simulink®. The dead time for PWM modulation with the t_m= 2 [μs] was also taken into account for the proper control of the inverter. The few selected results of studies of a unipolar modulation system (better frequency properties) and the shape of a sinusoidal current of 15 A are shown in fig.2. The corrector of the closed feedback loop system was chosen in manner to achieve the narrowband features of

* Corresponding author: adam.gulczynski@put.poznan.pl

the system, hence the lack of carrier components in the current waveforms. The presence of low-frequency components for the LCL filter is the result of the dead time.

4 Laboratory prototype tests

Experimental studies of the physical power source system in the 1-phase version were carried out on the basis of a converter with the IPM PM50RSA120 transistor module, controlled by the ALS-G3-1369 starter kit with Analog Devices ADSP-21369 SHARCTM floating-point signal processor. The voltage supply to the inverter is a laboratory power supply with a voltage of 50 V and a current capacity of 15 A.

The control algorithm has been implemented in the microprocessor system. The block diagram of the control system is shown in figure 3.

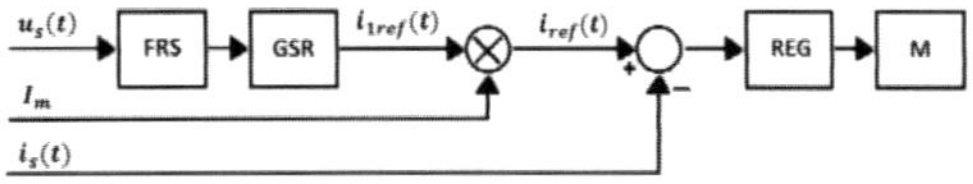

Fig. 3. Block diagram of the grid current control system.

Synchronization of the current of the transformer's secondary side (grid) with the mains voltage was performed using a moving averae as a low-pass filter. The voltage of the $u_s(t)$ was sampled, then filtered through the moving average filter and stored in a circular register (FRS block). The samples of a shifted in phase sine wave with respect to the grid voltage were obtained. The obtained samples were given on the peak value detector (GSR block). Next, the scaling of this waveform and the phase correction (compensation of phase characteristics of the average mobile filter) were made. Finally, a unit input signal for the current $i_{ref}(t)$ was obtained - figure 4.

The amplitude of the grid current is the result of the set power that should be transfered to the grid. The reference current is compared to the actual grid current, and then, as a control error, is fed by the regulator (corrector) to the modulator that generates switching signals for the inverter transistors.

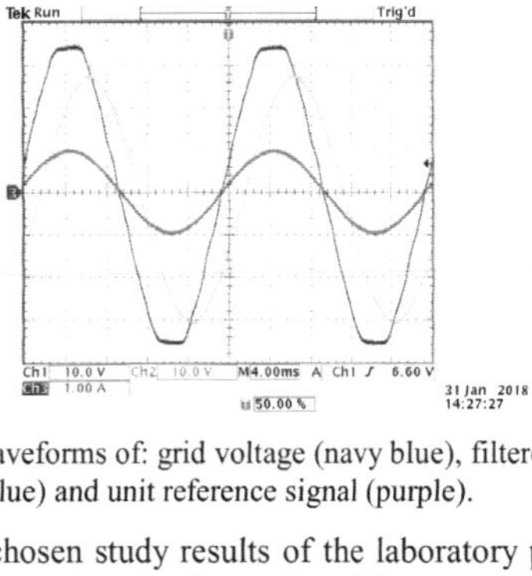

Fig. 4. Waveforms of: grid voltage (navy blue), filtered grid voltage (blue) and unit reference signal (purple).

The chosen study results of the laboratory prototype were presented on the figures 5 and 6.

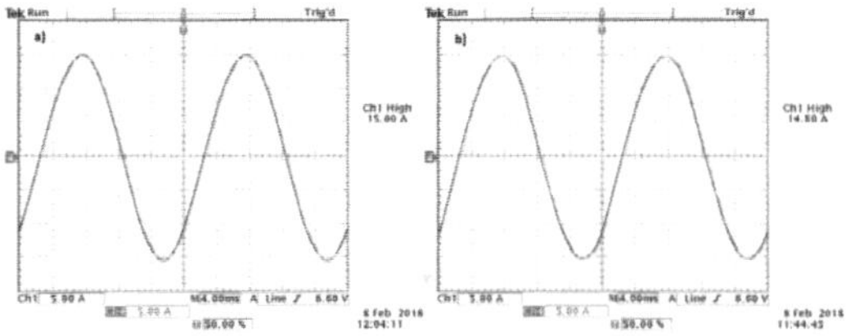

Fig. 5. Transformer's primary side current waveforms for the system a) without the LC filter ; b) with LC filter.

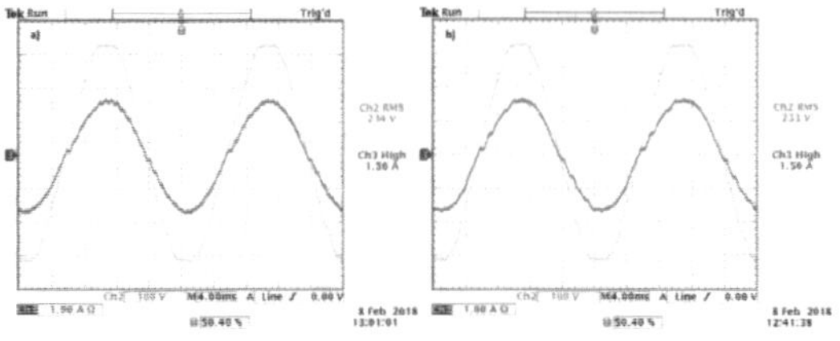

Fig. 6. Grid's voltage and current waveforms for the system: a) without the LC filter ; b) with LC filter.

The tests were carried out for two versions of the passive demodulator - series inductance L and T type LCL and unipolar modulation. In the practical system, the value of deformation of the current transfered to the grid in both cases has a similar value (<5%), which is an acceptable value in real life applications. A positive aspect of the obtained results is the low content of high frequency components in the current waveforms.

5 Summary

The results of laboratory tests indicate the need to perform some changes in the corrector system, controlling the physical system. The use of an LCL filter at the output of the inverter has little influence on the level of harmonic current distortions, however, it significantly changes the shape of the voltage of the transformer primary winding, which can affect the energy efficiency of the entire energy conversion path.

References

1. W Grega, *Methods and algorithms of digital control in centralized and expanded systems (in polish)*, UWND AGH (Kraków, 2004)
2. N. Mohan, T.M. Undeland, W.P. Robbins, *Power Electronics: Converters, Application and Design*. JWS (New York, 2001)
3. R. Porada, Pozn. Univ. Technol. Acad. J. Electr. Eng. **87**, 313-322 (2016)
4. R. Porada, A. Gulczyński, Pozn. Univ. Technol. Acad. J. Electr. Eng. **87**, 225-233 (2016)

Analysis of efficiency of photovoltaic bifacial cells

Dariusz Kurz[1,*], *Kamil* Lewandowski[1], and *Martyna* Szydłowska[1]

[1]Poznan University of Technology, Faculty of Electrical Engineering, Institute of Electrical Engineering and Electronics, St. Piotrowo 3a, 60 – 965 Poznań, Poland

Abstract. The paper presents the characteristic features and parameters of photovoltaic bifacial cells such as *BGE – Bifacial Gain Energy* and *BR – Bifacial Ratio*. Simulation test results of power yields and efficiency from bifacial panels for different values of irradiation and *BGE* ratio were presented.

1 Introduction

The improvement of the efficiency of the photovoltaic conversion is one of the major challenges for manufacturers of PV cells. The bifacial cell technology which has been known since the 80's of the previous century has become more and more popular in the recent years, and the manufacturers of photovoltaic panels introduce modern bifacial panels into the market [1,2].

The bifacial technology allows for the conversion of direct sunlight, which reaches the front part of the panel, and the radiation reflected from the surface and dispersed, reaching the back side of the panel. Panels manufactured in this technology may be installed on the ground, flat roofs, mast or solar tracking systems. The provision of optimal conditions for the operation of cells and the proper estimation of the real energy yield from the bifacial installation is necessary for the proper selection of energy storages [3-6].

The basic parameters which define the bifacial cells include [2,7,8]:

- ***BGE*** [%] (*Bifacial Gain Energy*) – the ratio which expresses the additional energy generated by the rear part of the module, referred to the energy generated from its upper part:

$$BGE = (Rear/Front) \qquad (1)$$

where:

Rear – the measured energy generated from the rear surface of the module (measured in standard test conditions without the participation of the front part) [kWh],

Front – the measured energy generated from the front surface of the module (measured in standard test conditions without the participation of the rear part) [kWh],

- ***BR* [%]** (*Bifacial Ratio*) – the ratio which expresses the relationship between the nominal power of the rear part of the module (obtained in standard test conditions) to the power of the front part:

$$BR = 100 \cdot (P_R / P_F) \qquad (2)$$

where:

P_R – the nominal power of the rear part of the module received in standard test conditions [W],

P_F – the nominal power of the front part of the module received in standard test conditions [W].

2 Tests and simulations of bifacial cells

In literature on this subject, it is possible to find many publications regarding the bifacial cell testing, depending on many variables such as e.g. the height of the panel installation, the angle of inclination, the surface reflection coefficient, the latitude, the deviation from the south, etc. [2,8-10]. Figure 1 presents the tests conducted by the authors of the paper [2] in the year 2014, in the U.S., using three Canadian Solar CS6P-245M monofacial panels and 2 Prism Solar B245 bifacial panels installed at the height of 0.2 m, inclined at an angle of 20° to the surface with the albedo (reflection coefficient) equal to 70%.

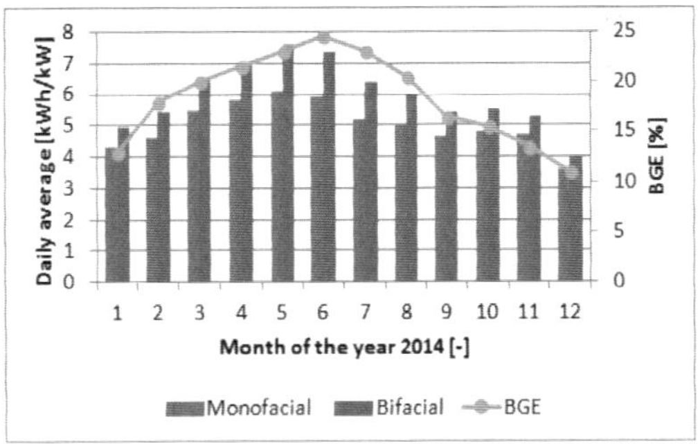

Fig. 1. Average daily energy yields and BGE, obtained in the tests conducted by the authors of the paper [2].

The panels selected for the comparison have the identical rated power in STC conditions, however, in view of the high albedo of the surface, the installation comprising bifacial panels during the best measuring day in June generated almost 25% more of the energy in comparison to the traditional models. The lowest values

* Corresponding author: dariusz.kurz@put.poznan.pl

of *BGE* were observed during the winter season, however its daily average value is higher than 10%.

The simulations of power yields from LG NeON2 BiFacial LG300N1T-G4 bifacial panels were performed using the Matlab/Simulink software [11], for different values of the *BGE* at the constant value of irradiation *E* (table 1 and fig. 2) and for variable values of *BGE* and *E* (table 1 and fig. 3). Descriptions of the current-voltage curves and power curves for different simulation conditions (presented in fig. 2 and fig. 3) are included in table 1. Based on the presented results, it is possible to notice the linear relationship between the values of the current generated by the panel and the irradiation, which is the sum of currents generated from the front and rear parts of the panel. The value of efficiency of the photovoltaic conversion increases by more than 33% (for *BGE* = 30% as compared to the monofacial cells, at *E* = 1000 W/m^2).

Table 1. Simulation parameters for the LG NeON2 BiFacial LG300N1T-G4 panel.

	E [W/m^2]							
	1000				700		300	
	BGE [%]							
	0	10	20	30	0	20	0	20
Curve on fig.2 and fig.3	A	B	C	D	E	F	G	H
P_{max} [W]	284,57	318,34	347,21	379,78	198,23	241,43	82,09	99,70
I_{MPP} [A]	8,95	9,92	10,82	11,75	6,27	7,58	2,69	3,25
U_{MPP} [V]	31,79	32,09	32,09	32,33	31,61	31,85	30,53	30,71
I_{SC} [A]	9,65	10,68	11,65	12,64	6,76	8,16	2,90	3,50
U_{OC} [V]	40,01	40,13	40,19	40,37	39,23	39,35	37,25	37,37
η [%]	17,35	19,41	21,17	23,16	12,09	14,72	5,01	6,08

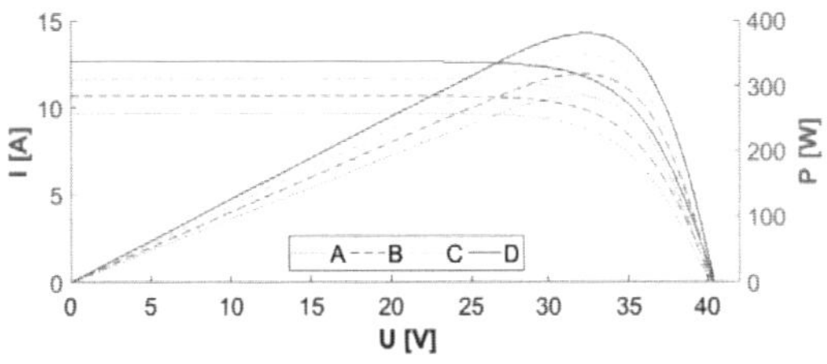

Fig. 2. Current-voltage characteristics and power characteristics of the LG300N1T-G4 bifacial panel for different *BGE* values.

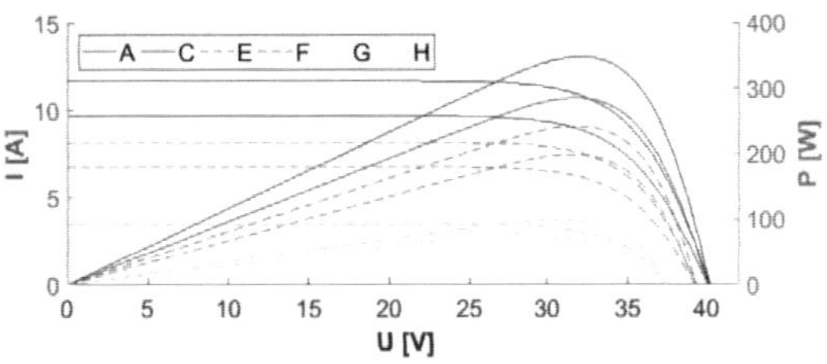

Fig. 3. Current-voltage characteristics and power characteristics of the LG300N1T-G4 bifacial panel for different *BGE* and *E* values.

3 Conclusions

The presented test results and the performed simulations indicate the possibility of obtaining additional energy, by means of photovoltaic bifacial modules in comparison with the monofacial ones. There are relationships between the parameters of the bifacial installation and the annual additional energy yield from a bifacial module. The main parameters which affect the value of *BGE* are: the surface reflection coefficient, i.e. albedo, the angle of inclination of the modules in relation to the surface and the height of the installation.

The use of bifacial cells may reduce the investment costs for PV installations and decrease the demand for the installation surface in view of the achieved higher energy yields as compared to the traditional one-sided PV panels, even up to 15-20% per year.

References

1. A. Cuevas, A. Luque, J. Eguren, J. D. Alamo, Solar Cells **3/4**, 337 (1981)
2. J. E. Castillo-Aguilella, P. S. Hauser, IEEE Access **4**, 498 (2016)
3. G. Frydrychowicz - Jastrzębska, A. Bugała, Energies **8**, 1025 (2015)
4. G. Trzmiel, Eksploat. Niezawodn. **19/4**, 516 (2017)
5. A. Bugała, K. Bednarek, L. Kasprzyk, A. Tomczewski, *International Conference EEMS – Energy, Environment and Material Systems*, (EEMS, E3S Web of Conferences 19, 01002, 2017)
6. D. Głuchy, L. Kasprzyk, Prz. Elektrotech. **93**, 99 (2017)
7. C. Deline, S. MacAlpine, B. Marion, F. Toor, A. Asgharzadeh, J. S. Stein, IEEE Journal of Photovoltaics **7/2**, 575 (2017)
8. D. Kurz, K. Lewandowski, M. Szydłowska, Pozn. Univ. Technol. Acad. J. Electr. Eng. **94**, 215 (2018)
9. C. Erben, J. B. Heng, Z. Xie, J. Fatehi, B. Yang, *42rd IEEE Photovoltaic Specialists Conference,* (PVSC, 1-3, 2015)
10. L. Kreinin, A. Karsenty, D. Grobgeld, N. Eisenberg, *43rd IEEE Photovoltaic Specialists Conference*, (PVSC, 2688-2691, 2016)
11. LG300N1T-G4 panel data sheet: http://www.lg-solar.com/downloads/products/LGE-Data%20Sheet-LG300N1T-G4-EN-08.2016.pdf, access: 04.06.2018

The use of computer simulations and measurements in determining the energy efficiency of photovoltaic installations

Artur Bugała [1,*], and *Karol* Bednarek [1]

[1]Poznan University of Technology, Institute of Electrical Engineering and Electronics, Piotrowo 3a Street, 60-965 Poznań, Poland

Abstract. The paper presents an analysis of the energy efficiency of a photovoltaic installation connected to the AC power grid. Forecasting of energy yield was carried out in two ways: with the use of PVSol software, as well as physical measurements of daily electricity production. On that basis, a statistical correlation between the results obtained from measurements and computer calculations was determined.

1 Introduction

Electricity is used in all areas of human business and private activity, therefore its rational production, storage and use is particularly important [1-3]. Most human activities are carried out in to achieve the best results of taken initiatives due to selected criteria [4-8].Various types of deterministic or stochastic optimization methods are used, as well as computer simulations and physical tests, in order to achieve high efficiency in the field of raw materials and energy management, object sustainability management, quality of supplied energy, check the profitability of undertaken investments or determine the profitability of production [4-14].

The paper deals with determining the energy efficiency of a photovoltaic installations [14-20]. Analyzes in this area were carried out in two ways: on the basis of computer calculations, using PVSol software and on the basis of physical measurements of daily electric energy from photovoltaic conversion [21]. The aim of the considerations is to develop tools (computer simulations) for the implementation of economic calculations and estimation of the return time of investment outlays related to the analysis of the legitimacy of using ecological energy sources.

2 Research object

The research object is a roof photovoltaic micro-installation with a nominal power of 3 kW located 96 km from Poznań in the north-east direction (Wielkopolskie voivodship).

The installation is equipped with 12 PV modules (Yingli Solar model YL250P-29b) with a power of 250 W, arranged in two strings. Photovoltaic modules are inclined at an angle of 30° to the horizontal plane, while the receiver azimuth angle is about 10° (south-west direction). The DC/AC power conversion was carried out using Steca Stecagrid 3000 inverter.

3 Research and simulation results

The on-grid photovoltaic installation was connected to the power grid in 2015 and enables the production of electric energy in the settlement system consisting in its transmission taking into account the energy consumption in a given balancing period. The obligation to purchase electricity arises from the first day of its connection to the distribution network and lasts for the next 15 years.

The presented measurement results, registered using prepared system consisting of a wireless communication gateway, DC/AC inverters, an external data server and a private user profile, are a measurement samples from the period July 2016 – June 2017. In order to compare the measurement results with the estimated values, a computer Valentin PVSol software was used [21, 22]. In order to improve the accuracy of the simulations, data of solar irradiance from the meteorological station located in the city of Piła was implemented.

Figure 1 shows the annual electricity production for the analyzed photovoltaic installation including measurement results and computer simulations.

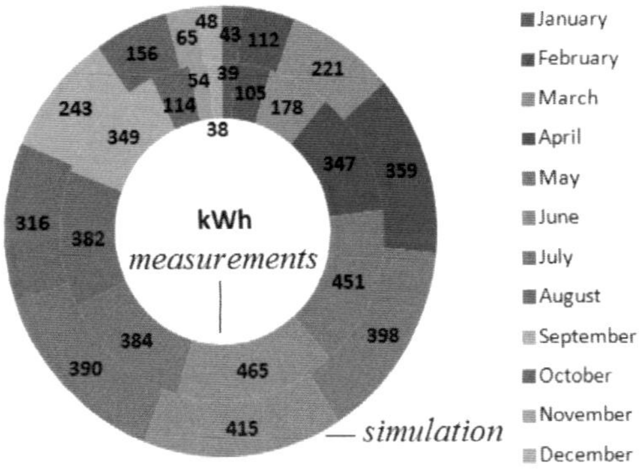

Fig. 1. The annual value of electricity from photovoltaic conversion for an installation with a nominal power of 3 kW.

---
* Corresponding author: artur.bugala@put.poznan.pl

4 Statistical analysis

The assessment of correlation of the measurement results and computer simulation was carried out using selected statistical tools in the form of root mean square error (*RMSE*), mean bias error (*MBE*) and Pearson correlation coefficient *k* [21, 23-26]:

$$RMSE\% = \frac{\sqrt{\frac{\sum (C_i - M_i)^2}{n}}}{\bar{M}} 100\% \quad (1)$$

$$MBE\ \% = \frac{\frac{\sum (C_i - M_i)}{n}}{\bar{M}} 100\% \quad (2)$$

$$k = \frac{\sum_{i=1}^{N} (C_i - \bar{C})(M_i - \bar{M})}{\sqrt{[\sum_{i=1}^{N} (C_i - \bar{C})^2][\sum_{i=1}^{N} (M_i - \bar{M})^2]}} \quad (3)$$

where: M_i – measured value of the electric energy, C_i – calculated value of the electric energy, n – sample size, M – average value of the measured quantity, C – average value of the calculated quantity. The results of the calculations are presented in Table 1.

Table 1. Results of statistical analysis including RMSE%, MBE% and Pearson correlation coefficient.

RMSE%	MBE%	k
[%]	[%]	[-]
21,05	-4,450	0,95

5 Conclusions

In the case of the analyzed installation, the results of the simulation turned out to be beneficial for the investor due to the increased electric energy production in relation to the value assumed at the design stage. The exception are the months of October and March, in which the value of electricity production is about 37% and 24% lower than estimated.

The average value of electricity, determined for a full measurement year, based on the results of measurements and simulation analysis, is respectively 242.2 kWh and 230.5 kWh. Based on the conducted analysis, 4.5% underestimation of the value of electricity in relation to the measured value was observed. The value of the RMSE% parameter, exceeding 21%, indicates the occurrence of months for which there are significant discrepancies between the results of measurements and calculations (May, September, October).

References

1. J. Jajczyk, A. Dobrzycki, M. Filipiak, D. Kurz, E3S Web of Conferences, **19**, 01027 (2017)
2. J. Jurasz, A. Piasecki, E3S Web of Conferences, **14**, 01017 (2017)
3. L. Kasprzyk, Eksploat. Niezawodn. **19**, 229-236 (2017)
4. K. Bednarek, R. Nawrowski, A. Tomczewski, *International Conference on Parallel Computing in Electrical Engineering* (PARELEC, 218-222, 2000)
5. J. Jajczyk, *Computational Problems of Electrical Engineering,* 1-3 (IEEE Xplore, Sandomierz, 2016)
6. L. Kasprzyk, A. Tomczewski, K. Bednarek, Prz. Elektrotechniczny **87/12b**, 82-85 (2011)
7. L. Nowak, Ł. Knypiński, C. Jędryczka, K. Kowalski, COMPEL **34**, 496-504 (2015)
8. R. Wojciechowski, Archives of electrical engineering **65/3**, 601-611 (2016)
9. K. Bednarek, Int. J. Occup. Saf. Ergon. (JOSE) **16**, 357-368 (2010)
10. L. Kasprzyk, A. Tomczewski, K. Bednarek, A. Bugała, E3S Web of Conferences **19**, 01030 (2017)
11. M. Lebioda, J. Rymaszewski, E. Korzeniewska, Journal of Physics Conference Series **494**, 012018 (2016)
12. Ł. Putz, D. Typańska, Prz. Elektrotechniczny **90/3**, 111-114 (2014)
13. J. Szymenderski. D. Typańska, *Computational Problems of Electrical Engineering,* 1-3 (IEEE Xplore, Sandomierz, 2016)
14. G. Trzmiel, Eksploat. Niezawodn. **19**, 516-521 (2017)
15. C. Augustine, M. Nabuchi, The Pacific Journal of Science and Technology **1**, 693-700 (2009)
16. A. Bugała, G. Frydrychowicz-Jastrzębska, D. Janczak, J. Dach, P. Boniecki, *International Multidisciplinary Scientific Geoconference* (SGEM, 337-344, 2016)
17. A. Bugała, G. Frydrychowicz-Jastrzębska, D. Janczak, W. Czekała, J. Dach, M. Zaborowicz, *International Conference on Energy and Environment*, (ICEE, 721-727, 2015)
18. A. Bugała, G. Frydrychowicz-Jastrzębska, Z. Zbytek, J. Dach, D. Janczak, *International Conference on Frontiers of Sensors Technologies* (ICFST, 2016), *MATEC Web of Conferences*, **59** (2016)
19. G. Frydrychowicz-Jastrzębska, A. Bugała, Energies **8/2**, 1025-1041 (2015)
20. D. Głuchy, D. Kurz. G. Trzmiel, Prz. Elektrotech. **90/4**, 78-80 (2014)
21. A. Bugała, K. Bednarek, Pozn. Univ. Technol. Acad. J. Electr. Eng. **94**, 235-244 (2018)
22. www.solargis.info
23. A. Bugała, K. Bednarek, L. Kasprzyk, A. Tomczewski, E3S Web of Conferences, **19**, 01002 (2017)
24. G. S. Maddala, *Ekonometria* (PWN, W-wa, 2014)
25. M. Sobczyk, *Statystyka* (PWN, Warszawa, 2016)
26. A. Zeliaś, *Metody statystyczne*, (PWE, W-wa, 2000)

Active and reactive power regulation in doubly fed asynchronous generator

Cezary Jędryczka[1,*], *Jacek* Prościak[1]

[1]Poznan University of Technology, Institute of Electrical Engineering and Electronics, ul. Piotrowo 3a, 60—965 Poznan, Poland

Abstract. The paper deals with active and reactive power regulation in doubly fed induction generator (DFIG) installed in the wind energy conversion system (WECS). The mathematical model of the studied machine has been proposed and suited for implementation of the field oriented control algorithm (FOC). The control strategy for decoupling the active and reactive power regulation has been proposed and implemented in Matlab/Simulink environment. Selected results of simulations have been presented and discussed.

1 Introduction

Increasing global energy consumption and conscious about environmental impact and the depleting reservoirs of fossil fuels are the driving force of progress in exploitation of renewable power resources. The number installed and operated WECS is continuously rising. Nevertheless the exploitation of the wind power is connected with problems of the power system stability and energy quality [1, 2]. As the percentage of WECS power starts to be remarkable against other sources in the power systems the methods of controlling of active and reactive power generated by WECS are imminent need [2].

Due to the improved power quality, lower cost of power electronic converter, high energy efficiency and controllability the variable speed wind turbines with DFIG are consequently used as an alternative to the direct drive turbines using permanent magnet synchronous generators (PMSG). The WECS with DFIG has been schematically illustrated in Fig. 1.

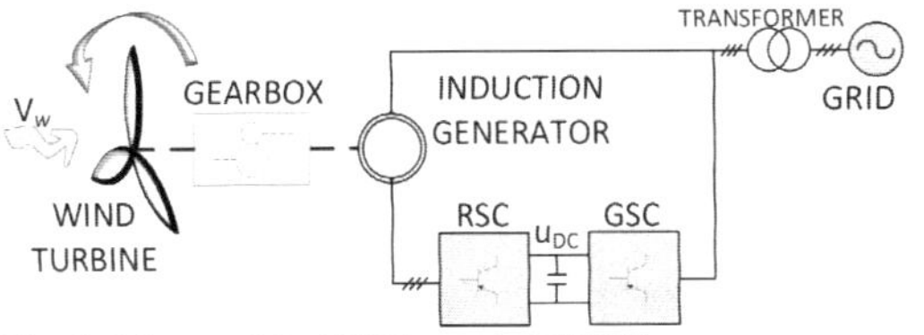

Fig. 1. Scheme of the DFIG operated WECS.

As stated above one of the crucial advantages of using DFIG in WECS is controllability. By changing frequency of currents in the rotor windings such system can operate in wide range of the turbine speed. Taking into account that most of the high power wind turbines are equipped with blade pitch control system the application of DFIG allows to optimize the system efficiency in wide range of the wind speeds using complex maximum power point tracking (MPPT) algorithms [3]. Moreover, in contrast to PMSG operated WECS the power controllability is achieved by power electronic converters of fairly low power rating about 20 to 30% of total machine power.

2 Model of DFIG operated WECS

There are number of approaches of different computational complexity and accuracy which have been utilized for modeling of DFIG operated WECS [1-5]. Most of them concern electromagnetic models including power electronics converters which are suitable for the detailed study of the power conversion system and its control strategies.

This paper proposes a simplified model of DFIG operated WECS including the wind turbine model, mechanical equilibrium equation, electromagnetic model of the DFIG and power control system. The grid and rotor power electronic converters (GSC and RSC in Fig. 1, respectively) are simulated in simplified manner i.e. as a ideal voltage source controlling the rotor current and frequency according to known orientation of the stator flux. The developed model of the machine and control system of DFIG operated WECS has been schematically illustrated in Fig. 2. Detailed description of the developed model has been discussed in [4].

3 Active and reactive power control

Elaborated model has been supplemented by the control system consisting of Power and Current controllers, respectively.

* Corresponding author: cezary.jedryczka@put.poznan.pl

https://doi.org/10.1051/itmconf/20181901022

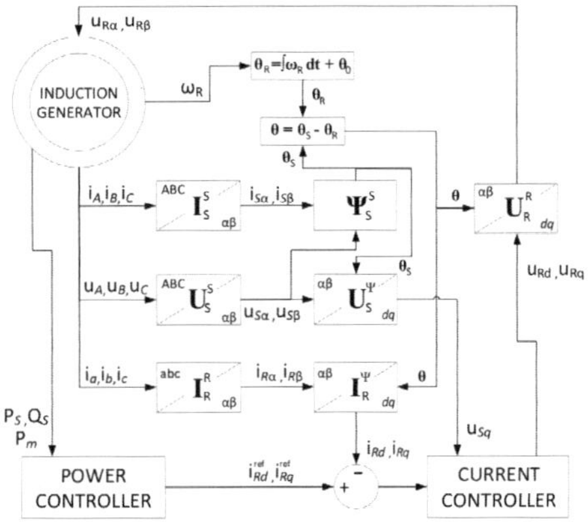

Fig. 2. Scheme of the developed model and control system.

The diagram of Power controller and Current controller has been shown in Fig. 3a, 3b and 3c, respectively.

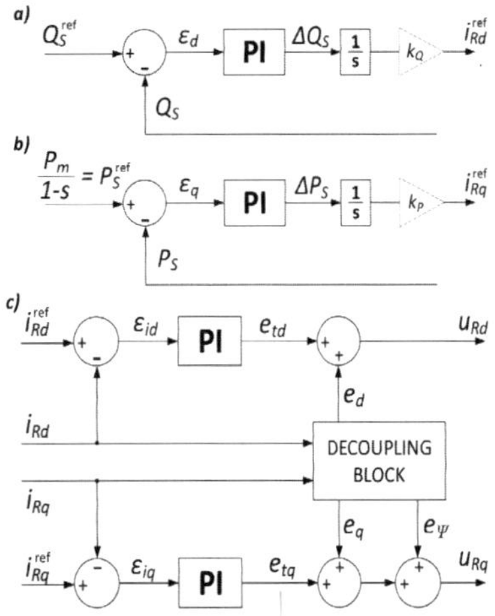

Fig. 3. Block diagrams of Power controller (a, b) and Current controller (c).

The current controller consists of decoupling block allowing for independent control of direct and quadrature currents [4, 5]. The active power controller has been tested for operation of WECS at different wind speeds assuming constant blade pitch angle of the turbine. The reference and response signal of the active power at forced wind speed waveform (green curve) has been shown in Fig 4.

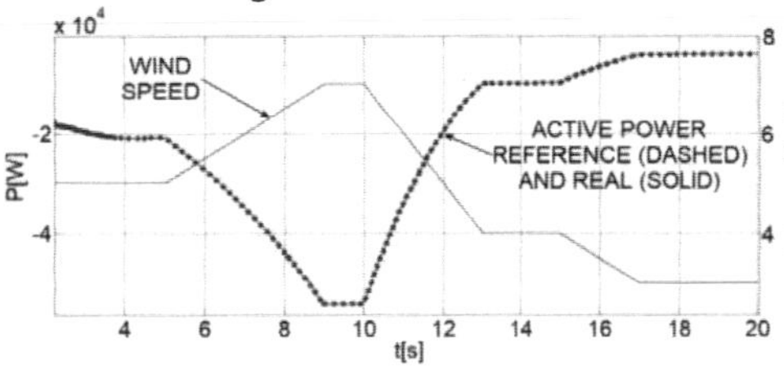

Fig. 4. Simulation results for active power controller.

The reactive power controller has been validated for the test reference signal shown in Fig 5. Additionally rotor power and rotor currents have been presented in Fig. 6. to illustrate response of machine for power control at transition from sub- to super-synchronous speed.

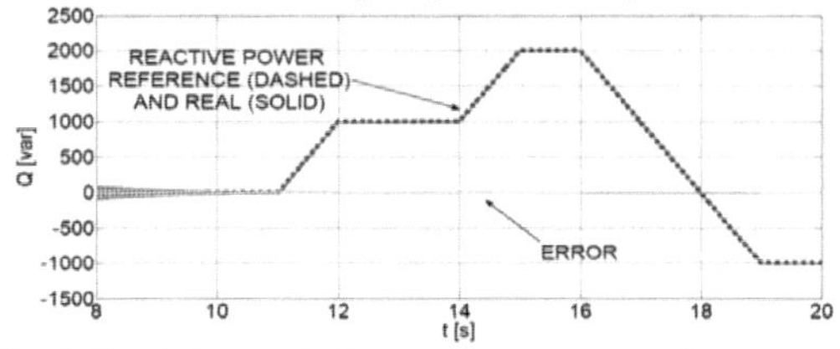

Fig. 5. Simulation results for reactive power controller.

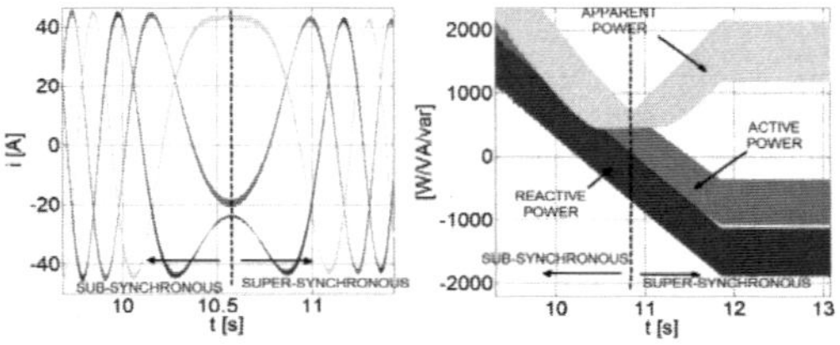

Fig. 6. Simulation results for sub- to super-synchronous operation moment – rotor currents (left), rotor power (right).

4 Conclusions

This paper discuss a simplified model of DFIG operated WECS including the wind turbine model, mechanical equilibrium equation, electromagnetic model of the DFIG and power control system.

Active power of the DFIG system depends on machine torque and rotor speed, whereas reactive power of the DFIG can be in independently controlled by core magnetization. Comprehensive power control is achieved by controlling machine electromagnetic torque and machine flux by rotor current space vector in quadrature axis and direct axis respectively, in reference to the stator flux. The DFIG can operate in both, sub- and super-synchronous modes. During transition between those modes the change of energy flow direction through rotor windings and reverse rotor currents phase shifting can be observed.

The capability of DFIG system to produce controllable active and reactive power is beneficial in terms of optimal wind energy conversion and power grid supporting during the disturbances.

References

1. Y. Lei, A. Mullane, G. Lightbody, R. Yacamini, IEEE Trans. on Energy Conversion **21**, 257-264 (2006)
2. H. Xu, X. Ma, D. Sun, Jour. of Power El. **15**, 235-245 (2015)
3. L. Sun, Z. Mi, Y. Yu, T. Wu, H. Tian, SUPERGEN '09,1-6 (2009)
4. C. Jędryczka, J. Prościak, Pozn. Univ. Technol. Acad. J. Electr. Eng. **94**, 26 (2018)
5. HC. Chen, PH. Chen, Appl. Math. Inf. Sci. **8**, 117-124 (2014)

* Corresponding author: cezary.jedryczka@put.poznan.pl

Comparison of different configurations of the solar and wind power supply system with energy storage using Matlab

Damian Głuchy[1], *Tomasz* Jarmuda[1,*], *Andrzej* Tomczewski[1]

[1]Poznan University of Technology, Piotrowo 3A, 60-965 Poznan, Poland

Abstract. In the study the hybrid model of the solar and wind power supply system with electrochemical energy storage developed in MATLAB & SIMULINK and MS Visual Studio environments was presented. Simulation tests of the system with rated power of 60 kW were conducted in different configurations of connections with the receiver with the set load characteristics. For each configuration of the system the length of periods with no power supply of the receiver was calculated along with the value of the energy consumed and given to the power grid in the case of application of the electrochemical storage and its lack.

1 Introduction

Generation of electrical energy in the systems using a single wind or solar source has a stochastic character resulting from the randomly changing weather conditions. One of the ways of mitigating a restless character of their operation is the application of hybrid systems with energy storage. Electrochemical storage systems are the most popular among them due to big energy density and simple use.

2 Modelling of a Hybrid System

The analysis of operation of the hybrid system requires development of its mathematical and numerical model. It is also significant for the model to combine two characteristics: accuracy relevant for the scientific tests and considerable speed of calculations connected with the use of great number of input data (irradiation time series and wind speed) [1, 2].

PV module models (2-diode model), wind turbines (discrete power characteristics) and electrochemical storage system (circuit model with one RC branch) [3, 4] were developed in Matlab and MS Visual Studio environments. Values of instantaneous power supplied from the hybrid source were calculated and included in the load curve using measurement data of irradiation and wind speed from a specific location. On that basis the periods of energy deficit were determined (energy intake from the storage or from the power system) along with the periods of overproduction (storage of energy in the energy storage system or its introduction to network) [5, 6, 7, 8].

3 Simulation of Hybrid System Operation under Real Load

The hybrid system with the total power of 60 kW constructed of PV modules type BVM6612P 310 W manufactured by Boviet and Excel 10 wind turbines manufactured by Bergey Windpower Company in three configurations was subject to simulation tests (Table 1).

Table 1. Variants of connection configurations of the solar and wind hybrid system with the power of 60 kW.

Name	Wind turbines section			PV modules section		
	No. of elem.	Power [kW]	Section power [kW]	No. of elem.	Power [W]	Section power [kW]
PV30 TW30	3	10.0	30.0	97	310.0	30.1
PV20 TW40	2	10.0	20.0	129	310.0	40.0
PV40 TW20	4	10.0	40.0	65	310.0	20.2

Load characteristics corresponds to the load curve of the office facility in which the increase in the demand for energy is visible in the afternoon hours. Assuming the identical character of load for the whole year, the annual demand for electrical energy amounts to about 58.9 MWh.

Lithium-ion storage with the capacity of 30 kAh was used in the system, which enables accumulation of energy equalling the average 16-hour demand of the implemented load. It was assumed that the storage operates in constant ambient temperature, close to the rated value, while the phenomenon of self-discharge of the cell and the memory effect were disregarded. The developed model of the tested system was presented in Figure 1.

Figure 2 presents the resultant power changes of PV30TW30 variant for the hybrid system (sum of solar and wind section power) and load of 8 January 2011.

* Corresponding author: tomasz.jarmuda@put.poznan.pl

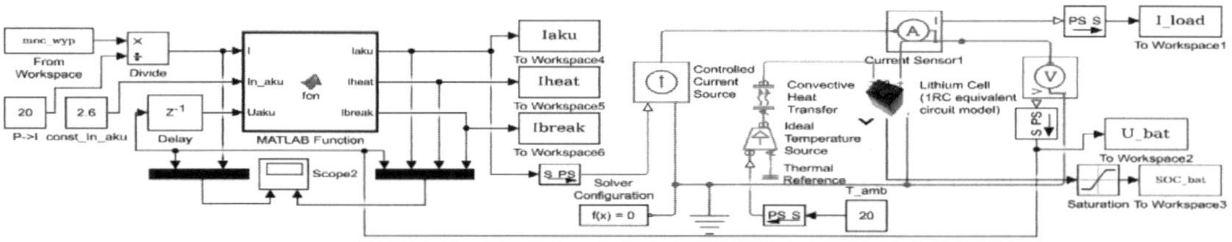

Fig. 1. The MATLAB & SIMULINK model of the controller and the energy storage cooperating with the hybrid power generation.

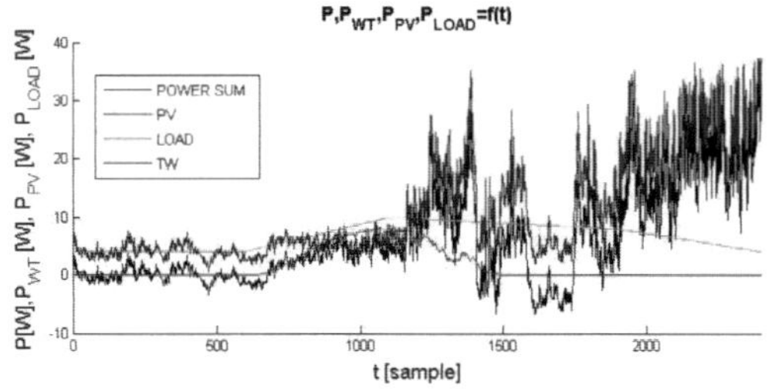

Fig. 2. Power changes: generated, load and resultant for the analysed system for measurement data of 08.01.2011.

Table 2 presents the results of simulation of the operation of the hybrid system conducted for three configurations of its connections. The prepared results cover the annual value: energy generated from wind turbines and photovoltaic modules, energy deficit and time of energy deficit for the system with the switched on energy storage and without the energy storage. The calculations were conducted with reference to the annual demand for electrical energy (58.9 MWh) resulting from the assumed load curve.

Table 2. Specification of generated energy and periods with energy deficit for three configuration variants.

	PV30 TW30	PV20 TW40	PV40 TW20
Energy WT [MWh]	38.67	51.55	25.78
Energy PV [MWh]	32.23	21.60	42.87
Energy balance [MWh]	11.91	14.16	9.65
Total energy taken from the grid without energy storage [MWh]	-20.65	-20.65	-21.98
Total energy supplied to the grid without energy storage [MWh]	32.56	34.81	31.63
Total period of energy deficit without energy storage [days]	218.60	218.60	228.60
Total energy taken from the grid **with energy storage** [MWh]	-9.02	-10.63	-9.15
Total energy supplied to the grid **with energy storage** [MWh]	19.26	25.03	18.94
Total period of energy deficit **with energy storage** [days]	85.80	103.79	86.89

4 Summary

On the basis of the results of the conducted simulations it may be found that the application of the hybrid system increases the stability and reliability of electrical energy production compared to the wind and solar systems that work independently. In the considered example, depending on the selected variant, the annual demand of 58.9 MWh was covered from the system with the power of 60 kW (without storage), obtaining the energy overproduction within the scope from 16 to 24%. However, these values do not reflect local energy deficits that last for as long as 220 days during the year. At the same time, during the year it was necessary to supply almost 35 MWh to the power grid during the periods of overproduction and take 20 MWh from the grid during the energy deficit periods for PV20TW40 variant.

Adding the energy storage allowed to improve the properties of operation of the hybrid system. In the considered case this allowed to shorten total period of energy deficit to 85 days. The use of energy storage allowed to reduce the amount of energy supplied to the power grid by 28% (25 MWh) and taken from the grid by 48% (10 MWh) in the worst from the considered configurations, that is PV20TW30. In the best case (PV40TW20), the energy balance was improved by 40% (9 MWh) and 58% (19 MWh), respectively.

From the conducted simulations it clearly follows that the use of energy storage for hybrid systems results in reduction of energy flow between the wind and solar sources, receiver and the power grid. This enables better local use of energy from renewable energy sources, with simultaneous shedding of the power grid, which is connected with the increase in the installation costs.

References

1. A. Tomczewski, The Scientific World Journal, Article ID 643769, 16 pages (2014)
2. D. Głuchy, L. Kasprzyk, Prz. Elektrotech. **12**, 99–102 (2017)
3. G. Trzmiel, Eksploat. Niezawodn. **19 (4)**, 516–521 (2017)
4. L. Kasprzyk, A. Tomczewski, K. Bednarek, A. Bugała, *International Conference Energy, Environment and Material Systems*, 91–92 (2017)
5. L. Kasprzyk, Eksploat. Niezawodn. **19 (2)**, 229–236 (2017)
6. S. S. Singh, E. Fernandez, Energy **143,** 719–731 (2018)
7. U. Akram, M. Khalid, S. Shafiq, IET Renewable Power Generation **12 (1)**, 72–80 (2018)
8. U. Westerhoff, K. Kurbach, F. Lienesch, M. Kurrat, Energy Technology **4**, 1620–1630 (2016)

* Corresponding author: tomasz.jarmuda@put.poznan.pl

Development time for initiating the mechanisms of electrical breakdown in vacuum

Grzegorz Twardosz[1,*], *Władysław Opydo*[2], and *Kazimierz Bieliński*[2]

[1]Poznan University of Technology, ul. Piotrowo 3A, 60-965 Poznań, Poland
[2]UTP University of Science and Technology in Bydgoszcz, Al. prof. S. Kaliskiego 7, 85-796 Bydgoszcz, Poland

Abstract. The paper presents the development time of the slowest basic physical phenomena occurring in the mechanisms initiating the electrical breakdown in vacuum. The phenomena mentioned above are for the most part decisive for the delay in initiating the electrical breakdown.

1 Introduction

In order to initiate and develop an electrical breakdown in the high voltage vacuum-insulation system, the following conditions must exist [1]: electrons or other carriers of electric charge must be introduced into the inter-electrode space and a sufficient amount of gas or vapour particles must appear in that space, which, after ionization, will cause an increase in the value of current until short-circuit conditions are created. Here, an important role is played by several physical phenomena, which initiate the breakdown by interacting with each other. Some of these phenomena take place relatively slowly and their duration is much longer than that of others. Thus, they determine the delay in the occurrence of an electrical breakdown. Such a delay causes differences between the electric strengths of the vacuum-insulation system at d.c. voltage, a.c. voltage or surge voltage.

Hypotheses for mechanisms initiating the electrical breakdown in vacuum may be categorised as follows [1]:

1. Hypotheses which assume the field emission of an electron beam by the microprotrusion of a cathode, whereby the said electron beam bombards a certain part of the anode area.
2. Hypotheses which assume the motion of small charged lumps of material – micro-particles – through an inter-electrode gap under the influence of the electric field.
3. Hypotheses which assume the occurrence of a layer of adsorbed gases on the internal surfaces of the vacuum-insulation system. The discharge develops in gases desorbed from these surfaces.

2 Basic dependencies

The hypotheses for mechanisms initiating the electrical breakdown through field emission of electrons may, in turn, be divided into two groups. In the first group, it is believed that the determinant initiating the breakdown is the resistance heating of the microprotusion which emits the electron beam (the cathode mechanism), and in the second group, the heating of the anode area bombarded with the electron beam (the anode mechanism). The heating processes which are present here are characterised by the longest duration in the mechanisms initiating the electrical breakdown.

Dependencies of time constants of the heating of microprotrusions made of steel, copper or aluminium, with the shape of a truncated cone finished with a spherical cap, having three different values of the form factor, defined as the quotient of the value of microprotrusion base radius and the spherical cap radius which constitutes its finishing, that is: $g = r_p/r$, are presented in Fig. 1 [2].

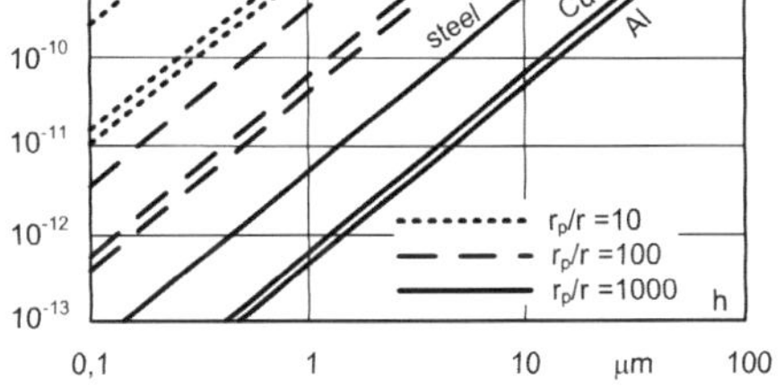

Fig. 1. Dependency of time constants for the heating of steel, copper or aluminium microprotrusions and the height of microprotrusions with different values of the form factor $g = r_p/r$ amounting to 10, 100 and 1000 [2]

* Corresponding author: grzegorz.twardosz@put.poznan.pl

On the other hand, the dependencies of the time constants of the heating of the anode area (made of aluminium, steel and copper) bombarded with the electron beam, on the values of voltage at terminals of the vacuum-insulation system are presented in Fig.2 [1].

Micro-unevenness of the electrode surface of the high-voltage insulation system or a small lump of material, i.e. a micro-particle on that surface, with voltage at the system terminals, has a certain electric charge. Thus, it is affected by the electrostatic force, which may detach it from the electrode and cause its motion towards the opposite electrode. The effects of the motion of the micro-particles between the electrodes of the vacuum insulation system and their hitting against the surface of the opposite electrode have become the basic phenomena in several hypotheses regarding the initiation of the electrical breakdown in vacuum [1].

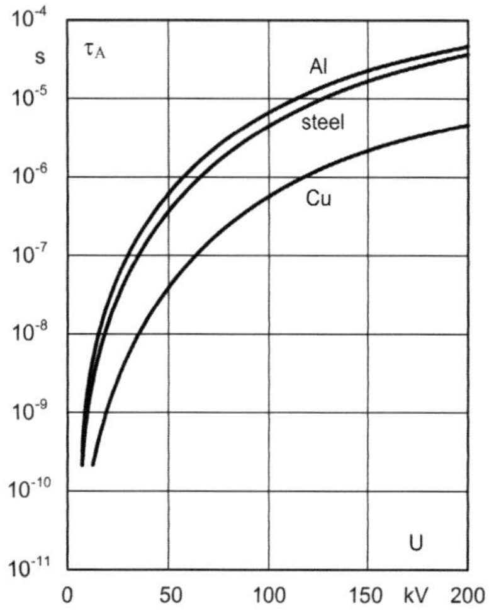

Fig. 2. Dependency of the time constants for the heating of the anode area (made of aluminium, steel or copper) bombarded with an electron beam, on the values of voltage at terminals of the vacuum-insulation system [1]

The delay time in the occurrence of the electrical breakdown in the vacuum insulation system, initiated by a micro-particle, is mainly caused by the time of its motion between the system electrodes. This time is much longer than that of other physical phenomena which the micro-particle initiates.

Based on work [2], calculations of the time of motion of spherical micro-particles made of copper and aluminium through a 5 mm vacuum gap were performed. The calculations were performed for 50 kV and 100 kV voltages. They demonstrated that in the case of the 50 kV voltage, the time of motion of copper micro-particles with radii of 0.1 μm, 1 μm and 10 μm was 45 μs, 143 μs and 452 μs respectively, and in the case of similar aluminium micro-particles – 25 μs, 79 μs and 250 μs.

In the year 1966, Tarasova [3] formulated the hypothesis regarding the desorption mechanism of initiating the electrical breakdown in vacuum. In that hypothesis, she concluded that at the pressure of 10^{-2} … 10^{-5} Pa, the surfaces of electrodes of the insulation system are covered with a layer of adsorbed gases. Under the influence of high voltage, neutral particles and ions are desorbed from these surfaces. At a certain number of gas particles in the inter-electrode space, ionization and discharge development take place.

The likelihood of occurrence of this mechanism is reduced with the removal of adsorbed surface gases and pollution from system electrodes in the conditioning process. The time of the repeated total coverage of the vacuum-clean surface with the monomolecular layer of main air components – nitrogen and oxygen, may be determined based on the formula [4]

$$\tau_c \approx 4 \cdot 10^{-5}\, T_p^{1/2}\, p^{-1} \quad [\text{s}] \qquad (1)$$

where: T_p – surface temperature in K, p – pressure in Pa.

By means of formula (1), it was calculated that the time of the total coverage of the vacuum-clean surface with the temperature of 300 K, with a monomolecular layer of nitrogen and oxygen at the pressure of 10^{-2} Pa, amounts to about 0.07 s, and at the pressure of 10^{-4} Pa – about 7 s.

3 Conclusions

The following conclusions can be drawn based on the paper:

1. In vacuum insulation systems, with vacuum whose pressure is 10^{-2} … 10^{-4} Pa, tested with surge voltage, the role of the desorption mechanism in initiating the breakdown seems unquestionable.
2. While analysing the options for initiating the breakdown in the vacuum insulation system, at the a.c. voltage, by electron field emission, it is possible to make an attempt at indicating whether the breakdown in the given conditions is initiated by the cathode mechanism (the heating of the microprotrusion which emits an electron beam), or the anode mechanism (the heating of the anode area bombarded with an electron beam).
3. The delay time in the occurrence of the electrical breakdown in the vacuum insulation system, initiated by a micro-particle, is caused mainly by the time of motion of the micro-particle between the electrodes. For instance, at the voltage of 100 kV, the time of motion of spherical copper micro-particles with the radii of 0.1 μm, 1 μm and 10 μm through a 5 mm inter-electrode gap was 23 μs, 72 μs and 226 μs respectively, and in the case of similar aluminium micro-particles – 13 μs, 40 μs and 125 μs.

References

1. W. Opydo, J. Ranachowski, *Właściwości elektryczne próżniowych układów izolacyjnych przy napięciu przemiennym* (WN PWN, Warsaw – Poznan, 1993)
2. G. Twardosz, W. Opydo, K. Bieliński, Pozn. Univ. Technol. Acad. J. Electr. Eng **94**, (2018)
3. L. V. Tarasova, Doklady AN SSSR **167** (1966)
4. A. Hałas, *Technika próżni* (Oficyna Wydawnicza Politechniki Wroclawskiej, Wrocław 2017)

Simulation and experimental model of power electronics UPS converter with the possibility of active parallel compensation

Michał Krystkowiak[1,*], *Łukasz* Ciepliński[1]

[1]Poznan University of Technology, Electrical Department, 60-965 Piotrowo 3a, Poland

Abstract. In the article the elaborated simulation and experimental models of the power electronics UPS converter with the possibility of active parallel compensation were described. The power circuits, control algorithms and the principle of working of presented UPS structure were presented. Also the chosen simulation and experimental results were analyzed.

1 Introduction

The work presents a structure of a power stage and a control system of the one-phase UPS with VFI structure [1], which additionally has an ability to compensate phase shift between fundamental harmonics of the voltage and current in power grid and reduction of higher harmonics generated by other energy loads connected to the common grid's node.

Phase shift compensation for the described UPS depends on the consumption of current with the opposite phase angle in relation to the resultant current drawn by other loads. The function of higher harmonics compensation forces the input current of the UPS to be deformed in the manner that its sum with the currents of the cooperating loads gives the resultant signal, which is characterized by the lowest possible content of undesired harmonics in the considered frequency band.

1.1 Operating principle of the UPS

The block diagram of the system is presented in Fig. 1. The UPS is powered from a power grid together with the other loads. Loads which needed a high parameters supply are powered from the UPS.

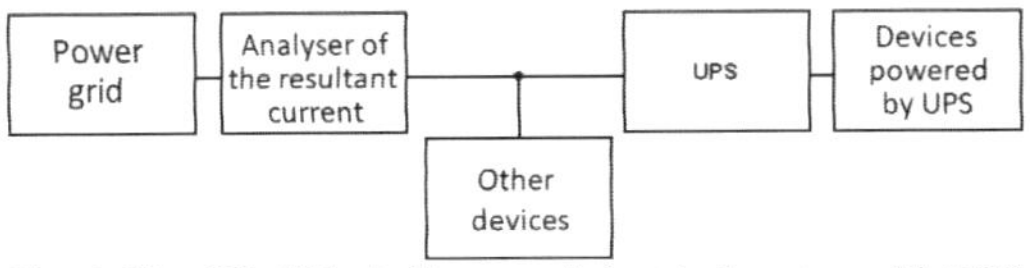

Fig. 1. Simplified block diagram of electrical system with UPS, cooperating with other loads connected to power grid.

The input stage of the UPS was designed on the basis of a fully controllable transistor bridge with an induction filter [2]. The DC/DC impulse converter, which enables the charging of a battery pack, is based on the DC/DC BUCK converter [3]. The output module operates as a closed-loop control system and worked as a controlled voltage source. The block diagram of the UPS with VFI structure is presented in Fig.2.

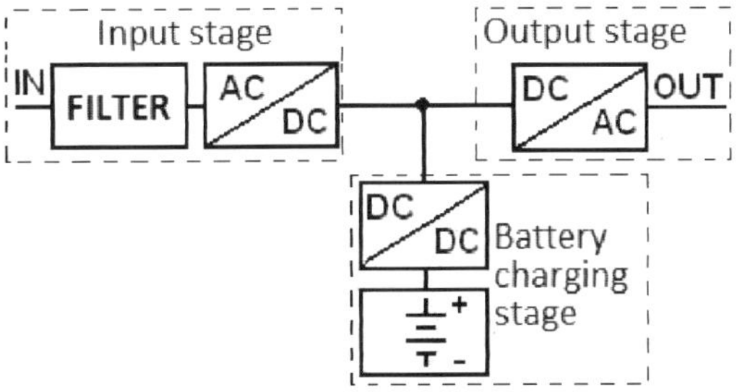

Fig. 2. Block diagram of the UPS based on VFI structure.

2 Structure of the UPS input stage

2.1. Simulation model

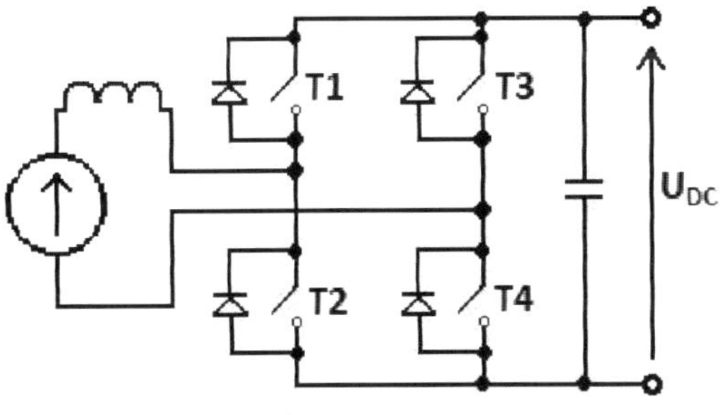

Fig. 3. Diagram of UPS input stage.

The task of the UPS input stage in the described solution is stabilization of the voltage on the DC bus and active phase shift and higher harmonics compensation of the resultant grid current.

The proposed solution does not need to use additional modules in the form of passive or active filters to improve the quality of the grid current [4, 5].

* Corresponding author: michal.krystkowiak@put.poznan.pl

The block diagram of the control system of the UPS input stage is presented in Fig.4. A master PI voltage regulator on the DC bus was used. As a slave regulator, the PI current regulator was implemented [6].

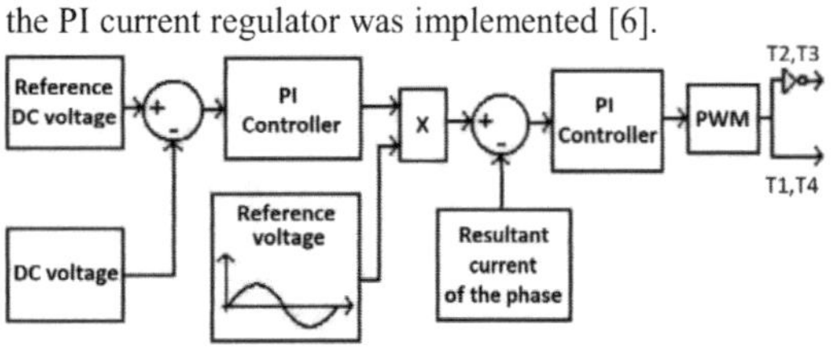

Fig. 4. Block diagram of the control system of the UPS input stage.

2.2 Experimental model

The input stage of the UPS was designed on the basis of ALFINE TIM's P3-5.0/550MFE LABINVERTER [7] with additional input choke. The block diagram of the LABINVERTER is presented in Fig. 5.

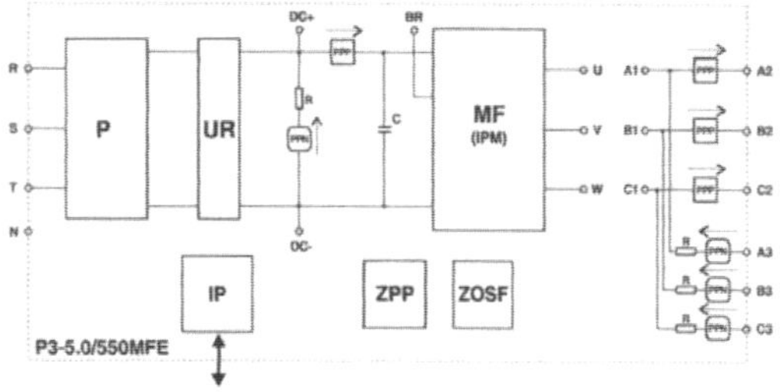

Fig. 5. Block diagram of P3-5.0/550MFE LABINVERTER.

The converter is based on two power electronics components: a three-phase integrated diode rectifier (P) and a 3-phase intelligent power module with Mitsubishi's PM50RSA120 IGBT keys, which is a component of the voltage inverter (MF) module. The input rectifier (P) was not used during the implementation of the laboratory model, just like the system (UR), which enabling pre-charging of the intermediate circuit capacitors. In the analyzed case, one leg of the MF module was not used.

The digital control system for the keys of the transistor rectifier was implemented based on the ALFINE TIM's ALS-G3-1369 evaluation board [8] with the Analog Device's third-generation SHARC signal processor family of type ADSP-21369.

3 Simulation and experimental researches results

Research of the UPS simulation model was carried out in the Matlab environment. A summary of the obtained simulation and experimental research results is presented in Fig. 6 and Fig. 7.

During the initial tests of the physical system, the function of active parallel compensation of the system was deactivated.

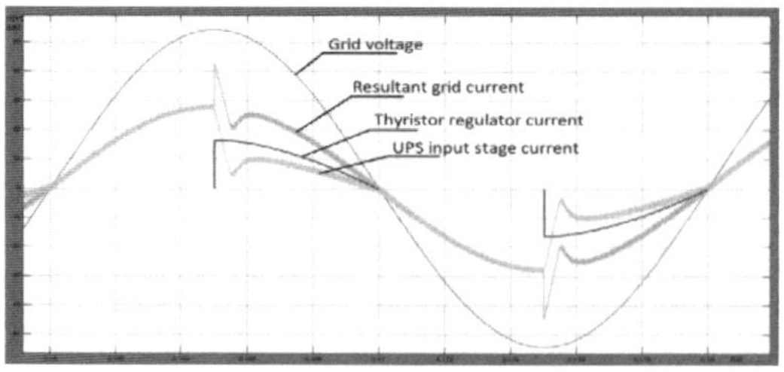

Fig. 6. Currents and voltage in power grid while additional load as thyristor rectifier with resistor at output.

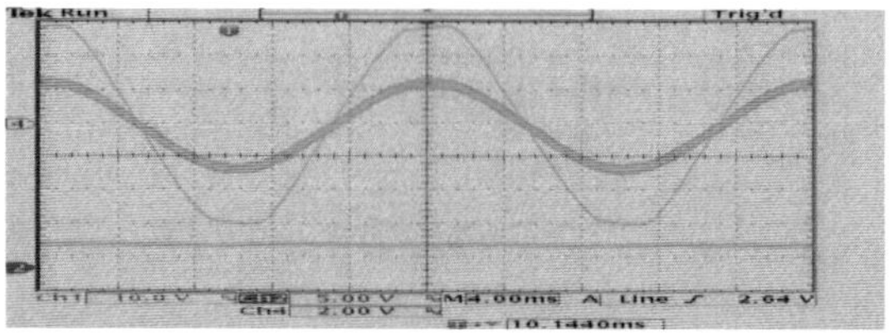

Fig. 7. Grid voltage (yellow signal), rectifier input current (green signal), and DC bus voltage (blue signal).

4 Conclusions

The paper presents the power and control stage of a one-phase UPS converter with the possibility of active parallel compensation. The use of such a solution makes it possible to reduce the investment costs associated with the installation of classic passive filters, or active parallel compensators.

References

1. S. Karve, Three of a kind [UPS topologies, IEC standard], IEE Review **46**, 27-31 (2000)
2. A. Dmowski, Warszawa, Wydawnictwo Naukowo-Techniczne, (1998)
3. K. Bednarek, and L. Kasprzyk, Pozn. Univ. Technol. Acad. J. Electr. Eng. **69**, 199-207 (2012)
4. E.W. Gunther, IEEE Transactions on Power Delivery **10**, 322-329 (1995)
5. F.Z. Peng, H. Akagi, and A. Nabae, IEEE Transactions on Industry Applications **26**, 983-990 (1990)
6. Z. Jędrzykiewicz, *Teoria sterowania układów jednowymiarowych*, (Kraków, Uczelniane Wydawnictwo Naukowo-Techniczne, 2004)
7. datesheet for LABINVERTER, Alfine TIM
8. datesheet for ALS-G3-1369, Alfine TIM

Measurements and calculations of capacitances of BJT and SJT made of silicon carbide

Joanna Szelągowska[1,*] and *Janusz* Zarębski[1]

[1]Gdynia Maritime University, Dept. of Marine Electronics, Morska 83, 81-225 Gdynia, Poland

Abstract. In the paper the results of capacitance-voltage (C-V) characteristics measurements of the current controlled BJT and SJT transistors were presented, for which a programmable measuring system manufactured by Keithley was used. The results of measurements was compared with results of the calculations obtained by using the commonly used Gummel-Poon model. For comparison, the results of the measurements found in the literature and in the datasheets of the considered devices were presented as well. The temperature impact on the shape of the considered characteristics was also investigated.

1 Introduction

The rapid development of electronic technology makes silicon carbide (SiC) one of the most promising materials for producing high power semiconductor devices with relatively short switching times [1,2]. This group of devices includes current controlled transistors such as classic SiC BJT (Bipolar Junction Transistors) offered by TranSiC [3] and modern SJT (Silicon Carbide Junction Transistor) with a relatively high current gain factor, offered since 2011 by GeneSiC [4]. The paper presents the form of the Gummel-Poon model and an evaluation of the accuracy of this model in determining the capacitance-voltage characteristics of arbitrarily selected BJT and SJT made of silicon carbide. The results of the calculations were compared with the results of the measurements. The temperature impact on the shape of considered characteristics was also investigated.

2 Gummel-Poon model form

In practice, modelling characteristics of a current controlled transistors is most often realised by using the Gummel-Poon model [5, 6]. The popularity of this model is evidenced by the fact that the considered model is implemented in many well-known computer programs for analysis of electronic circuits such as SPICE software [7]. Moreover, manufacturers of semiconductor devices usually provide parameter values for the mentioned model in the devices datasheets. The capacitances C_{bc} and C_{be} are responsible for modelling the non-linear capacitances of the base-collector and the base-emitter transistor junctions. The considered capacitances are described as follows [7]:

$$C_{bc}=C_{tbc}+area\cdot XCJC\cdot C_{jbc} \quad (1)$$

$$C_{be}=C_{tbe}+area\cdot \quad (2)$$

A detailed description of the analytical dependencies of the Gummel-Poon model, is available for example in work [7].

3 Results of the measurements and calculations

The paper presents the results of C-V characteristics measurements of the arbitrarily chosen transistors: SiC BJT (BT1206AC) and SJT (2N7635-GA). The measurements were performed using the Keithley 4200-SCS programmable system [8] in a wide range of an ambient temperature. In the case of the SiC BJT, a set of parameter values, obtained during the estimation procedure [9,10], was used in the calculations while in the case of the SJT, the calculations were performed using a set of parameter values, taken from the device datasheet [4]. Figure 1 depicts the $C_{bc}(v_{BC})$ characteristics of the SiC BJT where a filled points represent the results of an author's measurements, an unfilled points represent the results of measurements included in research paper [5] and a solid lines represent the results of calculations using Gummel-Poon model.

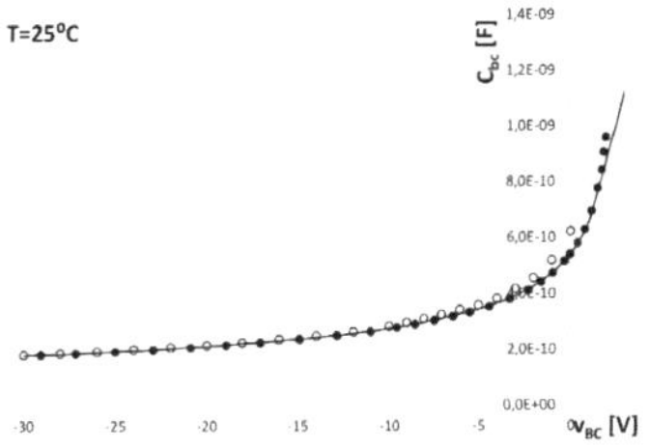

Fig.1. $C_{bc}(v_{BC})$ characteristics of the BT1206-AC transistor at the ambient temperature equal to 25°C.

As seen (Fig. 1), both the qualitative and quantitative agreement of the calculation results and measurements,

[*] Joanna Szelągowska: j.szelagowska@we.am.gdynia.pl

in the v_{BC} voltage range below 1.8 V, was obtained, which proves the high accuracy of the Gummel-Poon model in this operation range. Figure 2 presents the temperature impact on the $C_{bc}(v_{BC})$ characteristics. It turns out that in case of the SiC BJT, the influence of an ambient temperature on the considered C-V characteristic is barely perceptible for the bias in the reverse direction.

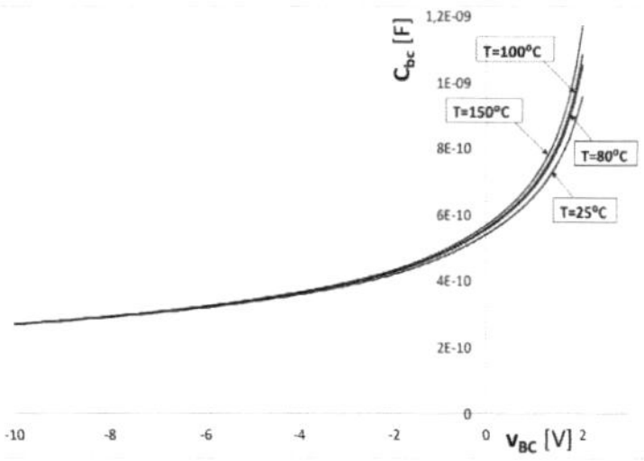

Fig.2. $C_{bc}(v_{BC})$ characteristics of the BT1206-AC transistor in a range of the ambient temperature from 25°C to 100°C.

Figure 3 shows the $C_{iss}(v_{SD})$ and $C_{rss}(v_{SD})$ characteristics of the considered SJT transistor at a fixed value of the base-emitter voltage equal to 0 V. A filled points represent the results of an author's measurements, an unfilled points represent the results of measurements taken from device datasheet [4] and solid lines represent the results of calculations using Gummel-Poon model. The capacitances C_{iss} and C_{rss} are described as follows [4]:

$$C_{iss}=C_{be}+C_{bc} \tag{3}$$

$$C_{rss}=C_{bc} \tag{4}$$

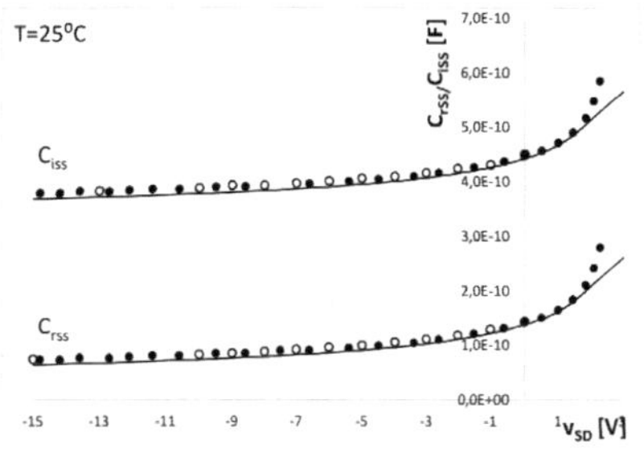

Fig.3. $C_{iss}(v_{SD})$ and $C_{rss}(v_{SD})$ characteristics of the 2N7635-GA transistor at the ambient temperature equal to 25°C.

In the case of presented $C_{iss}/C_{rss}(v_{SD})$ characteristics, a very good agreement between the results of measurements and calculations is observed in the range of v_{SD} voltage below 1.6 V. It confirms that the Gummel-Poon model can be also successfully used for modelling the C-V characteristics of SJTs. The slight temperature effect is visible on considered $C_{iss}/C_{rss}(v_{SD})$ characteristics presented on Figure 4. For example, with the increase of the ambient temperature by 150°C, a value of the C_{rss} capacitance increases for only about 20 pF for the base-collector junction biased in reverse direction and for about 50 pF for the polarity in the direction of conduction.

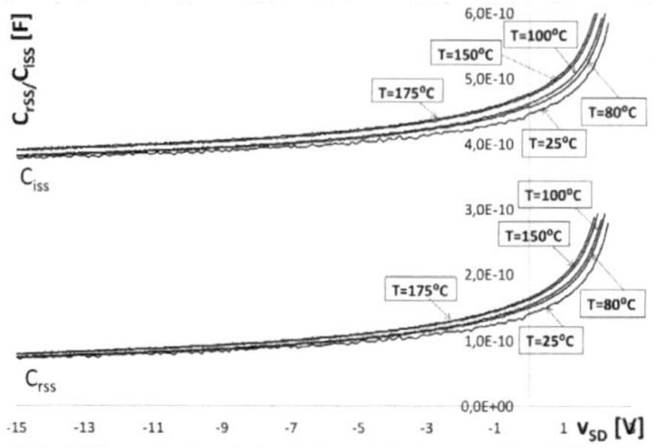

Fig.4. $C_{iss}(v_{SD})$ and $C_{rss}(v_{SD})$ characteristics of the 2N7635-GA transistor in a range of the ambient temperature from 25°C to 175°C.

4 Summary

The presented results of an experimental verification of the Gummel-Poon model show a very good agreement between the results of the measurements and calculations of C-V characteristics, which means that the considered model can be successfully used to model these characteristics for both considered classes of transistors. In addition, the ambient temperature has a small impact on capacitance-voltage characteristics of the SiC BJT and SJT. Moreover, the measured capacitances between the base and emitter and between the base and collector of the SJT junctions have a several times lower values in comparison with the values of considered SiC BJT capacitances which means that the SJT transistors can potentially be used in systems operating at higher signal frequencies.

References

[1] K. Bargieł, J. Zarębski and D. Bisewski, *SPICE-aided modelling of high-voltage silicon carbide JFETs*, 39th International Microelectronics and Packaging, (2015)

[2] K. Bargieł, D. Bisewski, *Modelling of silicon carbide JFET in SPICE*, 41st International Microelectronics and Packaging Poland, (2017)

[3] http://www.dacpol.eu

[4] http://www.genesicsemi.com

[5] Y. Huang, S. Cheng, W. Zhou, K. Sheng, *Modeling of a 1200 V 6 A SiC BJT*, Energy Conversion Congress and Exposition, (2013)

[6] J. Patrzyk, *Modelowanie tranzystorów mocy*, SJ GMU **95**, 168-176 (2016)

[7] PSPICE A/D Reference Guide Version 15.7

[8] http://tespol.com.pl

[9] D. Bisewski, *Estimation of parameters of GaAs and SiC MESFETs using genetic algorithm*, 45th International Conference on Microelectronics, Devices and Materials, 81-84 (2009)

[10] D. Bisewski, *Parameters estimation of SPICE models for silicon carbide devices*, 21st European Microelectronics and Packaging Conference (EMPC) & Exhibition, 1-4 (2017)

https://doi.org/10.1051/itmconf/20181901027

Evaluation of accuracy of SiC-JFET macromodel

Kamil Bargieł[*], *Damian* Bisewski

Gdynia Maritime University , Department of Marine Electronics, Morska 83-87 Gdynia, Poland

Abstract. In the paper, the results of experimental verification of the macromodel of UJN1208K JFET transistor made of silicon carbide fabricated by United Silicon Carbide, are presented. The macromodel form dedicated for PSPICE program is available on the manufacturer's website. The accuracy of the macromodel have been evaluated by comparison of selected calculated and measured static characteristics and C-V characteristics of the considered transistor. The influence of ambient temperature on the characteristics of the transistor has been evaluated, as well.

1 Introduction

Over recent years, technological progress in the field of semiconductor devices design has resulted in the appearance on the market of modern semiconductor power devices made of silicon carbide. This development trend also applies SiC-JFETs (Silicon Carbide Junction Field-Effect Transistors) often used in e.g. power electronics systems for generation and conversion of electrical energy [1-4].

Currently, in the process of designing and analysing of electronic circuits, appropriate computer programs containing reliable models of electronic components, are needed. In recent years, SPICE (Simulation Program with Integrated Circuit Emphasis) [5] has commonly been used as a comfortable CAD tool for the analysis of electronic circuits. A large number of passive and active devices models are built-in in SPICE, including a modified Shichman-Hodges [6] model of JFET.

On the other hand, semiconductor devices models (so-called macromodels) developed by manufacturers, are available, as well. A macromodel is formulated as an independent sub-circuit and contains e.g. SPICE built-in model, additional current or voltage controlled sources described by a suitable set of analytical dependencies, as well as additional passive devices [7].

In the paper, the form and principle of operation of the SiC-JFET UJN1208K macromodel offered by United Silicon Carbide [8, 9] are discussed. The accuracy of this macromodel was evaluated by comparison of calculated current-voltage and C-V characteristics with the corresponding characteristics included in the datasheet of the transistor. In addition, an influence of the ambient temperature on properties and characteristics of the transistor was investigated.

2 Results of simulations

The results of macromodel characteristics simulations of considered transistor were compared with the results of measurements presented in datasheet [9]. In subchapters 2.1 and 2.2, a current-voltage output characteristics and C-V characteristics of the transistor at different ambient temperatures are presented, respectively. Points denote the results of measurements, whereas the simulation results are denoted by solid lines.

2.1. Current-voltage characteristics

The output characteristics of the SiC-JFET at two arbitrarily chosen ambient temperatures for different values of the gate-source voltage are shown in Fig. 1 and 2.

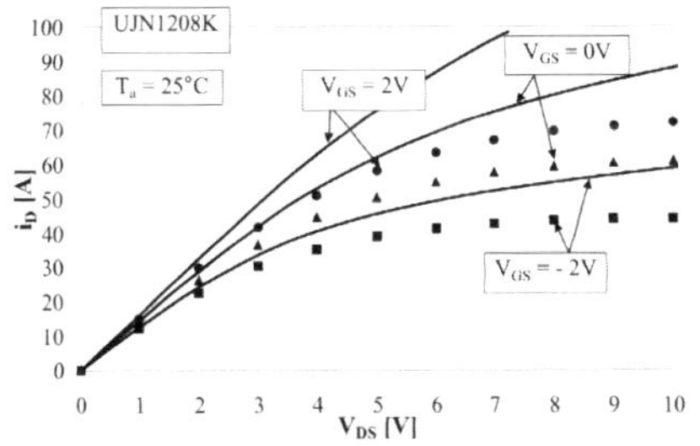

Fig. 1. Calculated and measured output characteristics of the transistor UJN1208K at 25°C.

[*] Corresponding author: k.bargiel@we.am.gdynia.pl

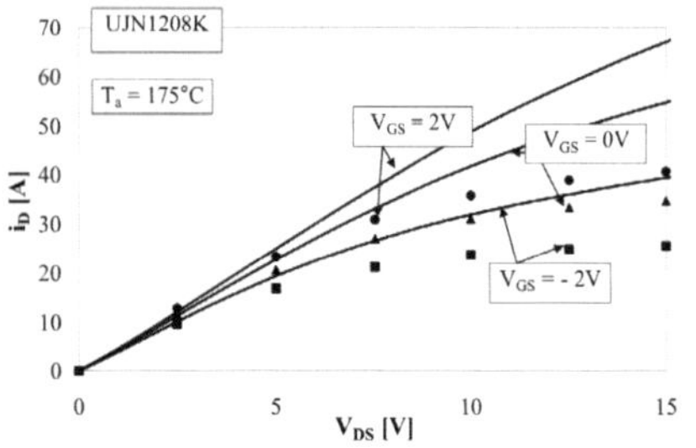

Fig. 2. Calculated and measured output characteristics of the transistor UJN1208K at 175°C.

As seen (Figs. 1 - 2), a good agreement between the results of simulations and measurements were obtained for the drain-source voltage not exceeding approximately 2.5 V at both considered ambient temperatures. For the higher values of the voltage V_{DS}, divergences between simulation and measurement results in the range from about 15% at temperature 25°C to even about 20% at 175°C, are observed, which indicates a high inaccuracy of the considered macromodel.

2.2. C-V characteristics

In the datasheet [9] of investigated transistor, C-V characteristics, such as: the input capacitance $C_{iss}(V_{DS})$, the output capacitance $C_{oss}(V_{DS})$ and the transfer capacitance $C_{rss}(V_{DS})$, are presented. The above mentioned capacitances express a suitable combinations of the transistor internal junction capacitances as follows [10]:

$$C_{iss} = C_{gs} + C_{gd} \tag{1}$$

$$C_{oss} = C_{ds} + C_{gd} \tag{2}$$

$$C_{rss} = C_{gd} \tag{3}$$

where C_{gs} - gate-source capacitance, C_{gd} - gate-drain capacitance, and C_{ds} - drain-source capacitance.

In case of simulations of C-V transistor characteristics, a special calculation circuits dedicated for SPICE [10], are used. An exemplary comparison of calculated and catalogue capacitance characteristics $C_{iss} = f(V_{DS})$ and $C_{rss} = f(V_{DS})$ of the SiC-JFET at fixed value of ambient temperature, are presented in Fig. 3.

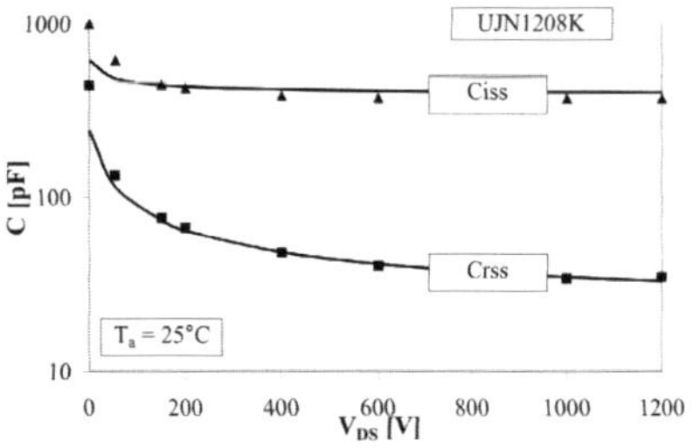

Fig. 3. Calculated and catalogue C-V characteristics of the transistor UJN1208K at 25°C.

As seen, a very good agreement between simulation and measurement results was observed, which proves the high accuracy of the macromodel in the case of transistor capacitance characteristics.

3 Summary

In the paper, evaluation of accuracy of the SiC-JFET macromodel of transistor UJN1208K is presented.

In the case of modelling of current-voltage characteristics, the considered macromodel is characterized by a relatively small accuracy, which leads to quite large discrepancies between the results of calculations and measurements.

On the other hand, a good agreement between the simulation and measurement results of C-V characteristics proves a high accuracy of the macromodel. In turn, the analytical description of the macromodel capacitance can presumably be used for modelling C-V characteristics of other JFETs made of silicon carbide.

References

1. X. Gong, A. Ferreira,. IEEE Energy Conversion Cong. and Exposition, 629-636 (2008)
2. S. Pan, L. Li and Z. Chen, Energy Procedica **16**, 1986-1993 (2012)
3. J. Patrzyk, J. Zarębski and D. Bisewski, *DC characteristics and parameters of silicon carbide high-voltage power BJTs*, 39th International Microelectronics and Packaging, 2015
4. J. Patrzyk, D. Bisewski, *Measurement and simulation of silicon carbide current-controlled transistors*, 41st International Microelectronics and Packaging, 2017
5. PSPICE A/D Reference Guide Version 10.0, Cadence Design Systems Inc., (2003).
6. P. Antognetti, G. Massobrio, *Semiconductor devices modeling with SPICE,* McGraw-Hill, 1988
7. J. Zarębski, D. Bisewski, Elektronika – konstrukcje, technologie, zastosowania **6**, 96-100 (2009)
8. http://unitedsic.com/wp-content/uploads/2016/02/UJN1208K.txt.
9. http://unitedsic.com/wp-content/uploads/2017/01/DS_UJN1208K.pdf.
10. J. Zarębski, D. Bisewski, SJ GMU **59**, 39-49 (2008)

A fast switched reluctance motor controller based on FPGA

Daniel Rataj[1], *Dennis* Slawik[1], *Krzysztof* Wrobel[1,*] and *Krzysztof* Tomczewski[1]

[1]Opole University of Technology, Faculty of Electrical Engineering Automatic Control and Informatics, Opole, Poland

Abstract. The paper presents the concept and practical implementation of a switched reluctance motor control system in an FPGA programmable device. The developed control system was designed for testing high-speed motors in order to limit the delays of output signals in relation to the signals from the encoder. The controller enables the values of commutation angles and PWM voltage to be set along with current limit values, measures the values of voltages and currents, and sends the results to the computer to be archived.

1 Introduction

Drives with switched reluctance motors (SRM) are characterised by a constant torque value over a wide speed range. However, achieving a high level of efficiency over the entire speed range requires the adjustment of commutation conditions to the machine's operating point [1]. Optimal relationships between rotational speed and commutation angles can be calculated using a mathematical model of the drive. The practical implementation of these relationships for high-speed drives is difficult, requiring the precise setting of output signals vs rotor position angle. Due to the rotor's high speed, the control system can cause delays resulting from the time required for calculations [2]. Therefore, when receiving high-frequency signals from the encoder, it may be necessary to limit their resolution. To avoid this, it is necessary to limit signal processing time; this is possible using hardware rather than software solutions.

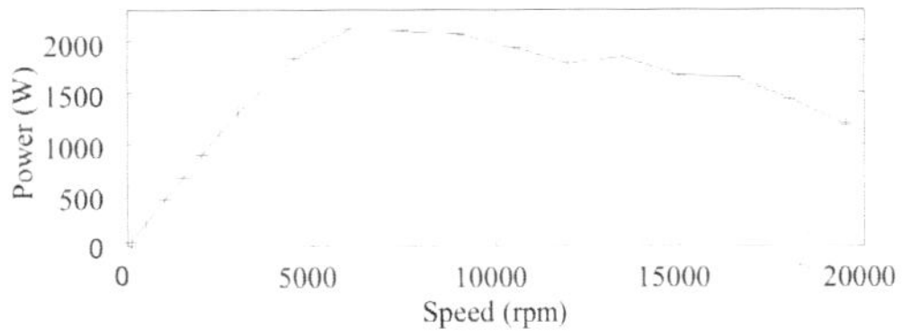

Fig. 1. The characteristics of the tested drive system as obtained from the simulation.

Determining the rotor position angle with an accuracy of 0.25 degree, at the maximum speed of the rotor, requires the calculation of outputs states at a frequency of 432 kHz. The execution time of the control algorithm must not exceed 2.3 μs. The proposed control system was based on an FPGA programmable device. FPGA topology is designed for concurrent execution of multiple tasks [3, 4].

2 SRM motor

The developed control system was designed mainly for testing a two-phase SRM drive, which had been optimised in terms of electromagnetic torque characteristics. The rotor of this motor is characterised by a non-cylindrical shape. The surface of the rotor teeth is described by 15 arches. The basic motor parameters are as follows: outer diameter of the stator magnetic circuit, 120 mm; package length, 80 mm; air gap diameter, 34.3 mm.

The characteristics of a drive with this motor obtained from the calculations are shown in Figure 1. According to the results of the simulation, the motor can operate over a speed range up to 18.000 rpm. In order to take measurements of its characteristics over the full speed range, it is necessary to minimise the time required to determine output signals.

3 Control system topology

For the implementation of the control system, an Xilinx Artix-7 FPGA was used. The system enables the control of machines from 2 to 6 phases, and contains two main modules: control and measurement. The former carried out the motor control and user interface functions. The latter performed measurements of currents and voltages during the control process; at the same time, this module transmitted the measurement results to a computer via a USB interface. The computer program archives the results of measurements in a text file. Descriptions of the basic controller structures were made using the VHDL language in the Xilinx ISE environment; the control system synthesis was performed in the Schematics module. The control module includes a user interface block with a serial menu which used a four-button keyboard and an alphanumeric display.

* Corresponding author: k.wrobel@po.opole.pl

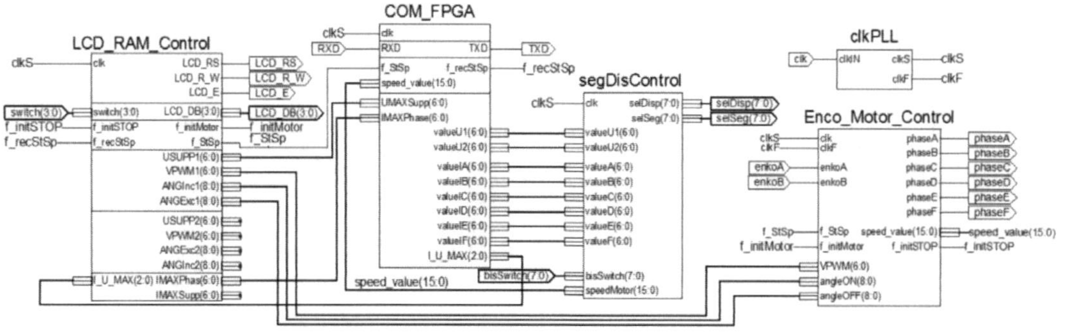

Fig. 2. Control module topology.

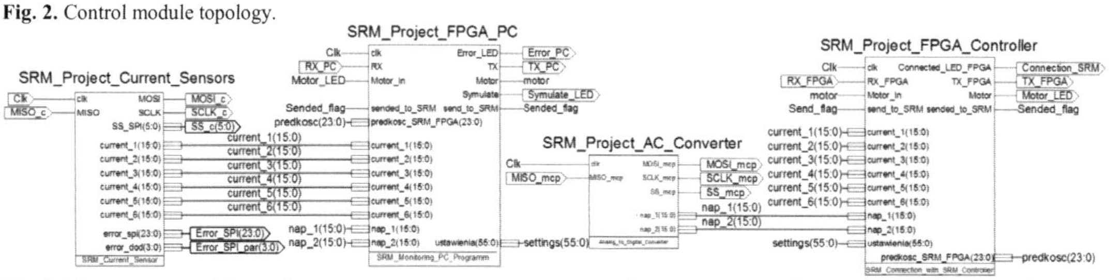

Fig. 3. Measurement module topology.

Due to the relatively large amount of data needed to operate the display, this module mainly uses the internal memory of the FPGA. Other modules, i.e. the central control system, PWM generator, current limit system, rotor position decoder, and control system of execution transistors, were based on the programmable structure and hardware DSP circuits. The developed architecture of the control module is shown in Figure 2.

The central control module was adapted to implement several SRM control algorithms intended for various power electronics systems.

To measure currents and voltages in the power electronics circuits, Hall sensors with ADC transducers with SPI output were used. Accordingly, the measuring modules SRM_Project_Current_Sensor and SRM_Projekt_AC_Converter were equipped with SPI interfaces with additional addressing outputs. These modules enable the measurement of 6 currents and 2 voltages. The measurement results are sent to the SRM_Project_FPGA_Controller control module via the UART interface. This solution was adopted because it enable the implementation of both modules in separate small FPGA devices. The second UART interface (SRM_Project_FPGA_PC), to which the USB converter is connected, was implemented for communication with the computer. In addition to the data archiving function, the computer program enable remote configuration and control of the system from a computer. The architecture of the measurement module is shown in Figure 3.

The maximal measured delay value of the output signal relative to the edge of the encoder signal was 406 ns. The UART transmission frequency between both main modules is 10 MHz, and between measurement module and the computer was 3 MHz.

At two-byte ADC measurement resolution with 1 byte label and 8 measured canals, as well as three-byte resolution with 1 byte label of rotor position angle or speed measurement, the maximum data transfer speed via USB interfaces was 3300 records each 9 values per second.

The maximum delay from initialising a current measurement to changing the state of the output ports was 130 μs. The results presented here refer only to FPGA structure, without peripherals such as drivers or power transistors

4 Summary

The developed structure makes it possible to execute the SRM control algorithm with delays shorter than the commutation time of the power transistors. This enables drive testing at very high speeds. The system enables the acquisition of measurement data such as currents, voltages, angular position of the rotor, and rotational speed. With a resolution of rotor position angle measurement of 0.25 degrees, the system can control a motor operating at 100.000 rpm.

References

1. K. Yasumura, Y. Inoue, S. Morimoto and M. Sanada, IEEE 12th International Conference on Power Electronics and Drive Systems, Honolulu, HI, 2017, 343-348
2. J. Gottschlich, B. Burkhart, C. Coenen and R. W. De Doncker, IEEE International Symposium on Sensorless Control for Electrical Drives and Predictive Control of Electr. Drives and Power Electr., Munich, 2013, 1-7
3. A. Stumpf, D. Elton, J. Devlin and H. Lovatt, 9th IEEE Conference on Industrial Electronics and Applications, Hangzhou, 2014, 12-17
4. H. Gürsoy, M. Önder Efe. IFAC-PapersOnLine **49**, 425-430 (2016)

Analysis of power system operation at asymmetrical load

Stefan Paszek[1], *Adrian* Nocoń[1], and *Piotr* Pruski[1],*

[1]Silesian University of Technology, Faculty of Electrical Engineering, 44-100 Gliwice, Akademicka 10, Poland

Abstract. The paper presents a mathematical model of a power system (PS) consisting of a generating unit (with a synchronous generator) connected by a high voltage (transmission) power line to a bus. The state and output equations of the generator are expressed in the coordinate system d, q, 0 and with the use of phase quantities of the generator stator, the bus and the power line, which is especially useful in the analysis of asymmetrical states. A disturbance of the steady state in the form of a two-phase short-circuit in the transmission line was taken into account in the made calculations. The influence of the excitation system and angular speed control system of the generator as well as the impact of selected generator model parameters on the waveforms were investigated.

1 Introduction

During the PS operation, primarily asymmetrical disturbances occur. The asymmetrical state of PS operation causes a number of unfavorable phenomena, including additional heating of the rotor surface and mechanical vibrations of machine elements [1].

Equations describing asymmetrical short-circuit processes of a synchronous machine are differential equations with periodically variable coefficients, which makes their solution difficult [2, 3]. In the case of stand-alone operation of a synchronous machine (without PS), it is possible to find a solution by approximate methods [2, 3, 4]. The analysis of the PS work with all its elements (including synchronous generators) is complicated and only practically possible using numerical methods.

In the investigations presented in the paper, it was assumed that the PS consisted of a generating unit (with a synchronous generator) connected by a transmission line to a bus. The state and output equations of the generator were presented in the coordinate system d, q, 0 and using the phase quantities of the generator stator and power line. A compact mathematical description of the whole PS was obtained and the waveforms of appropriate quantities for selected asymmetrical loads in transient and steady states were calculated.

2 The PS mathematical model

A mathematical model of the PS was developed in the Matlab-Simulink environment. First, a general model of the generating unit was created. In this model, using *Configurable Subsystem* blocks, it is possible to conveniently configure a model of the generating unit by selecting the model of: a generator, an excitation system, a turbine.

In the investigations, the GENROU synchronous generator model when taking into account possible subtransient asymmetry was used [5]. When analysing asymmetrical PS states, it is convenient to express the equations of stator currents and voltages, transmission line and bus with the use of phase quantities. The equations of Park transformation relating the quantities in the d, q, 0 coordinate system to those in the phase A, B, C coordinate system are then used [1, 5].

Due to the assumption of neglecting transformation voltages [1, 5], algebraic relations between the currents and voltages in the equations of the generator stator and transmission line were determined:

$$i_k(t+\Delta t_{k1}) = \frac{v_k(t)+v_{\mathrm{d}}(t)-v_{\mathrm{sc}}(t)}{|\underline{Z}_{k1}|}, \quad \Delta t_{k1} = \frac{\varphi_{k1}}{2\pi}\frac{1}{f}, \tag{1a}$$

$$i_{\mathrm{C}}(t+\Delta t_{\mathrm{C}}) = \frac{v_{\mathrm{C}}(t)+v_{\mathrm{d}}(t)-v_{\mathrm{sc}}(t)}{|\underline{Z}_{\mathrm{C}}|}, \quad \Delta t_{\mathrm{C}} = \frac{\varphi_{\mathrm{C}}}{2\pi}\frac{1}{f}, \tag{1b}$$

$$i_{k\mathrm{b}}(t+\Delta t_{k2}) = \frac{v_{\mathrm{sc}}(t)-v_{k\mathrm{b}}(t)}{|\underline{Z}_{k2}|}, \quad \Delta t_{k2} = \frac{\varphi_{k2}}{2\pi}\frac{1}{f}, \tag{1c}$$

$$i_{\mathrm{A}}(t)+i_{\mathrm{B}}(t)+i_{\mathrm{C}}(t)=0, \quad i_{\mathrm{A}}(t)+i_{\mathrm{B}}(t)=i_{\mathrm{Ab}}(t)+i_{\mathrm{Bb}}(t), \tag{1d}$$

where: i_l, $i_{l\mathrm{b}}$, v_l, $v_{l\mathrm{b}}$ – phase currents and voltages of the generator and the bus, v_{sc} and v_{d} – voltages in the short-circuit location and difference voltages of the star points of the bus and the generator, $\underline{Z}_j$, φ_j, – complex impedances and their phase angles in the transmission line, f = 50 Hz, k = A, B, l = A, B, C, j = A1, B1, C, A2, B2.

3 Exemplary calculations

In the paper, the results of calculations carried out for two cases are presented.

* Corresponding author: piotr.pruski@polsl.pl

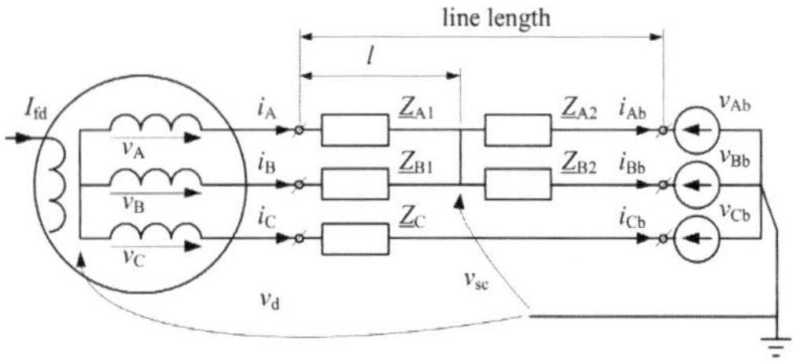

Fig. 1. Simplified diagram of the analysed PS for a two-phase short-circuit clear of earth.

In the first case, the stability of excitation voltage and angular velocity of the generator as well as the mechanical power of the turbine were assumed. It was assumed that the generator was loaded with low active and reactive power and its magnetization characteristic was linear. A long-term two-phase short-circuit in the transmission line located close to the generator terminals was modeled. In Tab. 1, there is compared the percentage content of higher harmonics in the steady state of the generator current in the short-circuited phase A (I_a), the generator voltage in the healthy phase C (V_c), and the generator excitation current (I_{fd}), with respect to the first harmonic for the stator quantities and with respect to the constant component for the field current.

Table 1. Harmonics amplitudes in the analysed waveforms in the steady state.

h	$X''_d \neq X''_q$			$X''_d = X''_q$		
	I_a, %	V_c, %	I_{fd}, %	I_a, %	V_c, %	I_{fd}, %
	0.0019	0.0065	100 (1.21 p.u.)	0.0023	0.0068	100 (1.21 p.u.)
1	100 (1.32 p.u.)	100 (0.56 p.u.)	0.0078	100 (1.40 p.u.)	100 (0.53 p.u.)	0.0078
2	0.0063	0.0045	87.029	0.0062	0.0046	86.275
3	9.1031	3.4390	0.0066	0.6228	0.2461	0.0066
4	0.0019	0.0009	2.9390	0.0024	0.0009	0.2119
5	0.3085	0.1160	0.0024	0.0025	0.0009	0.0026

In the second case, transient short-circuits (with a duration t_{sc} = 0.15 s) for the system at generator rated load, when taking into account the equation of motion and the impact of the excitation system and turbine were modeled. Fig. 2 shows the waveforms of the stator voltage and instantaneous power of the generator.

4 Conclusion

Based on the performed investigations one can state that:

– In the case of the synchronous generator subtransient asymmetry, in the steady state, during a long-term two-phase short-circuit in the transmission line, besides the fundamental harmonic, odd harmonics with significant amplitudes occur in the waveforms of the short-circuit current and voltage on the non-short circuited phase of the stator, in spite of the linear model of the system. In the steady state, the constant component, the second harmonic and higher even harmonics occur in the generator field current.

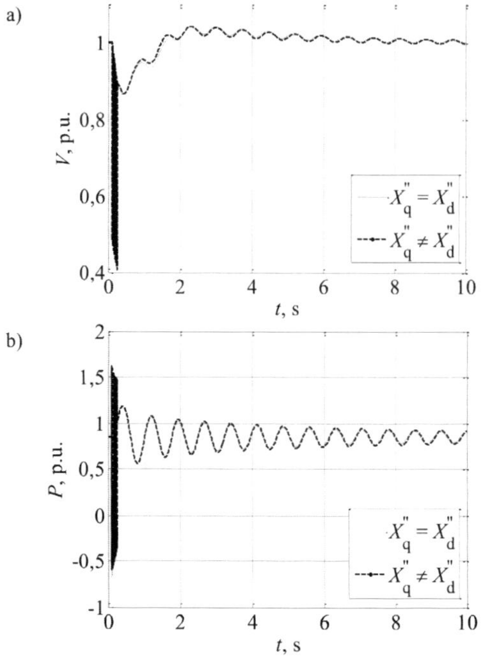

Fig. 2. Waveforms of the generator stator voltage (a) and instantaneous power (b) for a transient short-circuit.

– In the case of the generator subtransient symmetry, in the steady state, during a two-phase short-circuit, only the first harmonic in the short-circuit current and voltage on the non-short circuited phase of the stator as well as the constant component and second harmonic of the field current practically occur.

– In the case of short-term short-circuits, the generator subtransient asymmetry is of little importance. Its influence on the analysed waveforms can be observed when taking into account the impact of the excitation system and the turbine.

References

1. P. C. Krause, *Analysis of electric machinery*, McGraw-Hill (1986)
2. J.P. Chassande, E. Pillet, M. Poloujadoff, L. Pierrat, IEEE-PES **80**, 208-9 (February 1980)
3. Ch. Concordia, *Synchronous Machines. Theory and Performance*, (John Wiley & Sons, Inc., New York, 1951)
4. S. Berhausen, A. Boboń, Appl. Math. Computation **319**, 538-550 (2018)
5. S. Paszek, S. Berhausen, A. Boboń, Ł. Majka, A. Nocoń, M. Pasko, P. Pruski, T. Kraszewski, *Measurement estimation of dynamic parameters of synchronous generator and excitation systems working in the national power system* (in Polish), (Wydawnictwo Politechniki Śląskiej, Gliwice, 2013)

https://doi.org/10.1051/itmconf/20181901030

Analysis of vibration energy harvester with magnetic spring

Marcin Kulik[1,*], *Rafał* Gabor[1], and *Mariusz* Jagieła[1]

[1]Opole University of Technology, Faculty of Electrical Engineering, Automatic Control and Informatics, Opole, Poland

Abstract. In paper an electromagnetic energy harvester with two fixed permanent magnets and one moving suspended vertically by the magnetic interaction between them. The external force imposed on the system causes displacement of the magnet whose magnetic field induces emf in the coil wound around it. In order to obtain the resonance frequency around 25 Hz, the numerical optimisation was carried out. The measured frequency characteristics of the manufactured system compare well with results of computer simulation.

1 Introduction

In recent years, the problems involving obtaining electrical energy from the environment with its smart management have become research areas [1-3]. The process itself involves harvesting this energy from sources like wind, sunlight, heat or vibrations, and storing it in capacities or batteries [2]. This work concentrates on the mechanical vibrations.

2 Electromagnetic vibration energy harvester

Due to simplicity and relatively high induced voltage, the electromagnetic harvester shown in Figure 1 is proposed. It is a coreless system with the magnetic circuit composed of permanent magnets. The magnetic spring formed by the magnetically suspended central magnet ring brings a nonlinearity due to dependence of the magnetic force f_{mag} on displacement x which extends the operation frequency bandwidth of the considered system.

a) b)

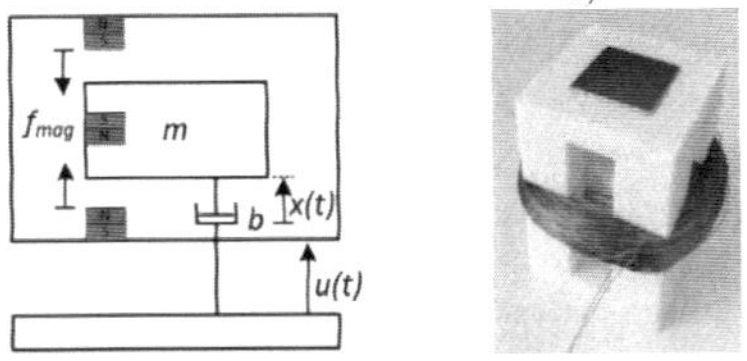

Fig.1. Vibration energy harvester, a) kinematic diagram, with b – damping coefficient, m – mass of moving element, $u(t)$ – displacement of the source of vibrations, b) manufactured prototype with coil wound around the moving magnet.

Under the influence of external vibrations the suspended magnet moves relative to the coil, and this induces emf in the coil. After linearization of the magnetic force, the equation of motion of the system in Fig. 1 reads

$$m\ddot{x}(t) = m\ddot{u}(t) - \bar{k}x(t) - b\dot{x}(t) \quad (1)$$

where: $\dot{x}$ and $\ddot{x}$ are velocity and acceleration of the mass m, whilst $\ddot{u}$ is the acceleration of force applied to the casing, and k is a magnetic stiffness linearized around $x = 0$. A more accurate analysis, should however take the k as a function of displacement into account, which would results in the occurrence of non-linear resonance [1, 3].

3 Designing of the system

The casing of the converter is manufactured of a plastic. The two fixed magnets are placed on the peripheries of the casing. In order to allow for the magnetic suspension of the moving magnet the poles are oriented as shown in Fig. 2. The moving magnet is also stabilised mechanically by the guides imprinted in the walls of casing.

a) b)

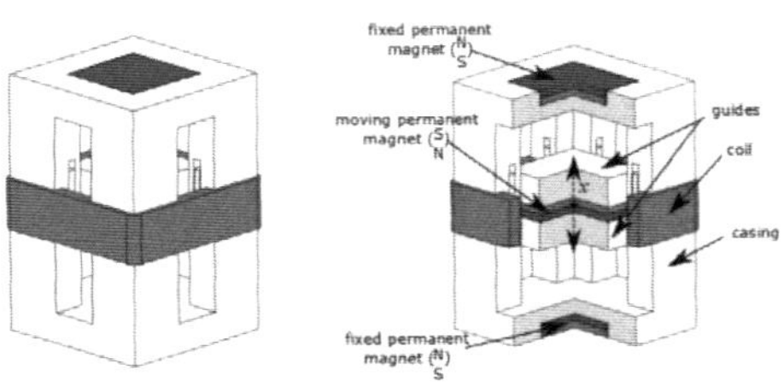

Fig.2. Tubular electromagnetic energy harvester model: a) CAD drawing and b) view of cross-section 3/4.

In the first stage, the converter dimensions were optimized in order to obtain the main resonant frequency equal to 25 Hz. The value of the stiffness coefficient necessary to meet the assumption can be determined from usual formula

* Corresponding author: marcin.kulik@doktorant.po.edu.pl

$$\bar{k} = (2 \cdot \pi \cdot f_{res})^2 \cdot m \tag{2}$$

where f_{res} is the resonant frequency, m = 0.01 kg, and

$$\bar{k}_{mag} = \left.\frac{df_{mag}}{dx}\right|_{x=0} \approx \frac{f_{mag}(\Delta x) - f_{mag}(-\Delta x)}{2\Delta x} \tag{3}$$

where f_{mag} is calculated from the Maxwell stress tensor method through the finite element analysis of the magnetic field distribution [4], Δx is the assumed virtual displacement the moving magnet. Optimization was carried out using the genetic algorithm from the Direct Search Matlab Toolbox [5]. The goal function was to obtain the value of $\bar{k}_{mag}$ that ensures minimum of square norm of the residuum of equation (2). The design variable was the distance between the fixed and moving magnets, which for the remaining dimensions of the system being constant, has the greatest impact on magnetic force. The variation of the variable was between 35 mm and 120 mm. After calculations, the optimal distance between permanent magnets was obtained, which was equal to 45 mm.

4 Computer simulation

The simulation of the tested system was carried with the purpose of determining its frequency-response characteristic. The latter was determined by solution of equation (1) within a time-interval of 400 s as the magnitude of the excitation system $\ddot{u}$ was kept constant while the frequency was swept within between 5 and 60 Hz. The variations of the flux linkage and force f_{mag} vs. displacement x were taken from the finite element analysis. The simulated frequency characteristics of the induced emf for different magnitudes of the excitation force $f_{exc} = m\ddot{u}$ are shown in Fig.3. It can be seen from figure that as the the magnitude of the external force increases, the resonant frequency shifts towards higher values, which is clearly the effect of rise of the magnetic stiffness of the system for large displacements. For the studied cases, the frequency range where the induced voltage is relatively large is between 18.2 and 25.4 Hz. The maximum magnitude of the induced emf was equal to 2.2 V.

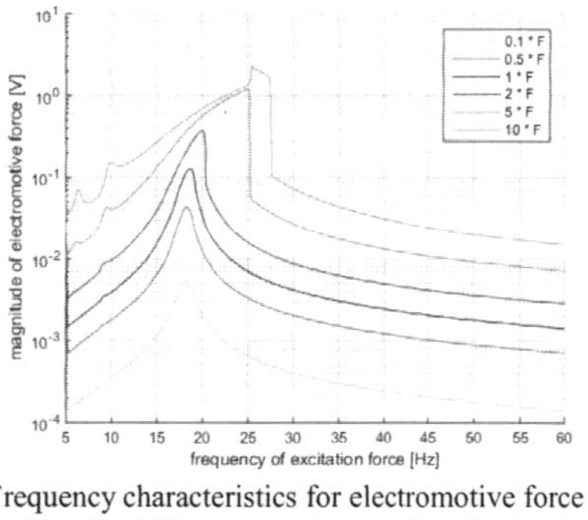

Fig.3. Frequency characteristics for electromotive force at no-load condition for different magnitudes of excitation force, where F = 0.0424 N.

5 Physical validation

The measurements were carried out on a laboratory test-stand shown in Fig. 4a. The voltage values were read at frequencies between 15 Hz and 30 Hz for the magnitude of the excitation equal to 0.0424 N. Fig. 4b compares the measured waveform with that obtained from simulation.

a)

b)

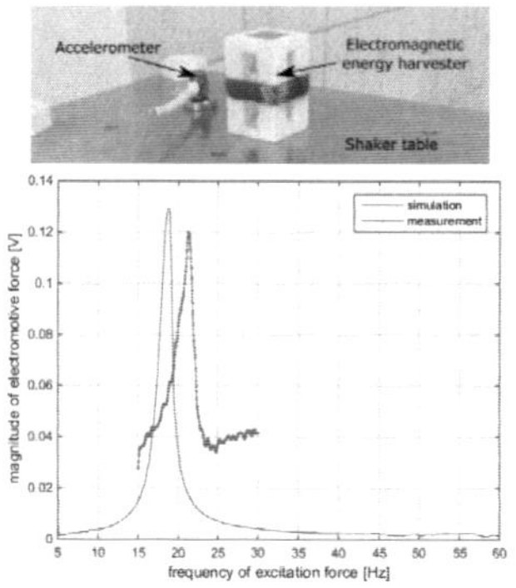

Fig.4. a) Laboratory test-stand, b) comparison of measured and simulated frequency characteristics of induced emf for magnitude of excitation force equal to 0.0424 N.

The comparison clearly shows the impact of the friction force, which is very difficult for identification due to complex type and event a discontinuity.

6 Conclusion

In this work an electromagnetic vibration energy harvester was designed and analysed. The magnetic spring contained in the system is capable to bring only the positive magnetic stiffness effect, and consequently the system should operate only in the low frequency range.

This work was carried out under project 2016/23/N/ST7/03808 of the National Science Centre, Poland

References

1. T. Kaźmierski, S. Beeby, *Energy Harvesting Systems, Principles, Modeling, Applications*, Springer, 2011
2. K. Kecik, A. Mitura, S. Lenci, J. Warminski, Int J Non Linear Mech, 1-7(2017)
3. M. Jagieła, M. Kulik, Prz. Elektrotech. 1(93), 311-315 (2017)
4. K. Adamiak, J. Mizia, G. Dawson, A. Eastham, IEEE Transactions on Magnetics **23**, 3005-3007 (1987)
5. D.E. Goldberg, *Genetic Algorithms in Search, Optimization & Machine Learning* (Addison-Wesley, 1989)

The influence of switched reluctance generator winding parameters on output power at different rotational speeds

Artur Sliwiński[1], *Krzysztof* Wrobel[1,*] and *Krzysztof* Tomczewski[1]

[1]Opole University of Technology, Faculty of Electrical Engineering Automatic Control and Informatics, Opole, Poland

Abstract. The paper presents the influence of the winding parameters of a switched reluctance generator on output power at different rotational speeds. All tested generators were designed on the basis of the same magnetic circuit. In the paper the influence of windings parameters on current and torque dependence on the rotor position angle are shown. The calculations were performed in the authors' own computing environment dedicated to optimisation, based on a two-stage genetic algorithm. A FEMM program was used for magnetostatic calculations, whereas the dynamic calculations were performed on the authors' own simulation program. The basic parameters of the tested generators were determined during the study.

1 Introduction

The annual electricity production of a wind generator depends on the wind speed distribution at the turbine's location [1]. The power output of a switched reluctance generator (SRG) at different rotational speeds depends on windings parameters and values of commutation angles [2, 3]. The optimal switch-on and switch-off angles values depends on rotational speed. The paper presents the results of a study on the influence of windings parameters on SRG output power at optimal dependencies of commutation angles vs rotational speed.

The calculations were performed in the developed computing environment based on a genetic algorithm [4]. The environment allows for magnetostatic and simulation calculations, based on autor's and external programs [5]. For optimisation, a genetic algorithm associated with the Matlab program was used. Magnetic circuit calculations were performed using the FEMM program, whereas the simulations were carried out in the authors' own simulation program. Optimisation was performed in two stages. In the first stage, the shape of the magnetic circuit was optimised. The main genetic algorithm (AG1) generates the geometric parameters of the magnetic circuit, on the basis of which the machine model is created in the FEMM program. This program calculates magnetics parameters of SRG.

In the second optimisation stage, a simulation program based on these characteristics was used. At this stage, the secondary genetic algorithm (AG2) optimises windings parameters and the values of commutation angles. This kind of two-stage optimisation limits the number of calculations of the magnetic circuit's variants, but enable faster calculation of optimal windings parameters and commutation angle values for various speeds.

The block diagram algorithm of the computational environment is shown in Fig. 1.

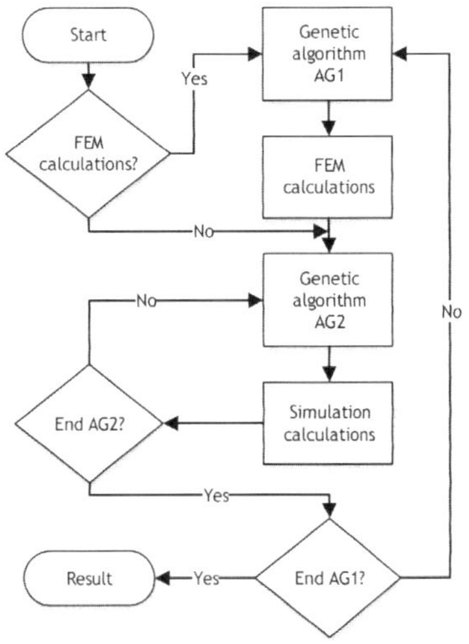

Fig. 1. Schematic diagram of the computational algorithm.

2 Computational results

The simulations were performed for a four-phase SRG with 8 stator poles and 6 rotor teeth. The magnetic circuit of the generator was characterised by an outer diameter of 120 mm, an air-gap diameter of 34.3 mm, and an active length of 80 mm. Variables are the diameter of wire Φ and the number of turns in phase windings N_{zw}. The objective function (1) maximises the difference between generated and consumed power (P_g - P_c), while limiting power losses in the windings (P_{cu}) and electronics elements (P_e) as well as the maximum current value (I_{max}) (2).

* Corresponding author: k.wrobel@po.opole.pl

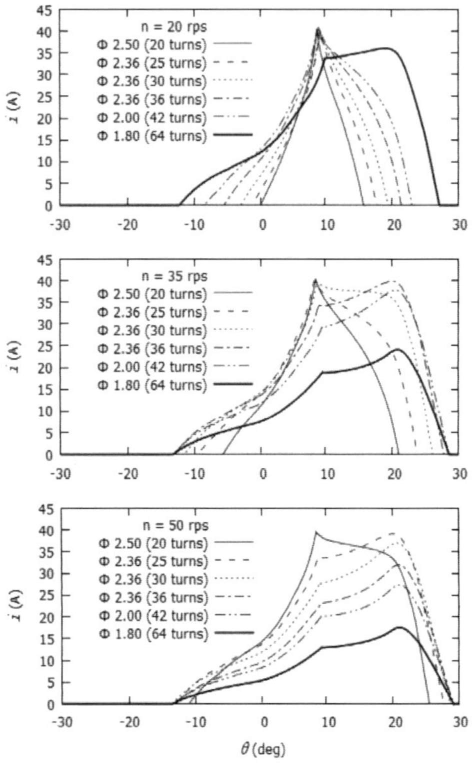

Fig. 2. Dependences of phase current vs rotor position angle for rotational speeds of 20, 35, and 50 rps.

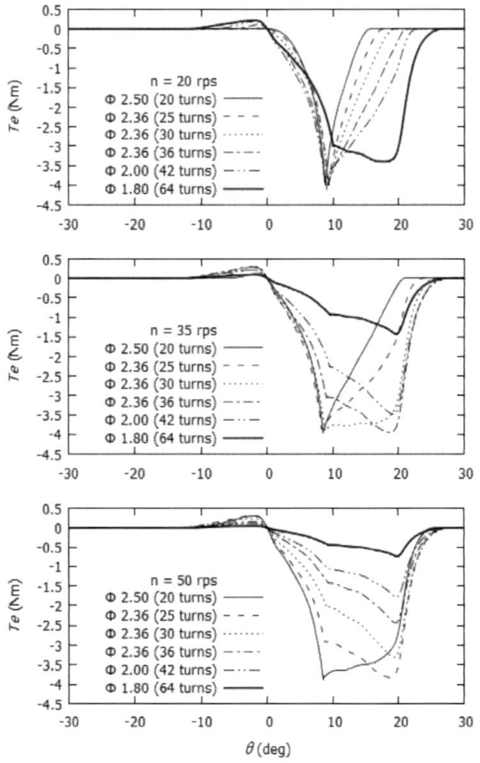

Fig. 3. Dependences of electromagnetic torque generated by one motor phase vs rotor position angle.

$$f = \begin{cases} P_g + P_{cu} + P_e < 1 & (P_g - P_c) f_c(I_{max}) \\ P_g + P_{cu} + P_e \geq 1 & \dfrac{P_g - P_c}{P_g + P_{cu} + P_e} f_c(I_{max}) \end{cases} \quad (1)$$

$$f_c(I_{max}) = \begin{cases} I_{max} < 40 & 1 \\ I_{max} \geq 40, I_{max} < 50 & -0.009(I_{max} - 40)^2 + 1 \\ I_{max} \geq 50 & 0.1 \end{cases} \quad (2)$$

Figures 2 and 3 present the dependencies of phase-current and electromagnetic torque produced by one motor phase at optimal values of commutation angles.

Table 1 presents: 1 - the number of turns in the phase windings; 2 - the diameter of the winding wire; 3 - the speed at which maximum power was obtained; 4 - the value of this power, 5-7 - the values of power obtained for the tested generators at different speeds.

Table 1. Power generated by the generators with different windings at different speeds.

1	2	3	4	5	6	7
N_{zw}	Φ mm	n_{Pmax} rps	P_{max} W	P_{20rps} W	P_{35rps} W	P_{50rps} W
64	1.8	22	409	**398**	298	228
42	2.0	35	505	234	505	367
36	2.36	35	548	183	**549**	444
30	2.36	45	555	116	474	521
25	2.36	50	548	77	307	**548**
20	2.5	59	**563**	46	128	448

3 Summary

The maximum value of output power was obtained for the SRG with 20 turns at a speed of 59 rps. The maximum power was obtained for different winding variants at different speeds. Therefore, the choice of generator should depend on the distribution of wind speed at the installation location of the wind turbine.

References

1. A. Tomczewski, The Scientific World Journal, **2014**, ID 643769
2. M. Korkosz, A. Powrozek, E3S Web of Conferences, **14**, 01037 (2017)
3. W. R. H. Araujo, C. A. Ganzaroli, W. P. Calixto, A. J. Alves, G. P. Viajante, M. R. C. Reis, A. F. V. Silveira, 13th International Conference on Environment and Electrical Engineering, 1-3 Nov (2013)
4. R. T. Naayagi, V. Kamaraj, Annealing IEEE Indicon Conference, Chennai, India, 11-13 Dec. (2005)
5. M. Heidarian, B. Ganji, Power Electronics, Electrical Drives, Automation and Motion, 1427-1432 (2016)

Analysis of cooling and heating system with Peltier cell

Wieslaw Lyskawinski[1,*], *Wojciech* Szelag[1]

[1]Poznan University of Technology, Institute of Electrical Engineering and Electronics, Piotrowo 3A 60-965 Poznan, Poland

Abstract. The article presents a developed cooling/heating system with a Peltier cell. This system is intended for local improvement of thermal comfort. The interaction between the Peltier module, a water block and the heat sink with a fan has been investigated. A thermal model of the cooling/heating system has been developed, as well as software for determining parameters of the Peltier modules and for analysis of the system operation conditions has been implemented. The obtained results of calculations were compared with the results of experimental tests.

1 Introduction

Peltier cells are thermoelectric elements in which, thanks to the use of the Peltier phenomenon, it is possible to absorb thermal energy through one side of the module and to extract it through the other side [1, 2]. The Peltier modules are used in households [3, 4], medicine, army, in space research, heat pumps, in air dryers or in cooling systems [5]. An interesting application of the Peltier modules, which uses both heating and cooling capacities of the cells, is thermally regulated clothing [6].

The article proposes the use of the cooling and heating capacities of the module for producing a small, temperature-controlled zone in its environment. The proposed solution may be an alternative to using large and expensive air conditioning systems in buildings.

In order to test the cooling and heating capacities of systems with Peltier modules, an algorithm and software for determination of the cell parameters, as well as for analysis and design of cooling/heating systems, have been developed. The algorithm and software have been verified by carrying out tests of the designed system on the built-in measuring stand.

2 Cooling/heating system

The developed prototype of a cooling and heating system is shown in Fig. 1. It provides for the possibility of cooling the hot side of the cell using a water block or a heat sink. In order to increase the thermal reaction speed of the system, low heat capacity heat sinks used in computer equipment for cooling the processors were applied. Two auxiliary copper blocks were placed on the built-in test stand to measure the thermal power consumed by and extracted from the Peltier cell. Temperature sensors PT 100 and the LabVIEW measuring system were used for temperature measurement.

3 System analysis algorithm

On the basis of the circuit model of thermal phenomena and Peltier module parameters, the cooling power P_c and heating power P_h of the cell can be determined [7]:

$$P_i = 2k[\alpha I T_1 + 0.5bI^2\rho/\sigma - \lambda(T_2 - T_1)\sigma] \qquad (1)$$

where: b=-1 for $P_i=P_c$, b=1 for $P_i=P_h$, I is the current, T_2, T_1 represent the temperature of the hot and cold surface of the cell, respectively, σ is the cell geometric factor, k is the number of pairs of semiconductor columns in the cell, α is the Seebeck coefficient, λ is the thermal conductivity, ρ is the resistivity. The values of the last three parameters depend on temperature.

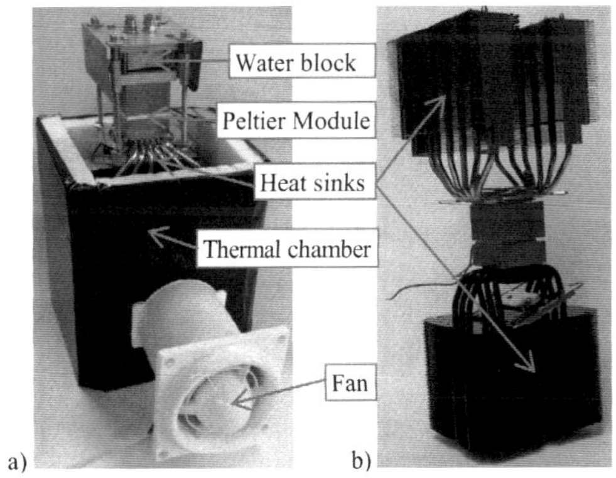

Fig. 1. Cooling and heating system with: a) heat sink and water block, b) two heat sinks.

To determine the temperature of both sides of the cell and selected components of the system, a circuit model of thermal phenomena has been used. The developed equivalent thermal circuit of the systems from Fig. 1 is shown in Fig. 2, where P_c, P_h represent the thermal power of the cold and hot cell sides, respectively; R_{thP}, R_{thCu}, R_{thR}, R_{thWB}, R_{thPar} are the thermal resistances of the thermal paste, copper block, heat sink, water block, thermal insulation of the sidewalls of the copper block,

* Corresponding author: wieslaw.lyskawinski@put.poznan.pl

respectively; T_1, T_2, T_A, T_c show the temperature of the Peltier cell surfaces, the temperature of the ambience and of the cold air at the output of the system, respectively. The method of calculating the equivalent circuit parameters is discussed in detail in [7].

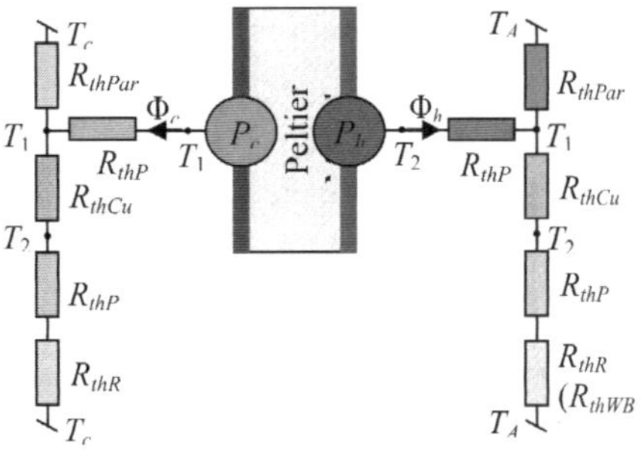

Fig. 2. Thermal equivalent circuit of cooling/heating system.

On the basis of the presented model of thermal phenomena, the software in the C# programming language for analysing a cooling/heating system has been developed. It allows the determination of parameters of the equivalent circuit diagram, the thermal input and output power of the Peltier module, as well as the temperature distribution and efficiency of the system. The view of the computer program interface is shown in Fig. 3.

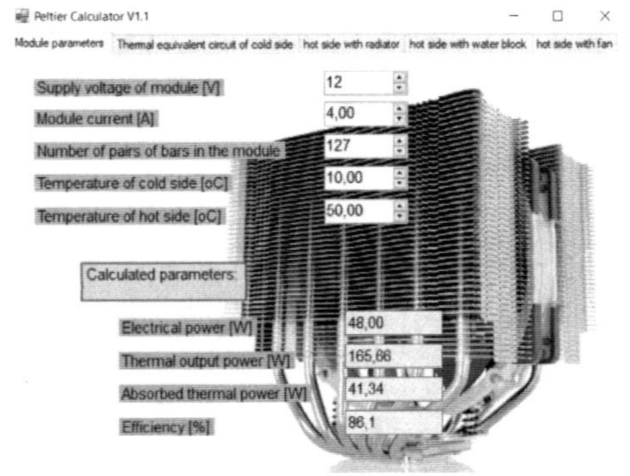

Fig. 3. Main form of the computer program.

4 Simulation and laboratory tests

The simulation and experimental tests of the cooling/heating system with Peltier modules of such types as TEC-127085, TES1-24106, TEC1-12726 have been carried out. Due to the limited volume of the article, only selected research results have been presented. Fig. 4 shows the comparison of the calculated and measured temperature dependences $T_1(I)$ and $T_2(I)$ on the cold and hot areas of the cell surface. During the tests, in the process of being cooled, the radiator was placed in the closed thermal chamber, and the hot side of the cell was cooled with a water block (Fig. 1a). Fig. 5 shows the cooling capacity of the same system, but with the air inlet and outlet of the thermal chamber being open. The influence of v_p air velocity on the temperature at the output of the system was investigated. The air speed at the output of the system was adjusted by changing the rotational speed of the fan. The measurements were repeated for two ways of cooling the hot side of the cell and the selected module types.

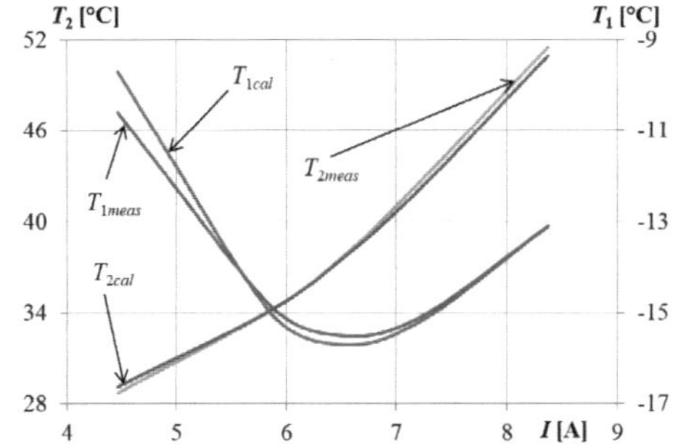

Fig. 4. Comparison of the calculated and measured temperatures T_1 and T_2 on the cold and hot sides of a TEC-127085 type cell.

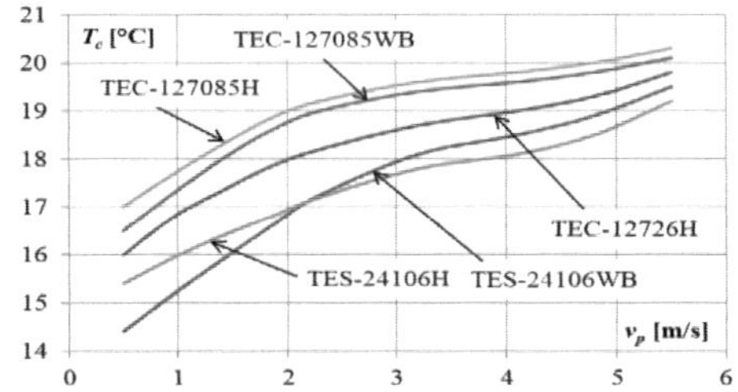

Fig. 5. Comparison of cooling capacity of exhaust air for the systems with a water block (WB) or a heat sink (H).

5 Conclusions

Good compatibility between the results of the calculations and experimental research has been obtained. Therefore, the usefulness of the developed algorithm and software for the analysis of thermal phenomena and the design of cooling/heating systems with the Peltier cell has been demonstrated. The performed tests confirm also the usefulness of the Peltier cells in microsystems to improve thermal comfort (local reduction/increase of temperature). The air temperature at the output of the system is regulated by changing the current of the Peltier cell and the rotational speed of the fan. The proposed system is cheap, quiet and ecological (no compressor and environmentally harmful coolant). For this reason, it can be an alternative to large and expensive classic air conditioning systems.

References

1. J. Goldsmid, Introd. to Thermoel., Springer, (2009)
2. J. Patel, M. Patel, J. Patel, H. Modi, Int. J. Sc. & Tech. Res. **5**, 73 (2016)
3. S. Manikadan, S.C. Kaushik, Elsevier **67**, 52 (2015)
4. D.M. Rowe, *Thermoelectrics Handbook – Macro to Nano* (Taylor and Francis, CRC Press 2006)
5. M. Jaworski, M. Bednarczyk, M. Czachor, Appl. Therm. Eng. **96**, 527 (2016)
6. K. K. Vistakula, Patent US8397518 B1 (2012)
7. W. Lyskawinski, W. Szelag, PUT Acad. J., Elec. Eng. **95**, 231 (2018)

Influence of electric vehicles on the electrical grid

Leszek Kasprzyk[1,*], *Robert Pietracho*[1]

[1]Poznan University of Technology, Institute of Electrical Engineering and Electronics, Piotrowo 3A, 60-965 Poznań, Poland

Abstract. The article discusses the issue of the development of electric energy storage and their impact on the power grid on the example of a charging station, to which a group of vehicles that have the capacity to transfer energy to the grid (V2G) is connected. An exemplary simulation of power distribution, energy losses in nodes of a standard IEEE 5 type network in two variants is presented: without and taking into account the impact of charging and discharging to grid the electric vehicles. The obtained results of power distribution in individual network nodes and power losses are presented in diagrams and commented.

1 Introduction

In recent years, one can notice the dynamic development of various types of energy storage, as well as systems powered from them, among which electric vehicles should be distinguished [1-5]. Although such vehicles are not designed to transfer energy to the grid, but due to the fact that many vehicles are used for 1-2 hours a day, and their energy storages are characterized by power of hundreds kW and energy capability of the order of hundreds kWh, they can be used as an intervention source of energy for the power system [6-8]. Currently, their number is not large, but it is expected that in the coming years the number of electric vehicles will increase. This will make real possibility of using V2G technology (vehicle to grid) and that makes a significant impact on the operation of the power grid [9-11]. The impact of a large number of vehicles can have two consequences - during charging it can cause excessive overload (reduction of voltage and transfer losses), but simultaneously supervised charging processes and possible discharge to the network can support the system (eliminate excessive voltage drops and power losses) [12-15]. Therefore, the selection of the optimal configuration of this type of structures requires advanced analysis as well as many technical aspects, and sometimes multi-aspect optimization. [16-25]. For this reason, in this work the analysis of the impact of charging and discharging a group of electric vehicles on the power grid was analyzed.

2 Example

As an example, a power flow analysis was carried out in the standard IEEE 5 type network with voltage level equal 20 kV for two cases: no electric vehicles and electric vehicles that act as energy storage, transferring energy to the grid. A daily electricity demand profile has been assumed for selected network nodes, which is shown in fig. 1. In the fig. 2, the network load in individual nodes is shown, including 4 groups of electric vehicles with different charging and discharging profiles. The values of generated power in individual nodes are: P_{N2} = 5 MW, P_{N3} = 7 MW, P_{N4} = 5 MW, P_{N5} = 8 MW.

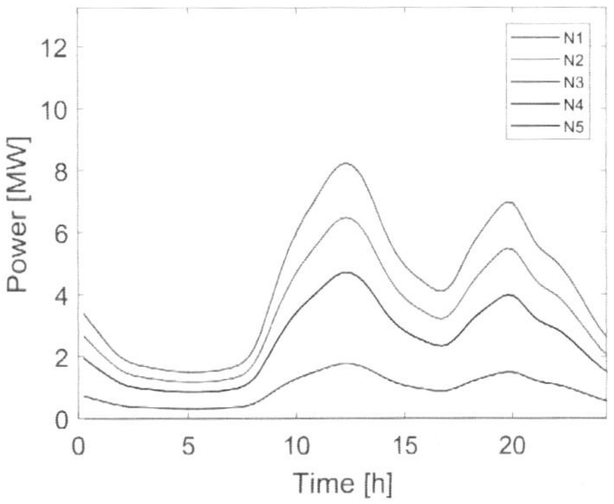

Fig. 1. Grid load characteristics without electric vehicles.

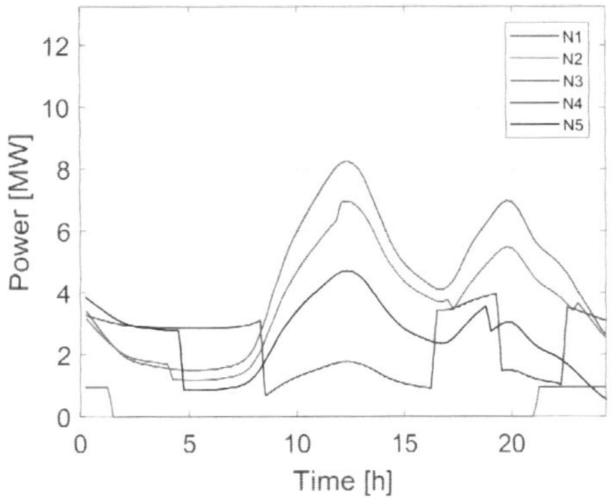

Fig. 2. Grid load characteristics with electric vehicles.

[*] Corresponding author: leszek.kasprzyk@put.poznan.pl

The fig. 3 and fig 4 show the total power and energy losses for all transmission lines in the examined case. It can be seen that the losses resulting from the incorrect generation match to the loads have been reduced using the power of the batteries of electric vehicles.

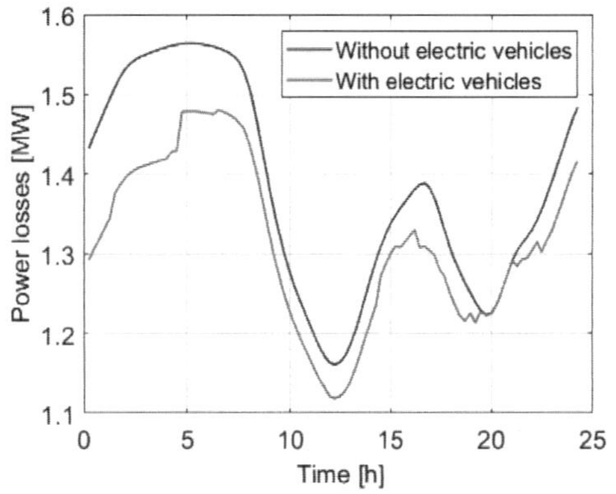

Fig. 3. Comparison of total power losses in the lines under consideration, without and with electric vehicles.

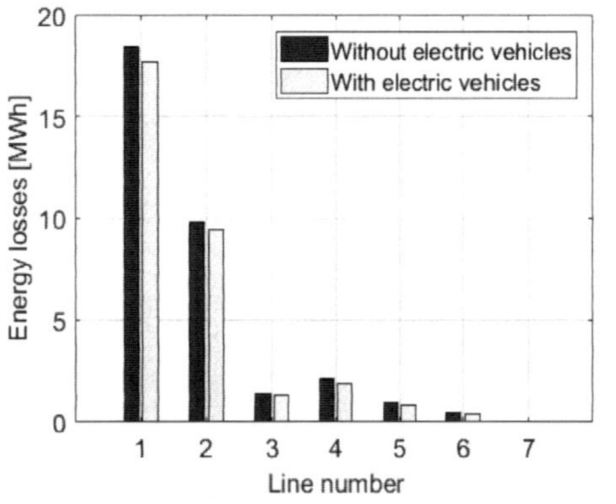

Fig. 4. Daily energy losses in the grid under consideration.

3 Conclusion

The simulation shows that electric vehicles can be used as additional energy storage and take part in regulatory processes of the power system. This regulation is based on local coverage of system losses due to load change at network nodes. In the case of using vehicles as intervention sources, one should also take into account the economic aspects of this solution, i.e. the impact of cyclic discharges on battery life and modernization of existing substations especially on the medium level to technology that would allow efficiently regulate energy flow to and from vehicles.

References

1. L. Kasprzyk, Eksploat. Niezawodn. **19/2**, 229-236 (2017)
2. D. Burzyński, L. Kasprzyk, E3S Web of Conferences, **14**, 01041 (2017)
3. S Balischewski, I Hauer, M Wolter, C Wenge, P. Lombardi, P Komarnicki, ISGT-Europe, IEEE PES, 1-6 (2017)
4. L. Kasprzyk, K. Bednarek, Prz. Elektrotech. **91/12**, 129-132 (2015)
5. B. Ohde, G. Ślaski, *International Automotive Conference* (Materials Science and Engineering) **148**, 012027 (2016)
6. J. Jajczyk, A. Dobrzycki, M. Filipiak, D. Kurz, E3S Web of Conferences, **19**, 01027 (2017)
7. D. Głuchy, L. Kasprzyk, Prz. Elektrotech. **93/12**, 99-102 (2017)
8. P. Komarnicki, P. Lombardi, Z. Styczynski, *Electric Energy Storage Systems: Flexibility Options for Smart Grids*, (Springer, 2017)
9. J. Alemany, P. Komarnicki, J. Lin, F. Magnago, Electr. Power Syst. Res. **140**, 363-377 (2016)
10. J. Alemany, F. Magnago, P. Lombardi, B. Arendarski, P. Komarnicki, Math. Probl. Eng., **1876934** (2017)
11. J. M. Alemany, L. Kasprzyk, M. Fernando, Electr. Power Syst. Res. **160**, 429-438 (2018)
12. L. Kasprzyk, A. Tomczewski, K. Bednarek, Prz. Elektrotech. **87/12b**, 82-85 (2011)
13. W. Opydo. A. Dobrzycki, Electr. Eng. **94/1**, 37-48 (2012)
14. J. M. Alemany, F. Magnago, D. Moitre, IEEE Latin Am. Trans. **11/1**, 421-425 (2013)
15. K. Bednarek, L. Kasprzyk, Prz. Elektrotech. **88/12b**, 236-239 (2012)
16. K. Bednarek, R. Nawrowski, A. Tomczewski, Prz. Elektrotech. **84/1**, 62-64 (2008)
17. L. Kasprzyk, Prz. Elektrotech. **88/7B**, 131-133 (2012)
18. Tomczewski, Sci. World J., 643769 (2014)
19. L. Kasprzyk, Prz. Elektrotech. **83/12**, 128-131 (2007)
20. D. Głuchy, D. Kurz, G. Trzmiel, Prz. Elektrotech. **89/6**, 78-80 (2013)
21. K. Skowronek, G. Trzmiel, Prz. Elektrotech. **83/11**, 108-110 (2007)
22. L. Kasprzyk, R. Nawrowski, A. Tomczewski, Studies in Computational Intelligence **119**, 21-29 (2008)
23. G. Trzmiel, Eksploat. Niezawodn. **19/4**, 516-521 (2017)
24. D. Kurz, Intern. Confer. Computational Problems of Electrical Engineering, 1-5 (2016)
25. L. Kasprzyk, K. Bednarek, Prz. Elektrotech. **85/12**, 65-68 (2009)

The economics of use of wireless power supply in electric buses

Michał Filipiak[1,*], *Jarosław* Jajczyk[1], and *Arkadiusz* Dobrzycki[1]

[1]Faculty of Electrical Engineering, Poznan University of Technology, Piotrowo 3A, 60-965 Poznań, Poland

Abstract. The article discusses the subject of wireless power supply for battery packs in electric buses. It presents the disadvantages and advantages of such a way to power the vehicle and charge the batteries. An attempt is made at analysing the economic legitimacy of use of this type of energy transfer method. The analysis is based on the annual course of the bus at the level of 70 000 km with the used battery pack whose capacity reaches 250 kWh. The assumed life of the system comprised of 2000 charging cycles. The characteristics of energy and losses was drawn up based on the entire life.

1 Introduction

Wireless power supply has gained more and more popularity mainly because mobile devices in which the transmitted power ranges between 5 and 120 W are becoming more and more widespread. This type of energy transfer method is also applicable in high power devices. One example here includes electric buses whose transmitted power reaches 200 kW [1]. In such cases, energy losses, while using inductive charging systems, may constitute a significant part of the energy transmitted into the vehicles (approx. 20%) [2]. Those losses result mainly from the necessity of using additional power electronic devices, and the lack of galvanic connection between the charging system and the receiver.

A reduction in losses may be obtained by way of optimization of the power supply systems as well as receiver and energy collection circuits [3, 4, 5, 6]. Care for their proper technical condition is important [7, 8, 9]. All the actions are aimed at ensuring reliability and the highest possible performance of the system, which will allow for the reduction in the energy demand.

Owing to the wireless charging, the batteries of electric vehicles can be charged while standing at bus stops. By using inductive charging, it is also possible to power and charge vehicles in motion, thus increasing the range and raising the comfort of use [1, 9, 10]. This requires the construction of special lanes on which the vehicles could move. An advantage of this solution is the lack of the necessity of a galvanic connection of the receiver with the power source and the concealment of the infrastructure of the charging system in the road surface.

The article analyses the legitimacy (from the economic point of view) of use of wireless battery charging systems in electric buses.

2 Operation of electric buses with wireless power supply

An increase in the number of sold electric vehicles has been noticeable for several years. This trend also refers to electric buses. In order to reduce the pollution coming from the burnt fuel, more and more cities decide to purchase electric buses. One example here is Warsaw, where 136 electric buses were ordered including the infrastructure containing 19 charging points [11]. Such a trend may in not a long time reach other cities in Poland.

The average annual mileage of buses on an urban route amounts to about 70 000 km. This translates into the daily mileage, which amounts to about 192 km. In order to extend the life of battery packs, they are charged once a day. Such a manner of operation allows for 5.5 years of their life during the whole warranty period which comprises 2000 charging cycles [12]. In order to cover this distance with a single charge, a bus must have batteries with the minimum capacity which amounts to about 250 kWh. The battery capacity used in buses ranges from 60 kWh up to even 660 kWh [13].

A number of variants of wireless power supply systems is used. Among the two-, three- and four-coil systems in vehicles, the two-coil systems are commonly used (often with a ferromagnetic core). An exemplary diagram of such a system is presented in fig. 1. It enables the transmission of high powers at the operating frequency of the system ranging from 20 kHz to about 40 kHz. This is a system with the serial-serial resonance on the primary side and serial compensation on the secondary side [10]. R_{odb} is a system which contains a controller and battery packs.

The implementation of the wireless power supply requires the construction or reconstruction of the power supply system in the bus per se and at the charging site. (e.g. a bus stop).

* Corresponding author: michal.filipiak@put.poznan.pl

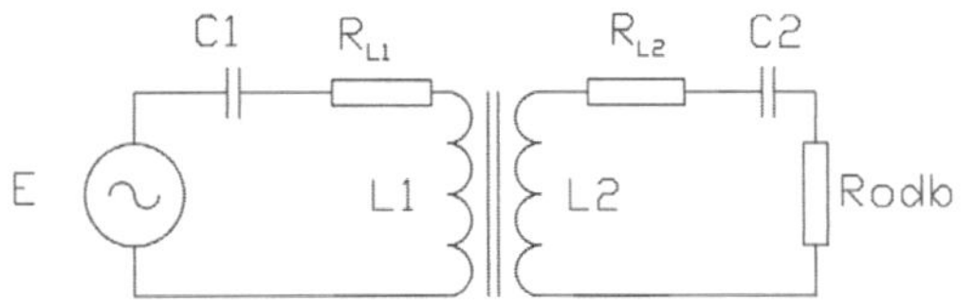

Fig. 1. Diagram of the system for the inductive energy transmission.

This entails the necessity of analysis and effective screening of electromagnetic fields, the impact of which will cover a bigger area than in the case of the conductive charging, especially in the case of the misaligned placement of transmitting and receiving coils [2, 9]. The imperfect geometry of the transmission system may be the source of additional losses, which leads directly to the necessity of detailed analysis of profitability of use of this solution. Neither can the energy effectiveness of the entire battery charging system be ignored. In the case of wireless systems, the aggregate energy losses are twice as high in comparison with the contact system [1].

3 Analysis of power losses at wireless power supply of an electric bus

During analysis of power losses at the wireless power supply of the electric bus, the assumed life was at the level of 5.5 years. With the assumption of the annual course of 70 000 km, we obtain the total distance of 385 000 km. Figure 2 presents the relationship between the energy supplied to the vehicle and the relationship between the energy losses and the covered distance. The conducted analyses demonstrate the energy losses related to the charging process at the level of about 120 MWh (fig. 2).

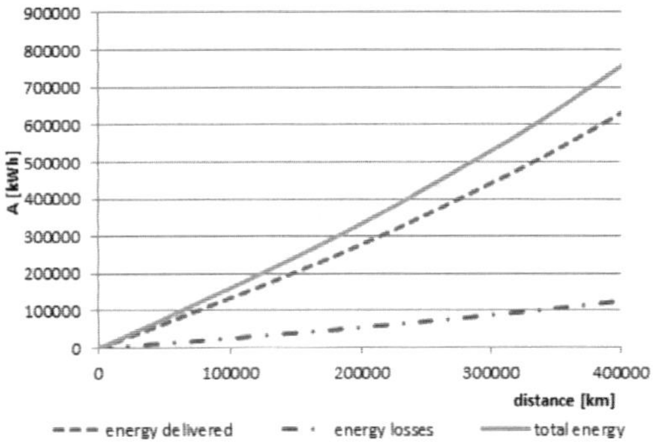

Fig. 2. Energy supplied to the bus and energy losses in the 5.5-year life cycle.

Such a way to ensure power supply, taking into account the actual electricity price at the level of 0.12 EUR/kWh, generates additional costs at the level of EUR 15 350. In comparison with the wireless system in which such extensive transmission losses do not occur, these costs will be higher by EUR 7 675.

3 Summary

The wireless power transmission technologies are subject to continuous development. Power transmission systems, which are characterized by greater and greater efficiency, are being constructed.

In the case of systems designed to charge the batteries of electric buses, there are problems omitted in the lower power systems, among others, those related to the electromagnetic impact. An important factor which increases the costs of operation is the significance of energy losses related to the powerless energy transmission.

In this paper, the additional costs related to the wireless power transmission throughout the assumed life were estimated at the level of EUR 7 675. The conducted analyses do not comprise the costs of construction and operation of the infrastructure. It is only the knowledge of aggregate investment and operational costs which will allow for the full estimation of the economic legitimacy of use of the wireless electric bus charging system.

References

1. A. Dobrzycki. M. Filipiak, J. Jajczyk,. Pozn Univ Technol Acad J, Electr Eng **92**, 25-35 (2017)
2. S. Ahn, J. Kim, *Antennas and Propagation (EUCAP), Proceedings of the 5th European Conference*, 3979-3982, IEEE (2011)
3. J. Jajczyk, L. Kasprzyk, 6th IASME/WSEAS (HTE'08), WSEAS Mechanical Engineering Series, 226-231, (2008)
4. J. Jajczyk, *IEEEXplore Electronic, CPEE 2016* (2016)
5. K. Bednarek, J. Jajczyk, *Prz Elektrotech.* **85**, 29-32 (2009)
6. L. Kasprzyk, *Eksploat Niezawodn* **19** (2), 229–236, (2017)
7. A. Dobrzycki, S. Mikulski and W. Opydo, *2014 ICHVE International Conference on High Voltage Engineering and Application*, 1-4 (2014)
8. W. Opydo, A. Dobrzycki, *Pozn Univ Technol Acad J, Electr Eng.* **94** (37), (2012)
9. J. Jajczyk, A. Dobrzycki, M. Filipiak, D. Kurz, *E3S Web Conf.* **19** 01027 (2017)
10. M. Filipiak, R. Nawrowski, *IEEEXplore Electronic*, CPEE 2017, 1-4, (2017)
11. Elektryczne autobusy w Warszawie. Docelowo 136 sztuk i 19 stacji do ładowania, http://warszawa.naszemiasto.pl/artykul/elektryczne-autobusy-w-warszawie-docelowo-136-sztuk, dostęp: 10.09.2017
12. M. Andersson, (2017). *UPTEC ES, ISSN 1650-8300 ; 17 002,* (2017)
13. https://www.proterra.com/products/40-foot-catalyst/ (access: 08.06.2018)

Analysis of the impact of quick charge technology on the charging process parameters of the lithium-ion storage at various temperatures

Damian Burzyński[1,*], *Damian* Głuchy[1], *Maksymilian* Godek[1]

[1]Poznan University of Technology, ul. Piotrowo 3A, 60-965 Poznan, Poland

Abstract. The paper deals with the subject of influence of the Quick Charge technology on the parameters of the charging process of lithium-ion cells. Tests of lithium-ion cell parameters during the charging process were performed at three different temperatures using conventional and accelerated charging. Also, the following paper comprises conclusions related to the conducted tests.

1 Introduction

The rapid technological development observed in recent years forces the analysis and creation of new solutions in the field of electricity storage [1-3]. It is the reason for the increase in energy consumption of mobile devices which prompts their producers to take actions aimed at preventing energy shortages. One example of such efforts is the development of quick battery charge technologies, which relatively contributes to the longer life of a device on a single charge[4].

2 Quick charge technology

In order to supply a bigger amount of energy to a device in a shorter time, the manufacturers provide the energy based on one of two standards available on the market. First of them only assumes an increase in the value of current and the other one links the changes in current with the changes in voltage with temperature. At present, the Quick Charge technology requires the application of appropriate modules in power supplies and receivers, closely cooperating with one another. At the same time, the power supplies and the chargers provided with this technology remain neutral towards devices which do not support this standard, acting at the same time like conventional chargers. Currently, Quick Charge in the 3.0 version is the most common variety of this technology and as well as the option of an increase in the value of current and voltage, it has the INOV (Intelligent Negotiation for Optimal Voltage) technology implemented in the charging algorithm. The adaptive control algorithm, depending on the surrounding conditions, adjusts the amount of the transmitted energy through a change in voltage in the range between 3.2 and 20 V with a step of 0.2 V including the appropriate adaptation of the value of current where the maximum possible value obtained by the charger is 3 A. Thankfully to INOV technology, during the charging process that uses Quick Charge 3.0 the power source as well as the device which is being charged are communicating with each other in real time. This increases the life of such a system and decreases the heat losses.

3 Testing a lithium-ion cell during the charging process using the Quick Charge technology

The Quick Charge 3.0 technology delivered by the Qualcomm company was subjected to tests. The technology is based on the possibility of free voltage and current control by the core of the operating system and the power supply source suitably prepared for this purpose.

The testing involved the use of the Sony Xperia X Compact smartphone, provided with the Quick Charge 3.0 technology and QNOVO (an optimisation which serves the purpose of extension of the battery life through the proper control algorithm). The battery in the tested device had the rated voltage equal to 3.8 V and the rated capacity equal to 2700 mAh. Each time, before proceeding with the measurements, the tested device was discharged. The charging process consisted of six measuring series: utilizing a conventional charger (5 V) and a charger that uses the Quick Charge 3.0 technology, for temperatures equal to 5°C, 20°C and 40°C.

3.1. Test results

The values of the measured voltages and currents during the charging process were used to determine the momentary power correlated with the changes in the cell temperature. The values of measurements and calculations were presented in figure 1.

* Corresponding author: damian.burzynski@put.poznan.pl

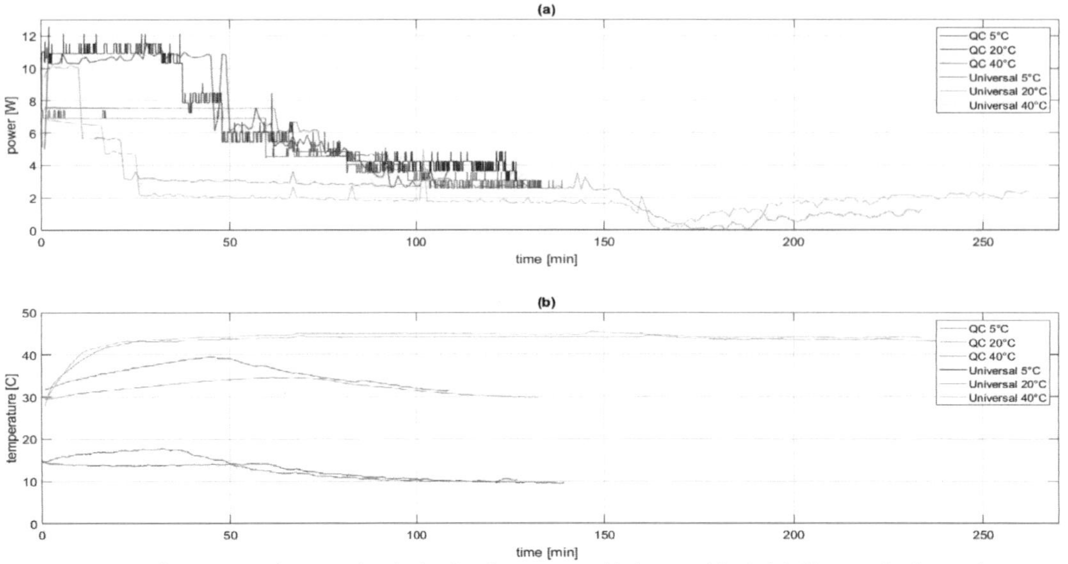

Fig. 1. Power (a) and temperature (b) versus time in the charging process, with the use of the Quick Charge technology and conventional charging, for three ambient temperatures.

3.2 Analysis of the obtained results

Using the Quick Charge technology in a comparison to conventional method of charging shortens the charging time by 22% (20°C), 12% (40°C) and 10% (5°C). At the same time, the applied technology caused an increase in temperature by 5°C in comparison with the conventional charging for measurements at 20°C. At 40°C, the difference amounted to 1°C, and in 5°C the difference was 3.5°C. It is possible to notice that at higher ambient temperature, the temperature difference between the two methods of charging is smaller and is caused by the limitation of power consumption which, in turn, is the direct consequence of the limitation in power consumption through a smartphone. At the same time this resulted in the longer charging time. On the other hand, at 5°C the charging time was increased as well in comparison to the ambient temperature equal to 20°C. Although, that the charging process increased the smartphone's temperature - which was unfavorably low for the device - it limited the energy flow comming from the charger in purpose of protecting the internal battery. Despite the fact that each charging time in 20°C in comparison to the ones in 5°C are different by almost a mere 5%, in case of a use of Quick Charge technology charging times differ by 17%.

The applied technology, in order to maintain the constant power level reaching the device, during the reduction in voltage by the above-mentioned system, forced an increase in the value of current which reached the battery. Such an activity directly contributes to an increase in the temperature during the charging process.

Quick Charge in cooperation with the charged devices, allows for a reduction in the temperature increase in order to avoid the battery damage, however in conditions where ambient temperature is significantly lowered it prevents the battery from being charged with unreasonably high charging currents in unfavourable conditions. Despite the limitation of power consumption throughout Quick Charge technology in various temperatures, in each of the cases a speed up of the charging process was noticed.

4 Summary

Increased voltage and current values during the charging process of mobile devices result in an unavoidable reduction of the lifespan of lithium-ion cells. Intelligent algorithms included in the Quick Charge technology allow for the smooth adjustment of charging parameters in such a manner as to make the charge of the device safe, efficient and faster than in the case of the conventional charge without significant disadvantage to the battery life. The Quick Charge technology leads to a compromise between the life and the battery charge time. Through the communication of the power supply source with the receiver, the optimization which led to an increase in the charging process efficiency was possible.

References

1. D. Burzyński, L. Kasprzyk, E3S Web of Conferences, **14** (2017)
2. L. Kasprzyk, Prz. Elektrotech. **88**, 7B (2012)
3. D. Sbordone, I. Bertini, B. di Pietra, M.C. Falvo, A. Genovese, L. Martirano, Electric Power Systems Research **120** (2015)
4. D. Burzyński, D. Głuchy D, M. Godek, Pozn. Univ. Technol. Acad. J. Electr. Eng. **95**, 309-320 (2018)

* Corresponding author: damian.burzynski@put.poznan.pl

Data bus modelling in city buses

Jarosław Jajczyk[1,*], *Wojciech* Lorkiewicz

[1]Wydział Elektryczny, Politechnika Poznańska, Piotrowo 3A, 60-965 Poznań, Poland

Abstract. The paper characterizes ICT networks used in urban buses. It describes the multiplex system manufactured by Continental VOD and the ELSY multicomputer system manufactured by Thoreb, Differences in the structure and functioning of both systems were presented. Based on the Thoreb system, a test station for the modelling of a complex data bus used in city buses has been designed and built.

1 Introduction

Information technology successfully enters different areas of our life. This is also true of areas connected with transportation. The progressive increase in traffic in urban agglomerations, observed in the last few years, encourages us to use public transport. The greatest benefits are seen in the introduction of public transport [1, 2, 3]. To make the passengers willing to use the urban transport system, it must provide them with several amenities. At present, the manufactured buses are equipped with a heating and air conditioning systems, audio-visual systems which provide information to the passengers, monitoring systems, ticket punchers, door controllers, passenger counting systems, USB ports which allow for the charging of mobile devices, lighting systems and Internet Access Points.. The interconnection of such a large number of devices is provided using computer networks and multiplex systems. They are based on the use of a computer, the control and diagnostic capacities of which are extended by devices called multiplexers. A multiplexer allows for an increase in the number of computer inputs and outputs. The communication between a computer and a multiplexer is most often executed with the use of a wire transmission medium. The connection of elements in the network is based on one of the known vehicle communication protocols – most frequently a CAN bus [4, 5, 6].

The design and manufacture of buses with the complex ICT structure is a difficult task which requires a whole range of tests and simulations. In such situations, systems for the modelling, simulation and testing of individual components and the entire system of the vehicle prove their usefulness. This paper presents a model of a multiplex network in a city bus.

2 Multiplex systems in vehicles

City buses among others are provided with systems connected with the passenger space (monitoring, ticket puncher system, passenger information system, door controllers or passenger counting system (Fig. 1)). Those systems are integrated and controlled by one, coherent multiplex system. The central unit communicates with the modules (multiplexes), which directly control the connected devices, via a CAN bus. Among the largest multiplex system manufacturers, one may list Continental VDO, Actia or Thoreb [7, 8, 9].

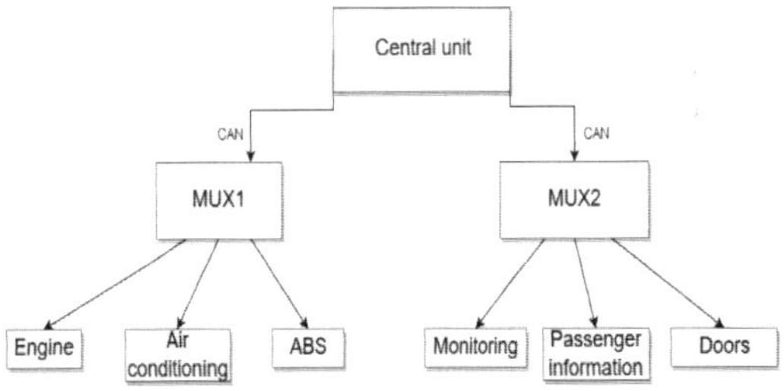

Fig. 1. Example of a structure of the bus multiplex system [7,8]

Several subsystems can be distinguished in a CAN bus of an urban bus, including systems responsible for the vehicle functions, e.g. PCAN (Powertrain CAN), ICAN (Instrumental CAN) or BCAN (Body CAN). The bus is controlled by a central processing unit, at the heart of which there is a microprocessor which executes instructions according to an uploaded software. A multiplexer is an element of the network, controlled by the central processing unit via the CAN bus. Owing to this, there is no need to have complex bundles of cables running to the central processing unit, which reduces the complexity of installation and its cost [5-9].

2.1 CONTINENTAL VDO Kibes32 system

The Kibes32 system from Continental VDO is a solution based on multiplexers. It consists of the ZR32-A central processing unit and MUX multiplexers (Fig. 2).

The computer has 6 CAN interfaces and enables the connection of up to 16 multiplexers. Its calculating power is defined by two 32-bit processors, which work independently. It complies with the SAE J1708/J1587 protocol (a communication standard used e.g. in trucks).

* Corresponding author: jaroslaw.jajczyk@put.poznan.pl

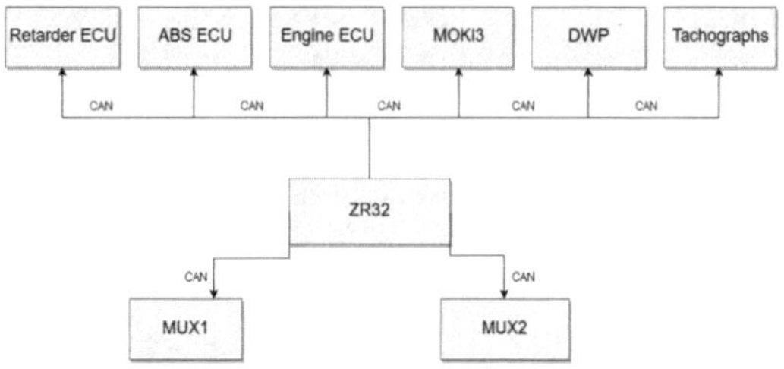

Fig. 2. Schematic diagram of Continental VDO system [7].

The diagnosis and programming are carried out via K-Line [7, 8].

2.2 Thoreb ELSY system

The ELSY system from the Swedish company Thoreb, the first version of which was developed already in 1986, is an alternative for the VDO multiplex system [8]. Contrary to the multiplex systems, Thoreb applies a different approach to the multi system control process. Instead of multiplexers and one computer, the system comprises of several equivalent computers connected via one common CAN bus. The use of several computers increases the reliability of the system in the case of a computer's failure and allows for the further operation of the whole system. The exemplary layout of computers in a bus is presented in Figure 3 [9, 10].

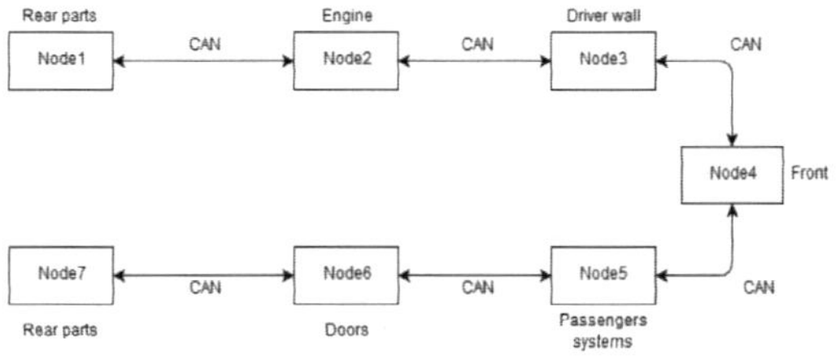

Fig. 3. Exemplary configuration of the ELSY system [9].

3 The model of a bus multiplex system

As part of the study, a test station based on the Thoreb system has been designed and built [9]. The developed solution ensures functionality which is similar to systems installed in buses. The station comprises of (Figure 4):

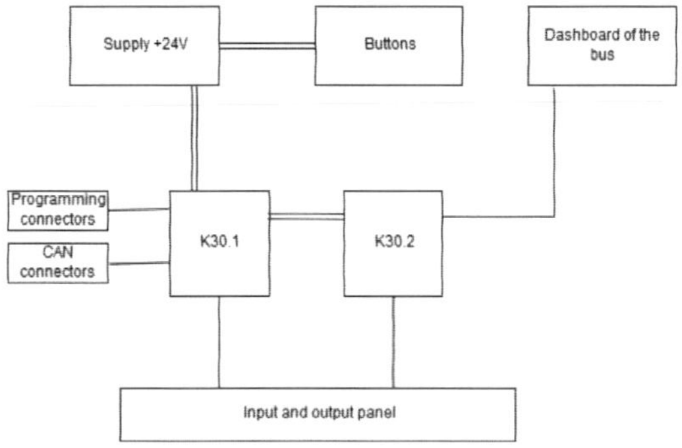

Fig. 4. Block diagram of the test station.

Thoreb K30 computers (connected via a CAN bus), +24V power supply, function buttons (KL15, desktop control), bus dashboard panel, connections used to program the computers and desktop, CAN bus connectors, the panel of input and output signal connectors (with LED diodes) [11].

As part of the study two programs controlling the selected devices (a three-way valve and a LED lamp) have been developed. The tests have proved correct functioning of the station. The communication between the computers is faultless and the inputs and outputs are correctly commanded [11].

4 Conclusions

Multiplex systems are complex systems which allow for the integration of independent controllers using a network which conforms with the CAN standard. The advantage of this architecture is that it is possible to diagnose the systems without interfering into the electrical system, and to freely program the system. The multiplex systems are popular among the manufacturers of city buses.

The performed studies and tests have allowed for the verification the behaviour of a multiplex system in different conditions. The station helped to analyse the behaviour of the communication bus of two computers by testing different variants of programs and performing a simultaneous analysis of the physical operation of the device (e.g. the signal condition switching rate). The built station allows for the test of the compatibility of the new solution with the existing bus system and the new software in a research laboratory. Advanced simulations performed on the test station save time and costs connected with the development of a reliable bus control software.

References

1. A. Dobrzycki. M. Filipiak, J. Jajczyk, *Pozn Univ Technol Acad J, Electr Eng* **92**, 25-35 (2017)
2. J. Jajczyk, A. Dobrzycki, M. Filipiak, D. Kurz, *E3S Web Conf.* **19** 01027 (2017)
3. L. Kasprzyk, *Eksploat Niezawodn* **19** (2), 229–236 (2017)
4. A. Herner, H. Riehl, *Elektrotechnika i elektronika w pojazdach samochodowych*, WKiŁ, (2013)
5. M. Frei, *Samochodowe magistrale danych w praktyce warsztatowej*, WKiŁ (2016)
6. J. Jajczyk, K. Matwiejczyk, *Pozn Univ Technol Acad J, Electr Eng* **79**, 31-39 (2014)
7. Continental VDO catalog notice.
8. Kibes-32 Software Documentation ZR32-A.
9. Technical documentation of Thoreb computers.
10. Educational materials of the ElsyGraf program
11. J. Jajczyk, W. Lorkiewicz, *Pozn Univ Technol Acad J, Electr Eng.* **95**, 321-332 (2018)

Constrained optimization using penalty function method combined with genetic algorithm

Łukasz Knypiński*, *Krzysztof* Kowalski, and *Lech* Nowak

Poznan University of Technology, Institute of Electrical Engineering and Electronics, 60-965 Poznan, Poland

Abstract. In the paper the way of adaptation of the penalty function method to the genetic algorithm is presented. In case of application of the external penalty function, the penalty term may exceed the value of the primary objective function. This means, that the value of the modified objective function is negative, while in genetic algorithm the adaptation must be of positive value, especially it in the selection procedure utilizes the roulette method. The sigmoidal transformation is applied to solve this problem. The computer software is developed in the Delphi environment. The proposed approach is applied to optimization of the electromagnetic linear actuator.

1 Introduction

Genetic algorithms (GA) fall within the group of non-deterministic methods of optimization [1, 2, 3]. In genetic algorithms, the optimization is performed using the mechanism of species evolution and natural selection. The basic mechanism of this method is a permanent adaptation of the population to the changes in the external environment. Within of the population, consisting of individuals with different adaptation, there is continuous rivalry. Just like in a natural environment, the stronger individuals survive the reproduction operation and become parents in the crossover. In case of solving the optimization problems, the population of individuals is a set of solutions of the analyzed task.

Genetic algorithms and particle swarm optimization algorithm (PSO) are very often used to solve optimization task with constraints [4, 5, 6]. The constraints are usually included by using the penalty function method. In case of including the constraints in the use of the external penalty function for the individuals situated far beyond the permissible area of the solved task, the value of the penalty can exceed the value of the primary objective function. In such case, the value of modified objective function is negative, while in genetic algorithm the adaptation must be positive. Therefore a sigmoidal transformation has been proposed to solve this problem.

2 Adaptation of the penalty function to genetic algorithm

The penalty function methods are used to solve optimization tasks with constraints using deterministic methods. In such strategy a modified objective function $h_k(\mathbf{x})$ is constructed. The $h_k(\mathbf{x})$ function is the sum of the primary objective function $f_k(\mathbf{x})$ and the penalty term $p_k(\mathbf{x})$ representing the penalty for overstepping boundary of permissible area. During the optimization process, the importance (weight) of the penalty is increased.

If in optimization process m constraints are imposed, the penalty term in the k-th penalty iteration has a form:

$$p_k(\mathbf{x}) = a_k \sum_{j=1}^{m} \lambda_j g_j(\mathbf{x}) \tag{1}$$

where $\mathbf{x}$ is the vector of design parameters, k is the number of penalty iteration, j is the number of constraints, λ_j are the weighting coefficients, a_k is the penalty coefficient.

In case of maximizing the objective function $f_k(\mathbf{x})$, the modified function is defined as:

$$h_k(\mathbf{x}) = f_k(\mathbf{x}) - [1 - \gamma \cdot \chi_k(\mathbf{x})] \tag{2}$$

where: $\gamma = \begin{cases} 1 & \text{for } g_j(\mathbf{x}) > 1 \\ 0 & \text{for } g_j(\mathbf{x}) \le 0 \end{cases}$

where $\chi_k(\mathbf{x}) = p_k(\mathbf{x})/f_k(\mathbf{x})$ is dimensionless penalty function [4].

In a genetic algorithm with a roulette procedure in the reproduction operation, the adaptation must be of positive value. In the k-th main penalty iteration, the adaptation is represented by the modified $h_k(\mathbf{x})$ function. In case of including the constraints, with the penalty function used for the individuals located far beyond the permissible area, in the space of the solved task, the values of the penalty $p_k(\mathbf{x})$ can exceed the value of the primary objective function $f_k(\mathbf{x})$. A direct use of the penalty function in the genetic algorithm can lead to mistakes in the operation of the program. In order to adapt the external penalty function to genetic algorithm the sigmoidal transformation has been proposed [4]. After the transformation the modified objective function has the form:

* Corresponding author: lukasz.knypinski@put.poznan.pl

$$h_k(\mathbf{x}) = f_k(\mathbf{x})\left[1-\left(1-e^{-\chi_k(\mathbf{x})}\right)\right] = f_k(\mathbf{x})e^{-\chi_k(\mathbf{x})} = \kappa_k(\mathbf{x}) f_k(\mathbf{x}) \quad (3)$$

The coefficient $\kappa_k(\mathbf{x})\leq 1$ represents the penalty for exceeding of the constrains which reduces the maximized objective function $f_k(\mathbf{x})$. If the designed devices fulfil all imposed constraints, then penalty term tends to zero. The coefficient $\kappa_k(\mathbf{x})$ achieve value 1.

3 Optimization of electromagnetic linear actuator

The optimization of the magnetic circuit of the axisymmetrical electromagnetic linear actuator was carried out. The structure of the device is presented in Fig. 1. The mathematical model of the actuator contains equations of the magnetic field with nonlinearity of the magnetic core.

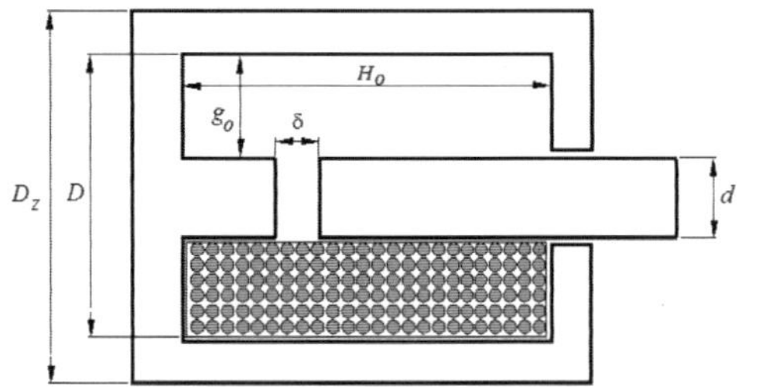

Fig. 1. The geometry of the axisymmetrical actuator.

The numerical implementation is based on finite element method. After determination of the magnetic field distribution, the value of the magnetic force was calculated using the Maxwell stress method.

The actuator structure is described by three design variables: $x_1=d$, $x_2=D/d$, $x_3=H_0/g_0$ – Fig. 1. Variables x_i constitute vector $\mathbf{x}=[x_1, x_2, x_3]^T$. The mass of the actuator has been assumed as the optimal criterion. Only the mass of winding cooper and mass of ferromagnetic material have been taken into account. The dimensionless objective function for i-th individual has a form:

$$f^i(\mathbf{x})=[m^i(\mathbf{x})/m_0]^{-1} \quad (4)$$

where m_0 is the average mass of the individuals after initiation procedure, $m^i(\mathbf{x})$ is the mass of the i-th individual (actuator).

Based on the preliminary analysis of literature and guidelines for the designing of this type of electromagnetic devices the ranges of variability of design variables were estimated [7]: $x_1\in(15\div 35)$, $x_2\in(1.3\div 2.3)$ and $x_3\in(2.5\div 7.5)$.

The optimization task consists in minimization of the objective function (4), while the constraint regarding the required force $F(\mathbf{x})\geq F_z$ has been imposed. The constraint function has been normalized into the dimensionless form:

$$g^i(\mathbf{x})=(F^i(\mathbf{x})-F_z)/F^i(\mathbf{x})\leq 0 \quad (5)$$

The course of the optimization process in selected genetic generations (n_g) is presented in Table 1. The constant number of individual in each genetic generation was equal 150. The following parameters of optimization procedure have been adopted: the number of genetic generations was 50, the probability of mutation p_m=0.005 and a=1.2. In a single penalty iteration related to the increasing penalty coefficient, the five genetic generations were executed. The permissible value of force $F_z\geq 90$ N has been imposed.

Table 1. The course of the optimization process.

n_g	x_1 [mm]	x_2 [-]	x_3 [-]	$h_k(\mathbf{x})$ [-]	a_k [-]	$F(\mathbf{x})$ [N]	$m(\mathbf{x})$ [kg]
0	25.58	1.98	4.26	0.9219	1.2	91.454	1.084
4	25.02	2.16	3.36	0.9292	1.2	90.013	1.076
7	23.88	2.08	4.56	0.9354	1.44	90.075	1.069
15	24.04	2.08	4.47	0.9360	1.72	90.017	1.068
30	24.04	2.09	4.39	0.9363	2.98	90.000	1.068
50	24.04	2.09	4.39	0.9363	6.19	90.000	1.068

Optimization calculations were repeated thirty times for random initial populations on two different computers. As a result of optimization process, similar variants of designed device were achieved. The obtained values of the objective function are similar, while the determined values of the design variables differ by a maximum of 1 to 3%.

4 Conclusions

The universal algorithm and computer software for the optimization of electromagnetic devices have been presented. The computational effectiveness of proposed approach has been verified by considering of the optimization task of electromagnetic linear actuator. In future research, it will be tested a new approach with reduction of the value of penalty coefficient during optimization process.

References

1. J. Vasconcelos, J. Ramirez, R. H. Takahashi, R. R. Saldanha, IEEE Trans. Magn. **37**, 1314 – 3417 (2001)
2. P. Di Barba, M. E. Mognaschi, P. Venini, S. Wiak, Archives of Electrical Engineering **66**, 607 – 623 (2017)
3. L. Kasprzyk, A. Tomczewski, K. Bednarek, Prz. Elektrotech. **87**, 82-85 (2011)
4. L. Nowak, Ł. Knypiński, C. Jędryczka, K. Kowalski, COMPEL **34**, 496 – 504 (2015)
5. R. M. Wojciechowski, Archives of Electrical Engineering **65**, 601-611 (2016)
6. C. Jędryczka, Ł. Knypiński, A. Demenko, J. Sykulski, IEEE Trans. Magn. **54**, 8102304 (2018)
7. Y. Nie, Y. Du, Z. Xu, Actuators **25**, 1-16 (2017)

The solutions used for long wave thermographic cameras designed for observing elements in SMD housings

Krzysztof Dziarski[1,*], *Joanna* Parzych[1]

[1]Division of Metrology and Optoelectronics, Poznan University of Technology, 3a Piotrowo Street, 60-965 Poznan, Poland

Abstract. The article presents example detector matrices used in long wave thermographic cameras facilitating observations of elements enclosed in SMD housings. Infrared radiation detector matrices parameters and an optical system used in modern long wave thermographic cameras are discussed. The criteria for selecting camera parameters and their impact on the performed measurement are considered.

1 Introduction

Obtaining the best possible temperature distribution visualisation for the surface of a surface mounted housing (SMD) requires the use of a thermographic camera equipped with an optical system and a matrix of detectors with appropriate parameters. Modern cameras feature an optical system (objective), a fixed FPA matrix comprising IR detectors and electronic amplification, processing and visualisation systems [5,6,13].

2 Spectral scope

The first parameter to be considered is the spectral range, within which the FPA matrix operates. Matrices operating in the MWIR (3 µm to 6 µm) and LWIR (6 µm to 15 µm) ranges are used most commonly [1]. This stems from the expected SMD housing surface temperature ranges. The housing temperature depends on the semiconductor junction temperature inside it and the ambient temperature. According to the authors' works, one should expect to observe temperatures in the 20°C to 160°C range, which corresponds to the 6.69 µm - 9.89 µm spectral range. It worth noting that this range spans the LWIR and MWIR threshold. The operating spectral range for the detectors making up the matrix depends on the detector type and material which it has been made out of.

3 IR and NEDT detectors

Single detectors used for observing SMD housings can be split into two groups: cooled and uncooled operating in ambient temperatures. Detectors with cooling take advantage of quantum effects to absorb infrared radiation. These can be categorised according to the material the semiconductors subsequently used to produce them are made of, into QWIP, MCT and T2SL detectors. The QWIP detector is a quantum well infrared radiation photodetector. It makes use of the quantum well effect in the structure of the two semiconductor bands with different bandgap levels. It mainly comprises AlGaAs and GaAs bands. The operating principle of an MCT detector is different. During its operation, minority carriers are moved by an external electrical field towards the signal electrode. Detectors made out of a number or MCT layers are often found in modern matrices [2]. A T2SL detector is made out of alternate GaSb and InAs semiconductor bands. Its operation is based on intra band carrier movement and tunnelling though a mulitiband quantum mechanical system [3].

Detectors without cooling (microbolometric) constitute a separate group of detectors. The operation of such a detector is based on a change of resistance as a function of temperature. Modern bolometric detectors comprise an absorber band absorbing the infrared radiation stream reaching the detector, a thermometer and thermal insulation.

NEDT thermal resolution is the last parameter. It determines the smallest detectable temperature difference between given points. For modern thermographic cameras, this value reaches 10-20 mK if using cooled quantum detector matrices and 40-100 mK if using uncooled bolometric detector matrices [2]. A matrix, together with an electronic system for reading and generating a signal is located in a vacuum housing with an objective, providing thermal insulation for the detector from its environment. This delivers high sensitivity and prevents the occurrence of temperature drift [2,4,5].

4 Optical system

The objective in a thermographic camera should only allow infrared rays to pass, damping visible spectrum radiation. That is why objectives used in thermography are made out of Ge, Si, ZnSe, ZnS single crystals and chalcogenide glass. Additionally, in order to increase IR radiation passage and VIS radiation damping, objectives are AR coated and may include bandpass filters. Sometimes special abrasion resistant anti-reflective

Corresponding author: krzysztof.j.dziarski@doctorate.put.poznan.pl

coatings are used with the stricture of a diamond, referred to as hard carbon.

To observe microelements in electronic systems, an objective is needed which will deliver high resolution (< 1mm) images of objects a few millimetres in size. It should feature a low IFOV value, appropriate geometric resolution and its focal range f should not be larger than the object - detector distance. Narrow-angle objectives, with f up to 50 mm (e.g. microscope, with an immersion lens) satisfy these requirements.

Most thermographic cameras feature a built-in objective, however in many cases it can be replaced or an additional one can be mounted. Additionally, modern objectives employ arrays of concave and convex lenses in order to eliminate defects such as spherical aberration or coma. [6] Intermediate rings may also be used to reduce MOD, minimum object distance. Unfortunately, heating up of the ring during a thermographic measurement results in an increase to the measured thermographic value and image distortion, and the longer the ring, the greater this effect. The effect may be reduced using software based non homogeneity correction, but this requires prior measurements using a temperature standard [7].

5 Comparison of parameters between selected thermographic cameras

Most thermographic cameras designed for observing microelements are equipped with an uncooled microbolometric matrix, and most often their spectral range spans from 7.5 µm to 14 µm. The spectral range of cameras with a QWIP or MTC detector is significantly lower, for example the FLIR Titanium SC7700L camera (8.1-8.7 µm) or the FLIR SC7750L camera (8.0-9.4 µm), which reduces the camera's usability for certain applications [8,9]. Whereas the spectral range of cameras with a cooled T2SL detector spans both MWIR, as well as LWIR, with lowest-order bounds wavelength of more than 9 µm (e.g. Pelican-D LW, 9.3 µm), and as such these can be useful for measurements at the boundary of the medium and long waves [10].

The thermal sensitivity of the available cameras stands at a few dozen or so mK (40 mK on average). Here only the VarioCam HD Research 900 (20 mK) camera, FLIR SC7000 (20-30 mK) series cameras or FLIR SC660 and FLIR T540 (30 mK) cameras stand out, however the difference in NEDT values is not that significant [8,11,12].

The measurement range for cameras with microbolometric matrices is quite broad, it spans temperatures from -40°C up to as much as +2000°C. Here, the FLIR ETS320 camera is noteworthy, with a narrower measurement range (from -20°C to +250°C), however one which is dedicated to measure temperature distributions in electronic systems (it has a special stand with adjustable object - objective distance) [11]. Whereas the measurement uncertainty for the available cameras stands at ±2°C measurement or 2% of the measured value (±1°C or 1% only sometimes), which today is a standard of a kind when it comes to thermographic camera measurements.

5 Summary

A thermographic camera with an objective and a matrix of detectors featuring appropriate parameters should be chosen to observe temperature distributions on SMD housing surfaces. The spectral range, within which detectors in the matrix receive radiation, should overlap as much as possible with the spectral range of radiation emitted by SMD elements' housing surfaces. Furthermore, the smaller the dimensions of an observed object, the more detectors should the used matrix hold. The NEDT value should not be overlooked - it should be as small as possible. On the other hand the selection of an appropriate objective impacts both the sensitivity and spectral range of a camera, as well as its image resolution. The materials which lenses are made out of determine the IR radiation transmission and VIS radiation absorbency. Whereas the focal length, FOV and IFOV parameters determine the minimum size of the observed area and the dimensions of the smallest object which a camera is able to distinguish.

References

1. K. Chrzanowski, K Firmanty, J. Bareła, PAK **7-8**, 34-36 (2005)
2. B. Więcek, *Wybrane zagadnienia współczesnej termowizji w podczerwieni* (Politechnika Łódzka, Instytut Elektroniki, 2010)
3. http://www.ir-nova.se/t2sl/ [07.01.2016]
4. H. Madura, T. Sosnowski, G. Bieszczad, Prz. Elektrotech. **9**, 5-8 (2014)
5. W. Minkina, P. Rutkowski, W.A. Wild, PAK **1**,. 11-14 (2000)
6. M. Vollmer, K-P. Möllmann, *Infrared Thermal Imaging. Fundamentals, Research and Applications*, (Willey-VCH, 2018)
7. M. Kałuża, PAK **10**, 1238-1241 (2011)
8. http://www.flirmedia.com [19.01.2017]
9. http://www.hoskinscientifique.com [19.01.2017]
10. P.C. Klipstein, E. Avnon, Y. Benny et al., Proc. SPIE **9451**, 94510K (2015)
11. http://www.flir.com [19.01.2017]
12. http://www.infratec-infrared.com [19.01.2017]
13. A Hulewicz, Elektronika – konstrukcje, technologie, zastosowania **7**, 107-110 (2012)

Use of cross-compiling in the programming of an intelligent device for measuring electrical quantities

Jakub Przybylski[1,*] and *Paweł* Idziak[2]

[1] Faculty of Mechanical Engineering and Management, Poznań University of Technology, 60-965 Poznań, ul. Piotrowo 3, Poland
[2] Faculty of Electrical Engineering, Poznań University of Technology 60-965 Poznań, ul. Piotrowo 3A, Poland

Abstract. A device for voltage and direct current measurement, built by coupling a Raspberry Pi microcomputer with an Arduino series microcontroller is presented in this paper. The structure of the device is presented and the method of implementing proprietary programs for both devices is described. A touch screen of the device allows the user to decide on the measurement mode (automatic or manual) and on the method of archiving and visualizing the effects of measurements. The application uses the so-called cross-compiling, thanks to which it is possible to effectively couple such different platforms as Raspberry Pi and Arduino.

1 Introduction

The digitization of practically all life areas forces the search for such techniques to measure various physical quantities that the measurement results could be: digitally processed into a form enabling their direct or deferred visualization, such as "stored" digital signals transformed (changed) into an analogue form and archived in an efficient way.

Modern instruments usually allow for measurement of several different physical quantities, e.g. current, voltage, temperature, frequency, sometimes power, condenser capacitance, resistance, etc. Depending on the measurement principle and device design, the measurement results are made available to the operator either in an analogue or in a digital form [1]. In a typical multimeter, the control elements placed on the front panel of the multimeter allow selection of the measurement mode and range of measured quantities, and the measurement configuration of the instrument remains unchanged [2].

2 Design of an intelligent multimeter

The intelligent multimeter presented here was built using the Raspberry Pi and Arduino platforms. In the original version, it allows you to measure DC voltage or current in one of three available modes [1]. Two of them will ensure an automatic measurement of the controlled quantity and registering it. In the automatic mode, the user has to declare the number of planned measurements - detecting changes in values and "capturing" data is the task of the multimeter system. In the manual mode, the user decides themselves on the number and time of measurements to be taken and recorded [1]. The touch screen is used to operate the instrument and to visualize the measurement values. The program realizing all functions of the multimeter allows you to export the measurements to a file and save the latter to a SD card.

An important feature of such an instrument is the possibility to reconfigure it and adapt it to the user's individual needs (change of the screen appearance, change of the measured quantities, etc.). This requires, however, the use of sufficiently efficient software.

The use of a touch screen requires the use of a suitably efficient control platform that allows you to design and program the user's interface in a relatively simple way.

In this project, a Raspberry Pi 3 microcomputer in version B was used. As none of the models of this device offers analogue inputs necessary to implement the foreseen algorithms, the measurement functions were separated from the screen operation.

In the project, a microcontroller from the Arduino family - Arduino Mega 2560, was used to measure DC voltage and current. It supports analogue inputs and is able to communicate with the Raspberry Pi platform via I2C or USB type communication modules. An additional advantage is the wide range of additional components and modules such as, for example, current sensors (required for the ammeter).

2.1 Block diagram of the device

For designing the architecture of the device using two coupled platforms, the priority was their reliable, mutual communication. Two different communication interfaces are used to control and transmit measured values. In the case of one common interface, the device would have to interrupt transmission of measured values to change the system's operating mode. This could result in problems at the stage of programming and developing the

* Corresponding author: pawel.idziak@put.poznan.pl

application, as well as undesirable, misleading measurements during the operation of the device.

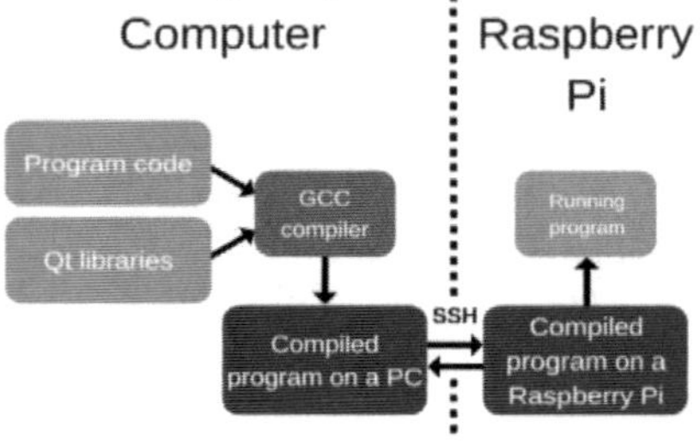

Fig. 1. Block diagram of an intelligent multimeter.

At a given moment, the Raspberry Pi provides an image display on only one output. It is not possible to run the application on the touch screen while operating the Raspbian system (an operating system edited for the microcomputer) via the image from the HDMI port. For this reason, for the purposes of developing and modifying application, a remote access to microcomputer files was provided through the SSH (Secure Shell) communication protocol, and the application itself was designed from the PC level using cross-compiling. The software used for it is open-source software.

3. Cross-compiling

The cross-compiling, supported by the Qt environment, allows programming and compiling applications in architecture other than the target platform architecture. This allows you to design applications from the level of a desktop computer, which is more efficient, and to reduce the share of the less-efficient portable target platform for testing the program code functioning. The realization of the same process on a desktop computer shortens the time of device configuration from a dozen or so to a few hours [3].

The program code along with the Qt libraries is compiled by the GNU Compiler Collection (GCC) and then sent via SSH protocol to the Raspberry Pi. It is possible to install Qt libraries together with the Qt Creator utility program in the Raspbian system, but the configuration process (realized partly in the Terminal) takes then a very long time [4].

Performing cross-compiling in the Windows environment succeeds only for the Raspberry Pi 1 and 2 models. Therefore, the tools from the Linux-Ubuntu system were additionally used for the design process. The structure is shown in Figure 2.

The key steps in configuring the cross-compilation are as follows: build a so-called "Qt Base" containing all basic libraries and upload them to the device by running scripts in Terminal. The whole process may last up to several hours, depending on the computer hardware possibilities. The information about the original and target architecture of platform, path names of previously created folders with Qt files for both of these platforms, and the name of the device for which the program is to be compiled are to be included into the project launch command.

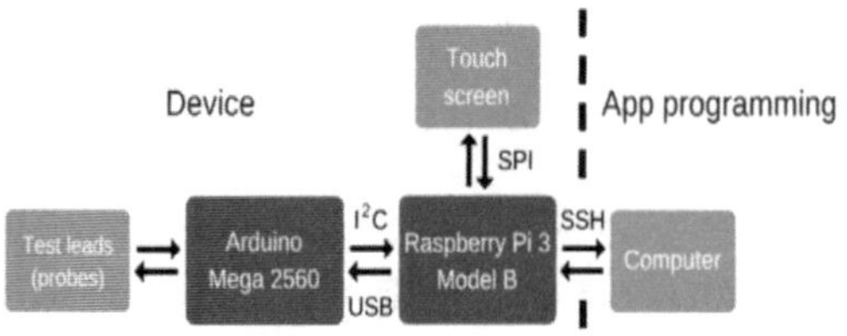

Fig. 2. Structure of the system during cross-compiling.

The command for the configuration of cross-compilation from Ubuntu 64-bit system for Raspberry Pi 3 Model B with 32-bit Raspbian system used in the multimeter structure is as follows [4]:

/configure -release -opengl es2 -device linux-rasp-pi3-g++-device-option CROSS_COMPILE=~/raspi/tools/arm-bcm2708/gcc-linaro-arm-linux-gnueabihf-raspbian-x64/bin/arm-linux-gnueabihf- -sysroot ~/raspi/sysroot -opensource -confirm-license -make libs -prefix /usr/local/qt5pi -extprefix ~/raspi/qt5pi -hostprefix ~/raspi/qt5 –v.

After setting up the GCC copmiler and debugger in Qt Creator as described in Qt's technical documentation, whole process has been completed, the application can be programmed from the computer level.

4. Concluding remarks

There are technical reasons to continue work on the development of an intelligent multimeter, to be used to measure not necessarily electrical quantities. The used separation of measurement and control functions to separate systems makes it possible to build a device with various measurement possibilities, operated by means of a touch screen.

This requires the use of adequately software, both in the area of communication inside the instrument as well as at the stage of design or modification of the latter.

The use of the mentioned cross-compiling significantly (several times) shortens the configuration process. By using this method the time necessary to perform the modification of the device can be shortened up to 10 times. The vast majority of used and necessary software is an open source environment.

References

1. The official Raspberry Pi documentation is available at https://www.raspberrypi.org/documentation/ (access 10/09/2017)
2. A. Kumar, What is a digital multimeter (DMM) and its working principle details, https://analyseameter.com/2015/09/digital-multimeter-dmm-working-principle.html (access 09.09.2017)
3. The official documentation of Qt libraries for version 5.10 is available at https://doc.qt.io/qt-5.10/ (access 24.01.2018)
4. M. Summerfield, Biblioteki Qt. Zaawansowane programowanie przy użyciu C++ *(Advanced programming using C ++)*, Gliwice: Helion (2014)

ITM Web of Conferences **19**, 01040 (2018) https://doi.org/10.1051/itmconf/20181901040
ZKwE'2018

Implementation of the lighting control algorithms in the KNX system

Sławomir Sowa[1,*], *Jarosław Gielniak*[1]

[1] Institute of Electric Power Engineering, Faculty of Electrical Engineering Poznan University of Technology, Poland

Abstract. There are many different ways of managing the lighting. The usage of appropriately selected controlling algorithms allows to increase the functionality, improve the comfort of using and introduces measurable benefits in the form of power consumption savings. In order to precisely apply the proper lighting control algorithms, it is important to know the distribution of light intensity in the room. This article is aimed at comparing different ways of lighting control and contains a control idea based on the KNX system, which is a popular building automation system. It is very useful for the implementation of lighting control criteria.

1 Introduction

Lighting is an important part of our lives. It affects the comfort of being in a room, the quality and work safety as well as our well-being. The need to maintain appropriate lighting parameters has been recognised in the legislative provisions. The possibility of ensuring the required parameters of lighting in rooms is possible because of the application of appropriate lighting control, which will ensure the required intensity of light throughout the room area. This may be achieved by controlling the lighting system by using algorithms that use information about the light distribution inside the room. The paper presents the application of algorithms controlling lighting in the room based on the information concerning the illuminance research and done with the use of KNX system.

1.1 Lighting regulations

1.1.1 European norms and standards

One of the guidelines is CEN/TC 169 N 0618 [1]. It defines the methods for assessing the availability of light and prescribes the conditions necessary to ensure a minimum level of light in the rooms. Since 2003, all EU members have adopted the common standard EN-12464-1 for workplace lighting requirements [2].

1.1.2 Legislation and regulations in Poland.

In Poland, the PN-EN 12464 [2] is used in the first place, and it is mandatory in all EU Member countries. It defines the values of light intensity and also defines a number of terms related to light in the interiors. In September 2017, a new version of the 15193 standard [3] was released. In this new version, the impact of daylight availability and control on energy efficiency was determined much more precisely than in previous versions.

1.2 Lighting control systems

This article examines only the automatic way of control, which can be implemented in three ways:
- switch on/off
- darken/lighten
- darken/lighten with daylight control.

The choice of an appropriate control method depends on the function of the room, its technical parameters and the location in the building. The first type of control will be limited only to switching on the entire lighting when the daylight intensity does not ensure the desired parameters of the room lighting. However, if the daylight intensity is satisfactory, the controls will switch off the lighting in the entire room. A more advanced, but also more effective way, is to control the darken/lighten type. It regulates the power of lighting fixtures topically so as to provide the required illumination on the reference surface and it is necessary to darken when the artificial lighting is at a lover value.

The third way of control, the most energetically and economically effective, is to use light intensity sensors, that will measure the light intensity values inside and outside the building. The results of the light distribution measurements have been presented in Figure 1 and are useful for assessing the savings in electricity consumption for lighting. Calculations prove that it is possible to achieve savings of up to 52% compared to energy consumption without lighting control [4].The method of implementation of all control versions in the KNX system is presented in point 3 of this article.

* Corresponding author: Slawomir@Sowa.poznan.pl

Table 1 The intensity of the light inside the room and the operating status of the light fixture.

Light intensity E [lux]	luminairies Row I	luminairies Row II	luminairies Row III
< 1200	ON	ON	ON
1200 - 2100	OFF	ON	ON
2100 - 3200	OFF	OFF	ON
> 3200	OFF	OFF	OFF

2 Light intensity inside the room

The light intensity of the room shall be maintained over its entire area. Naturally, by moving away from the window, the light intensity decreases. If the required light intensity is not provided in a particular room width, suitable luminaires with artificial lighting must be provided. The energy efficiency of an object can be improved significantly when artificial lighting is used. The lighting control shall be so designed that where the required intensity is provided, no additional artificial lighting shall be supplied. The study of such a distribution of light intensity allowed to develop appropriate criteria of regulation of light intensity.

2.1 The measurement of the light distribution

The studies were carried out over a period of 18 months, which made it possible to perform them in all seasons in various weather conditions. The diagrams of the light distribution in the rooms are shown in Fig. 2.
Measurements of the light distribution in the room show that the course of the light distribution curves is very similar for different weather conditions.
The research has also proved that the location of the room in relation to the parts of the world does not have a significant impact on the distribution of the light intensity [5].

2.2 Test results

The measurements of the light distribution in the room show that the course of the light distribution curves is very similar for different weather conditions. The research has also shown that the location of the room in relation to the parts of the world does not have any significant impact on the distribution of the light intensity [4].

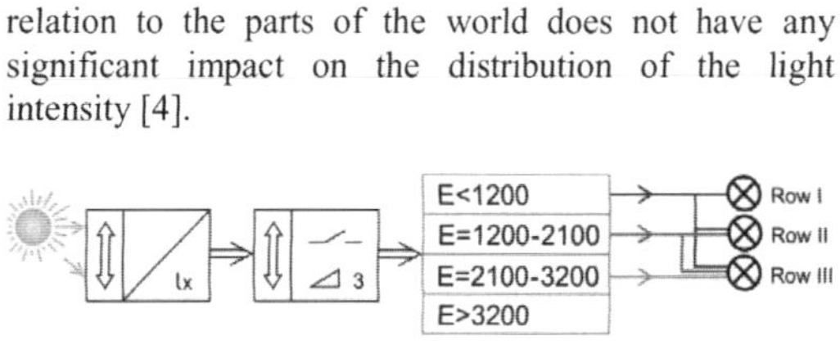

Fig. 1. An overview diagram of the lighting control in KNX system.

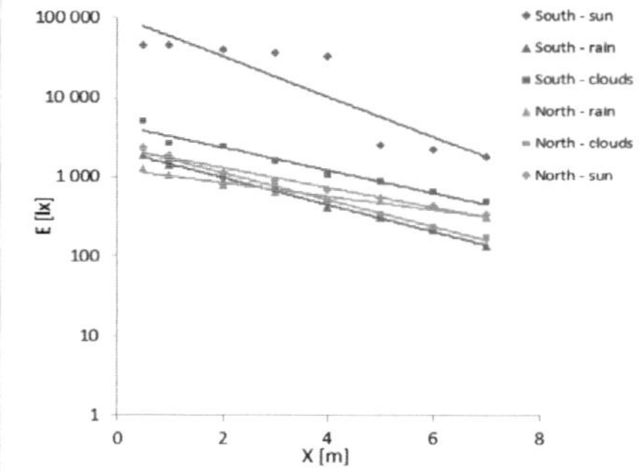

Fig. 2. Light distribution in the room from N and S for different weather conditions.

2.3 Test results and its usage

The obtained results of research into the distribution of light intensity in the room, allowed to develop algorithms for controlling artificial lighting in such a way as to ensure, as far as possible, uniform lighting intensity over the entire room. At the same time, an economic effect was achieved in the form of savings in energy consumption for lighting. The threshold values for the daylight intensity measured at the window inside the room are shown in table 1 and are directly related to the switching on and off of the respective lighting system rows in the room.

3 Controlling in the KNX system

Lighting control can be achieved with one of the many available building automation control systems. The KNX system is becoming increasingly popular and well known among hardware manufacturers and installers. Control in this standard will consist in switching on/off dimming and lightening the respective rows of light fixture. The algorithm is shown in Figure 1.

References

1. PrEN 15193: Energy performance of buildings - Energy requirements for lighting (2006)
2. PN-EN 12464-1:2012 Light and lighting - lighting at the workplaces - Part 1: Indoor workplace (2012)
3. PN-EN 15193:2017E Energy performance of buildings - Energy requirements for lighting (2017)
4. S. Sowa, A. Kamińska, Prz. Elektrotech. **2**, 193–197 (2018)
5. S. Sowa, Informatyka Automatyka Pomiary w Gospodarce i Ochronie Środowiska **3**, 78-81 (2017)
6. S. Sowa, J. Gielniak, Pozn. Univ. Technol. Acad. J. Electr. Eng. **96**, 153-162 (2018)

https://doi.org/10.1051/itmconf/20181901041

The control and visualisation system in an intelligent building

Rafał Nowak[1], *Aleksandra* Pietrasz[1], and *Grzegorz* Trzmiel[1,*]

[1]Poznan University of Technology, Faculty of Electrical Engineering, Piotrowo 3A, 60-965 Poznan, Poland

Abstract. This publication contains the description of the design of PLC-based comfort control system, interoperating with the safety system, whereby the said interoperation is subject to the master control and visualisation that uses the SCADA software. The introduction presents the description of the respective elements integrated into one system. Further on, the paper includes design assumptions and the principle of operation of the comfort control system. The article ends with conclusions.

1 Introduction

1.1 Programmable logic controllers

PLC's are microprocessor-based systems which are used to control processes and actuators in automation systems. Because of the wide array of applications and the easiness in the adaptation to the controlled process, they have gained much popularity [1, 2, 3, 4].

1.2 Intelligent building

The function of an intelligent building is to ensure the maximum efficiency in its functioning, as well as the comfort and safety of the user by making the most of the available resources, which entails the reduction in the costs of operation [5, 6, 7, 8].

1.3 SCADA systems

The term SCADA defines the software which ensures the possibility of master process control and data processing in real time. The visualisation of the controlled process or model in this type of software consists of the connection of the graphics on synoptic screens with the defined set of variables [1, 2, 9].

2 System design

2.1 Design assumptions

The function of the system is to ensure comfort and safety to users of a residential building. The task of the comfort management system is to control the lighting, heating, cooling and anti-burglary roller blinds, and it also cooperates with a separate alarm system – the intrusion and hold-up system with additional fire, gas and flood detectors. In the case of all the comfort control subsystems, there is an option of the master control, using the SCADA software [10,11].

2.2 Operation of the system

2.2.1 Lighting

The lighting is controlled using presence sensors, lighting intensity sensors and wall switches – the lighting is switched on in rooms depending on the condition of the three-position switch, therefore it is possible to switch on/off the lighting on a permanent basis and leave it in the automatic mode (fig.1) [11].

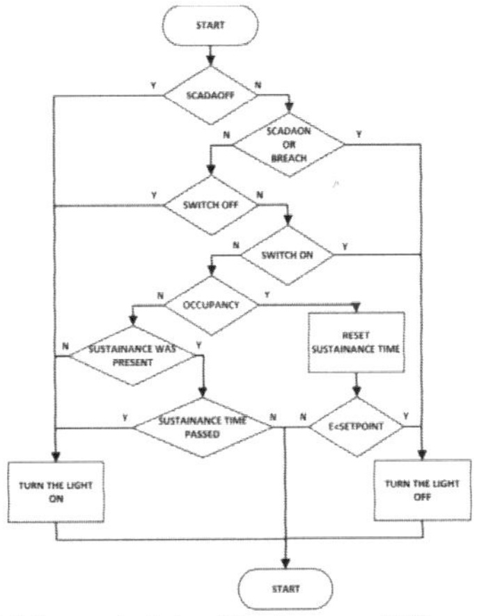

Fig. 1. Lighting control algorithm in rooms [11].

A mono-stable switch is used in other rooms, while in the bathrooms and in corridors, the lighting intensity criterion was not taken into consideration. Furthermore, the lighting is switched on in the case of violation of protected zones [11].

* Corresponding author: grzegorz.trzmiel@put.poznan.pl

2.2.2 Heating and cooling

The surface heating system uses coils with hot water installed in floors and walls of rooms, while the cooling system uses coils with cold water installed in ceilings (cooling ceilings). It is possible to support the operation of the cooling system by using anti-burglary roller blinds [11].

The heating and cooling systems are controlled using the pulse-width modulation (PWM) in the living room and the on/off modulation in other rooms. The algorithm presented in fig. 2 depicts the diagram of the cooling system operation in the living room [11].

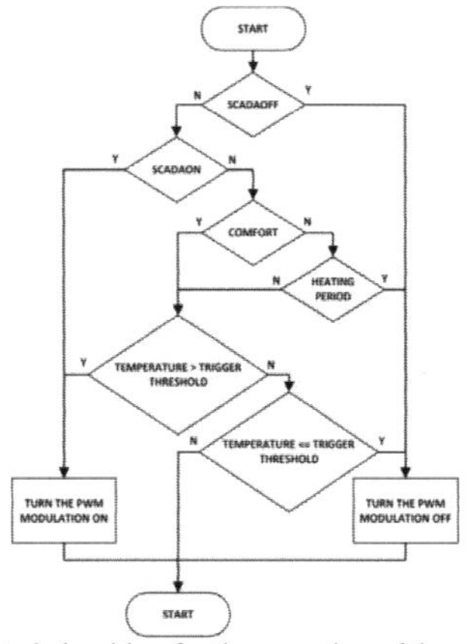

Fig. 2. Control algorithm for the operation of the cooling system in the living room. [11]

2.2.3 Roller blind control

The roller blinds are controlled using switches, signals from the alarm system, temperature and rain sensors, the current roller blind position and the hour taken from the real time clock built in the controller [11]. A part of the control programme responsible for the operation of the anti-burglary roller blinds was provided using the sequential function chart - SFC. The use of the SFC enables the creation of the control sequences based on steps, in which actions are performed, and transition – conditions of switching between the respective steps. In the case of such a type of control, the switching to a given step takes place only upon fulfilment of the condition specified in the transition. – by that time the programme may only perform an action described in the current step [11].

2.3 Visualisation

In order to monitor the system operation, the SCADA software with the visualisation based on synoptic screens was used. As well as the view of the current status of the comfort control system in the building, the SCADA software allows for the control of its respective functions, e.g. the positioning of the roller blinds in a certain manner, or the switching on of the lighting [10]. Owing to the creation of the users, the access control to the respective system functionalities is provided [10].

* Corresponding author: grzegorz.trzmiel@put.poznan.pl

3 Summary

The reliance of the comfort control system in the building on the PLC enables its adaptation to the individual needs of the user. On top of this, the universality of such a controller allows for its interoperation with other systems based on popular analogue and digital data transmission standards. All the subsystems interoperating in one control system may be covered by the visualisation, including the master control via the SCADA software. This shows that the systems, which were created for industrial purposes may easily be transferred to the commercial applications, which allows for the creation of the building automation system at a limited budget – the solutions designed taking into account the intelligent building are often more expensive and less universal.

4 References

1. J. Kasprzyk, *Programowanie sterowników przemysłowych*, (Wyd. Naukowo-Techniczne, Warszawa, 2006)
2. J. Kwaśniewski, *Sterowniki PLC w praktyce inżynierskiej*, (Wyd. BTC, Legionowo, 2008)
3. T. Legierski, J. Kasprzyk, J. Wyrwał, J. Hajda, *Programowanie sterowników PLC*, (Wyd. Pracowni komputerowej Jacka SKALMIERSKIEGO, Gliwice, 1998)
4. J. Jajczyk, A. Dobrzycki, M. Filipiak, D. Kurz, E3S Web Conf. **19**, 01027 (2017)
5. D. Clements-Croome, *Intelligent Buildings: Design, Management and Operation*, (Thomas Thelford Publishing, Londyn, 2004)
6. L. Kasprzyk, A. Tomczewski, K. Bednarek, A. Bugała, E3S Web of Conferences **19**, 01030 (2017)
7. A. T. P. So, W. K. Chan, *Intelligent Building Systems*, (Kluwer Academic Publishers, Norwell, 1999)
8. S. Wang, Intelligent Buildings and Building Automation, (Spon Press, Nowy Jork, 2010)
9. G. Trzmiel, Eksploatacja i Niezawodnosc – Maintenance and Reliability **19/4**, 516 (2017)
10. R. Nowak, *Wizualizacja sterowania procesami w budynku inteligentnym*, Master's thesis, Poznan University of Technology, Poznan (2017)
11. A. Pietrasz, *Sterowanie systemami komfortu w budynkach inteligentnych*, Master's thesis, Poznan University of Technology, Poznan (2017)

Forecasting long term lumen maintenance of LED lamps

Malgorzata Zalesinska[1,*], *Julita* Zablocka[1], *Krzysztof* Wandachowicz[1], and *Agata* Raczak[1]

[1] Poznan University of Technology, Institute of Electrical Engineering and Electronics, 5 M. Sklodowska-Curie Square, Poznan, Poland

Abstract. Due to the very high life of LED lamps, amounting to tens of thousands of hours, the life declared by the manufacturer is most often life determined on the basis of the method of forecasting the long term lumen maintenance. Life forecasting is based on operational measurements of the luminous flux drop over a period of at least up to 6000 h every 1000 h and extrapolation of the obtained results with an appropriate exponential curve. The article presents the results of measurements of luminous flux changes in the range of 0 to 9000 h of operation of light sources. The analysis of the obtained results was carried out and the life of the tested lamps was estimated.

1 Introduction

The control of LED lamp parameters in accordance with the regulations [1] is usually only limited to the initial parameters [2-4]. Measurements of the luminous flux maintenance are rarely carried out for 6000 h of lamp lighting [5], not to mention the luminous flux drop for longer times and checking the declared life on this basis.

The life L_x of a single LED lamp is determined by the time at which the light source provides at least the declared percentage of the initial luminous flux [6]. Measurements of the operational drop in the luminous flux of LED are time-consuming measurements, which is why a method for forecasting the long term lumen maintenance and estimating the life of LED [8] on this basis was developed. The luminous flux drop ($\Phi'(t)$) during operation is described in the publication [7] with an exponential curve:

$$\Phi'(t) = B \cdot exp(-\alpha t) \tag{1}$$

where:
t - operating time, B – projected initial constant, α – decay rate constant.

In order to determine the lumen maintenance life, the measurements should be carried out at least for the first 6000 h of lighting, every 1000 h. If the measurements are carried out for longer operating times (every 1000 h), all measurement results between the half and the end of the time considered should be taken into account in order to assess the life [7].

The method of LED lamp lumen maintenance life forecasting described in the publication [7] allows to calculate the life (L_p) for the assumed luminous flux drop percentage (p) based on the dependence (2):

$$L_p = \frac{\ln\left(100 \cdot \frac{B}{p}\right)}{\alpha} \tag{2}$$

* Corresponding author: malgorzata.zalesinska@put.poznan.pl

2 Description of test objects

In order to assess the actual luminous flux drop during the 9000 h lamp lighting and estimate the long term lumen maintenance in accordance with the procedure described in [7].

Six lamps from different manufacturers were selected for the tests. The basic information available on the packaging of the product as well as the results of measurements of the initial parameters of the tested LED lamps are described in the publication [8]. The appearance of the tested lamps is shown in Figure 1.

Fig. 1. The appearance of the tested LED lamps.

3 Measurement of luminous flu

The measurement stand and the measurement of the luminous flux are described in detail in [8, 9]. Relative changes in luminous flux of the tested lamps in [%] during the time from 0 to 9000 h of lighting are summarised in Table 1. On the basis of the measured luminous flux drop, the life forecast up to 70%, 80% and 90% of the initial value of the luminous flux was calculated for 6000 h of lighting. The results of calculations L_p are presented in table 2. Figure 2 shows the course of forecast curves of luminous flux drop up to 25,000 hours of lighting together with the actual measurement results.

Table 1. Relative changes in the luminous flux of the lamps.

t [h]	No. 1	No. 2	No. 3	No. 4	No. 5	No. 6
0	1,000	1,000	1,000	1,000	1,000	1,000
1000	0,977	0,784	0,951	0,947	0,890	0,994
2000	0,961	0,736	0,931	0,904	0,826	0,983
3000	0,959	0,733	0,945	0,880	0,800	0,996
4000	0,943	0,719	0,918	0,814	0,750	0,981
5000	0,943	0,716	0,917	0,783	0,749	0,981
6000	0,941	0,716	0,917	0,741	0,749	0,979
7000	0,936	-*	-*	0,703	0,745	0,978
8000	0,932	-	-	0,620	0,732	0,978
9000	0,927	-	-	0,422	0,730	0,975

* - the light source burnt out after 6000 h

Table 2. Results of lumen maintenance life.

Lamp	α	B	L_{70} [h]	L_{80} [h]	L_{90} [h]
No. 1	7,465 E-06	0,979	44960	27072	11293
No. 2	1,587 E-05	0,776	6456	-	-
No. 3	7,328 E-06	0,954	42231	24008	7935
No. 4	4,959 E-05	1,001	7220	4527	2151
No. 5	3,487 E-05	0,895	7053	3224	-
No. 6	2,780 E-06	0,995	126583	78556	36194

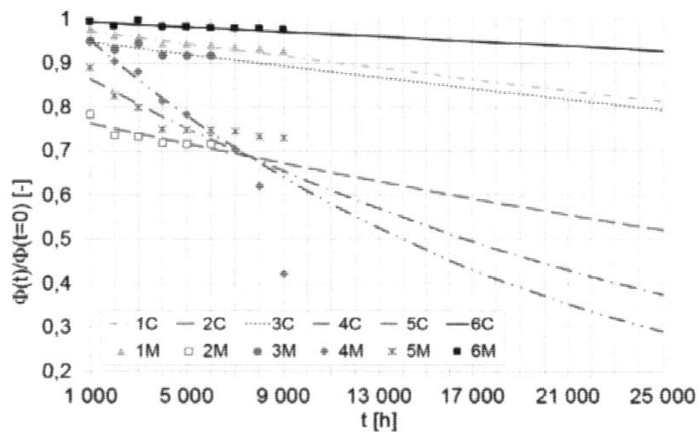

Fig. 2. Measurement results and curves extrapolated for obtained results. "C" from calculation, and "M" from measurements.

The forecast life was determined for all 6 tested lamps, although two LED lamps (no. 2 and no. 3) burnt out after 6000 h. In the case of lamp no. 2, it was impossible to determine the life for the assumed luminous flux drop up to 80% and 90% of initial value, and for lamp no. 5 for 90%. This was caused by a very large drop in the luminous flux at the beginning of operation. The luminous flux of lamp no. 2 during the first thousand hours of lighting dropped by over 21%, and of lamp no. 5 by 11%. In other cases, the forecast life was determined for all three luminous flux drops most frequently used in practice (70%, 80% and 90%).

Based on the measurements and calculations carried out, it was possible to divide the tested lamps into two groups. The first of them includes lamps with a low luminous flux drop during operation (no. 1, 3 and 6), and thus high life. In the case of lamps no. 1 and no. 3, life L70(6k) exceeded 40,000 h, and in the case of lamp no. 6 even 12,000. However, despite such good forecasts, lamp no. 3 burnt out after 6000 h. Due to the relatively low luminous flux drop within 6000 h of lighting, this lamp can be included in the group of good quality lamps. The second group are lamps that had a significant luminous flux drop during the first 6000 h of lighting. In each case, this drop was greater than 20%, and thus the lamps did not meet the requirements of regulation [1] regarding the required value of the luminous flux maintenance coefficient after 6000 h of lighting (≥80%). On the basis of such a large luminous flux drop, the forecast life was much lower than for the other lamps. Nevertheless, based on the example of lamp no. 2, it can be stated that forecasting life based on the first 6000 h of lighting does not always provide a good estimation. On the basis of the measurements for subsequent lighting times, it can be seen that the flux drop is much lower than it would result from the forecast values based on 6000 h (Fig. 2).

4 Summary

The measurements of the operational drop of the luminous flux were carried out only on single copies and it is not possible to generalise them for the whole production. Nevertheless, they confirmed the need to constantly monitor products on the market, and particularly to carry out tests after 6000 h in order to fully assess the quality of LED lamps. As the tests have shown, even though all the lamps met the criterion of the minimum initial value of the luminous flux [8], only half of them had a luminous flux maintenance coefficient higher than the required one [1]. The tests carried out also allowed to calculate the expected life of lamps based on the initial 6000 h of lamp operation and evaluation of the procedure described in the publication [7]. Based on the analysis of the measurement results, it can be concluded that the limit of the measurement time up to 6000 h [7] as a minimum sufficient to estimate the life of lamps may be insufficient in numerous cases. Confirmation of this thesis requires the authors to continue the tests and carry out verifications after at least 10,000 h of operation.

References

1. Commission Regulation (EU) No. 1194/2012
2. Pawlak, M. Zalesińska, Management Systems in Production Engineering **25**, 35-41 (2017)
3. St. Szwedek, M. Zalesińska, M. Górczewska, Pozn. Univ. Technol. Acad. J. Electr. Eng. **92**, 153-164 (2017)
4. T. Tabaka, Light & Engineering **23**, No 1, 79-86 (2015)
5. Zalesińska M, Zabłocka J, Wandachowicz K.: Prz. Elektrotech. **3**, 188-192 (2018)
6. *PN-EN 62612:2013.*
7. *IES TM-21-11.*
8. J. Zabłocka, M. Zalesińska, M. Górczewska, Pozn. Univ. Technol. Acad. J. Electr. Eng. **92**, 166-167 (2017)
9. J. Zabłocka, M. Zalesińska, K. Wandachowicz A. Raczak, Pozn. Univ. Technol. Acad. J. Electr. Eng. **96**, 209-218 (2018)

Applying the princigples of stage lighting in the illumination of the monument Państwa Podziemnego i Armii Krajowej in Poznan

Sandra Mroczkowska[1,*], *Małgorzata* Górczewska[1], *Krzysztof* Wandachowicz[1]

[1]Poznan University of Technology, Piotrowo 3a, Poland

Abstract . Designing the illumination of monuments requires an analysis of a number of determinants of their meaning and symbolism and the emotion which lighting should express. When choosing lighting solutions, the rules used in stage lighting may be helpful. Computer visualization of effects in different ways of illuminating an object facilitates the evaluation and choice of final lighting solutions.

1 Introduction

The illumination of sculpture and monuments is a very special task, because their size comparing to other building objects is usually much smaller. Mostly, sculpture and monuments are part of compositions, where one or main elements are human figures. Therefore, it may be helpful to use stage lighting rules when designing illumination of monuments.

Stage lighting system uses the following type of light sources:

• Key light, the basic lighting of the object or figure. Most often it is a stream of light directed from the front and from the side, within the angles 30 to 60 degree.

• Filling light brightens the shadows created by key light. Lighting direction may be different. Illuminance caused by filling light is always smaller than illuminance caused by key light.

• Contour light, illuminance of contour light is similar to illuminance of key light

• Background lighting brings out the outline of the elements of the illuminated object

• General lighting illuminates the entire surface evenly. Refering to illumination it may be assumed it is the light reflected from the bulidings and road surfaces neighboring with illuminated object. Value of general lighting is usually low.

• Special light, emphasizes mood and dramaturgy of illuminated scene.

All described types of light are rarely used in the stage lighting. Similary in the illumination of sculptures, it is mostly used a limited number of types of lighting, depending on the shape, size, location of an object, the effect the designer wants to achieve.

Described types of light sources allow to create illumination on different levels. It can be divided into high, low and medium "key lighting". High "key lighting" involves the use of lighting with small or very small contrast. The picture is bright . High contrast plays a major role in low "key light".The picture is shaded. Medium "key light" is a connection between high and low "key light".

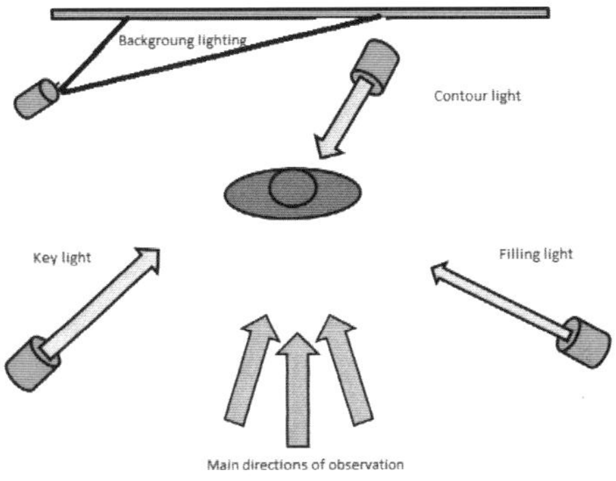

Fig. 1. Scheme of arrangement and direction of luminaires in stage lighting.

When choosing lighting equipment it is important to use the knowledge of vision psychophysiologist, what means impact on the visual experience:

• lighting level

• contrasts

• psychological interaction of light color

• vision adaptation

Proper exposure of illuminated objects requires obtaining adequate luminance level. It can be assumed the object, located in a park among trees, is in the low brightness environment and recommended lighting level corresponds to luminance 4 cd/m^2. While the object, located at the intensely lit street or building facade, is in the high brightness environment and the minimum recommended lighting level corresponds to luminance 12 cd/m^2. These lighting levels correspond to the observation conditions from a short distance. They should be accordingly increased if the object is observed from a bigger distance. The reception of the object illumination is also influanced by obtained contsrast, both contrasts of luminance and color. They are extremly impoortant means of expression, especially in relation to exhibitions that commemorate dramatic figures or events.

* Corresponding author: sandra.mroczkowska@put.poznan.pl

2 Illumination of the monument Państwa Podziemnego i Armii Krajowej in Poznan

The low lighting key uses high contrasts to emphasize the dramatic nature of presented events and evoking appropriate emotions. The monument Państwa Podziemnego I Armii Krajowej was illuminated according to these principles. A daily view of this monument is shown in the Figure 2.

Fig. 2. View of the monument during the day.

The ground part of the monument is made up of corroded steel plates, symbolizing the tomb - a shelter and a colonnade of stone blocks – "piles of memory", which are also "the gate of freedom open to eagles". The underground part, visible through the glass fragments of the wall, symbolizes ruins. From these ruins eagles fly to freedom.
When designing illumination of this monument, a special mood of reflection and reflections on the dramatic fade of Poles fighting for freedom, was to be given away. The preparation of the detailed design was preceded by creating visualizations of the proposed solutions.
When lighting the monument it was decided to use only key lighting with high contrast to emphasize the dramatic meaning of the composition of the monument's solid. It was also necessary to ensure legibility of the inscriptions on granite slabs of pillars.
The visualization of the monument's illumination was created in 3ds Max program. Based on architectural project, the geometry of an object with suitable textures on surfaces has been modelled. Next, based on adopted concept of illumination, light with real photometric parameters were placed. The visualization of illumination is presented in the Figure 3. The actual lighting effect of the monument is shown in Figure 4.
According to the assumptions, the elements of the monument with eagles flying out from the underground are illuminated and exposed on the dark background what emphasize the drama of the symbolized events.

3 Summary

Based on the example of the monuments lighting, the possibility of using stage lighting rules to create monuments illumination is presented. Finding a proper lighting equipment and their placing to achieve the desired lighting effects is facilitated by the use of computer visualization method. The ground part of the monument is made up of corroded steel plates, symbolizing the tomb - a shelter and a colonnade of stone blocks – "piles of memory", which are also "the gate of freedom open to eagles". The underground part

Fig. 3. Illumination of the monument.

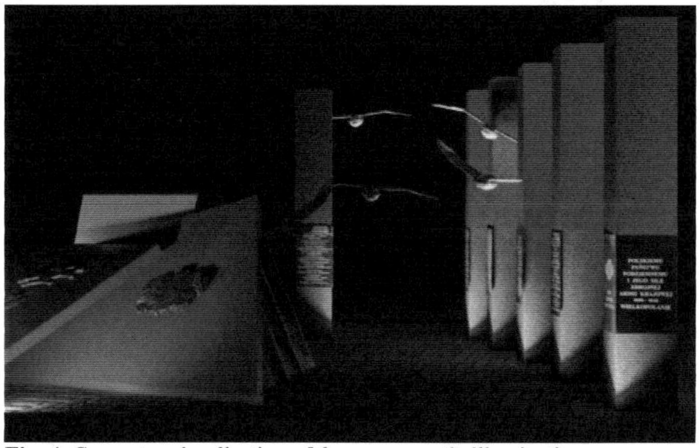

Fig. 4. Computer visualization of the monument's illumination.

References

1. M. Górczewska, Some a aspects of architectural lighting of historical buildings, (WIT Press, Southampton, Boston, 2011)
2. M. Górczewska, S. Mroczkowska, Prz. Elektrotech. **88**/5a, 173-176 (2012)
3. W. Żagan, R. Krupiński, Teoria i praktyka iluminacji obiektów, (Oficyna Wyd. Politechniki Warszawskiej, 2016)
4. F. Dybczyński, Oświetlenie sceniczne. Technika Świetlna, 132-140 (2009)
5. CIE Technical Report No 94 - Guide for Floodlighting

ITM Web of Conferences **19**, 01044 (2018) https://doi.org/10.1051/itmconf/20181901044
ZKwE'2018

Comparison of edge detection algorithms for electric wire recognition

Paweł Kowalski[1,*], *Maciej* Czyżak[2] and *Robert* Smyk[1]

[1]Gdansk University of Technology, 80-233 Gdansk, Poland
[2]The State University of Applied Sciences in Elbląg, 82-300 Elbląg, Poland

Abstract. Edge detection is the preliminary step in image processing for object detection and recognition procedure. It allows to remove useless information and reduce amount of data before further analysis. The paper contains the comparison of edge detection algorithms optimized for detection of horizontal edges. For comparison purposes the algorithms were implemented in the developed application dedicated to detection of electric line wires. The optimized algorithms were benchmarked on a set of images of electric wires.

1 Introduction

Detection and recognition of wires of electric lines in an image can be realized using shapes. The shape of a wire can be extracted using edges. Such approach is shown, for example, in [1, 2]. Accuracy and execution time of edge detection process can strongly affect the further image processing. In this paper we present and analyse a selected set of edge detection algorithms which are well suited for detection of edges representing electric lines in the image. We also suggest important modification that increases the performance of the wire detection. We have implemented individual algorithms and compared their execution time and accuracy.

In Section 2 a short review of selected edge detection algorithms is given and Section 3 contains the benchmarks and discussion of the results.

2 Review of edge detection algorithms

The digital image can be treated as a matrix with the entries that contain the pixels. In grayscale images small values represent dark pixels and large values bright. It is assumed that edges appear where there is a large difference in the values of neighboring pixels. Table 1 contains the sample data row with the highlighted edges.

Table 1. Sample data row.

10	9	11	10	15	140	141	145	140	40	35	37	39	38

The output of the edge detection algorithm is the matrix where edges are represented by relatively large values. The final step of the edge detection process is the thresholding which gives the binary image represented by an array of bits, where each bit corresponds to one pixel. The value of 1 represents the edge and 0 the area outside the edge. The core of algorithms is the two-dimensional convolution of the part of image called window $W_{x,y}$ with the appropriate mask M. An example of M can be 3x3 mask that can provide satisfactory results without imposing heavy computational burden. The convolution result $z_{x,y}$ can be expressed as

$$z_{x,y} = W_{x,y} * M\,, \tag{1}$$

where $W_{x,y}$ is the window from the image V, x and y are the coordinates of the left upper corner

$$W_{x,y} = \begin{bmatrix} v_{x,y} & v_{x+1,y} & v_{x+2,y} \\ v_{x,y+1} & v_{x+1,y+1} & v_{x+2,y+1} \\ v_{x,y+2} & v_{x+1,y+2} & v_{x+2,y+2} \end{bmatrix}, \tag{2}$$

and $v_{x,y}$ is the pixel of the input image V. The convolution result $z_{x,y}$ for mask 3x3 is calculated by using the following formula

$$z_{x,y} = \sum_{i=0}^{2}\sum_{j=0}^{2} m_{i,j} w_{i,j}\,, \tag{3}$$

where $m_{i,j}$ is the coefficient of the mask M and $w_{i,j}$ is the pixel of the window $W_{x,y}$.

In their basic form edge detection algorithms use the 3x3 mask to extract both vertical and horizontal edges. There are three types of basic edges: horizontal, vertical and diagonal oriented. For wire detection it can be assumed that wires are situated horizontally. It allows to simplify the algorithms that can be achieved by using a set of masks adjusted to horizontal edge detection. Below the directional masks of selected algorithms are shown. The masks with the highest sensitivity to horizontal edges have the following forms:

$$S = \begin{bmatrix} 1 & 2 & 1 \\ 0 & 0 & 0 \\ -1 & -2 & -1 \end{bmatrix}, P = \begin{bmatrix} 1 & 1 & 1 \\ 0 & 0 & 0 \\ -1 & -1 & -1 \end{bmatrix}, K_N = \begin{bmatrix} 5 & 5 & 5 \\ -3 & 0 & -3 \\ -3 & -3 & -3 \end{bmatrix},$$

$$K_S = \begin{bmatrix} -3 & -3 & -3 \\ -3 & 0 & -3 \\ 5 & 5 & 5 \end{bmatrix}, Sch = \begin{bmatrix} -3 & -10 & -3 \\ 0 & 0 & 0 \\ 3 & 10 & 3 \end{bmatrix}, \tag{4}$$

where S is Sobel[3] mask, P – Prewitt[4], K_N and K_S – Kirsch[5], Sch – Scharr[6] masks.

* Corresponding author: pawel.kowalski2@pg.edu.pl

An example of the operator that uses masks smaller than 3x3 is Roberts operator [7].

$$R_1 = \begin{bmatrix} 1 & 0 \\ 0 & -1 \end{bmatrix}, \qquad R_2 = \begin{bmatrix} 0 & 1 \\ -1 & 0 \end{bmatrix}. \tag{5}$$

Using these masks the new pixel value is calculated using the formula

$$z_{x,y} = \left| v_{x,y} - v_{x+1,y+1} \right| + \left| v_{x+1,y} - v_{x,y+1} \right|. \tag{6}$$

This algorithm has high sensitivity to all edges but the highest sensitivity to diagonal edges.

It can be shown that the simpler masks [9] can be used with the following form

$$P_{1x3} = \begin{bmatrix} 1 \\ 0 \\ -1 \end{bmatrix}, \; P_{1x2} = \begin{bmatrix} 1 \\ -1 \end{bmatrix}. \tag{7}$$

These masks provide relatively high sensitivity to horizontal edges and are insensitive to vertical edges.

3 Results

The comparison of edge detection algorithms has been carried out using the elaborated custom software for detecting of electric lines that uses OpenCV library[8] for elementary processing. The run-time environment included the PC based computer with i7 class four cores processor. It has been assumed that the basic assessment criteria are the noise level in the image and the algorithm execution time. We have applied as the figure of merit the efficiency function *eff*. This function computes the number of columns of the binary image in which the wire has been detected

$$eff = \sum_{i=1}^{n} \sum_{x=0}^{img\_width-1} f_i(x) \tag{8}$$

$$f_i(x) = \begin{cases} 1 & if \;\; \exists z_{x,y} \in L_{i,x} \\ 0 & if \;\; \forall z_{x,y} \notin L_{i,x} \end{cases} \tag{9}$$

The internal functions $f_i(x)$ in (8, 9) are equal to 1 when at least one pixel of the wire i in column x has been detected otherwise to 0. The full set of pixels of the wire i in the column i is represented by $L_{i,x}$. The function *eff* has been used to select individually the threshold for each of the considered algorithms. In effect, the thresholds are selected for each image and algorithm, which results in *eff* equal to 90% of the maximum attainable value.

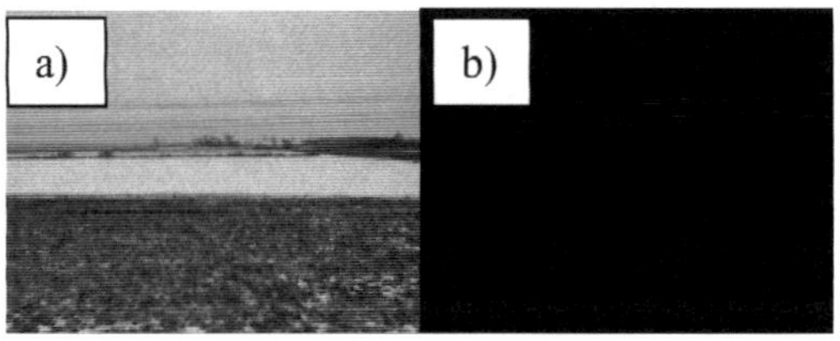

Fig. 1. a) Input image in gray-scale, b) Result of edge detection using mask K_n.

The accumulated noise value N_v was calculated as the count of pixels detected outside any wire. The noise level was calculated as N_v divided by the image resolution. The 1% noise in the 10Mpx image means that 100 000 pixels are recognised outside all wires. Fig. 2 and Fig. 3 presents the comparison of the influence of the individual masks on the noise level.

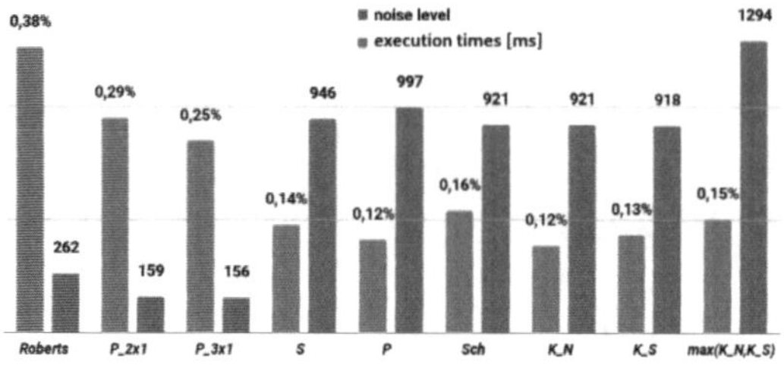

Fig. 2. Average noise in presented algorithms and times of execution in milliseconds on 10Mpx image.

Roberts, 2x1 and 3x1 algorithms was significant faster than other algorihtms. The fastest alorithm (3x1) is eight times faster than the slowest (Kirsch with 2 masks).

4 Conclusion

The paper contains the analysis of performance of selected edge detection algorithms which are well suited for detection of electric wires in images. The execution times and accuracy for individual algorithms have been shown. As well certain modifications have been proposed to increase the efficiency detection of wire treated as horizontal edges.

References

1. C. Weiran, Z. Linlin, H. Jianda, W Tianran, D. Yingkui, IEEE/ASME Int. Conf. AIM, 554-558 (2013)
2. J. Candamo, R. Kasturi, D. Goldgof, S. Sarkar, IEEE Transactions on Aerospace and Electronic Systems **45**, 3, 937-949 (2009)
3. I. Sobel, G. Feldman, An isotropic 3x3 image gradient operator, Stanford Artificial Intelligence Project (SAIL), (1968)
4. J.M.S. Prewitt, Object Enhancement and Extraction, Picture processing and Psychopictorics, Academic Press,1970
5. R. A. Kirsch, Computers and Biomedical Research, **4**, 3, 315-328 (1971)
6. H. Scharr, Optimal Operators in Digital Image Processing, PhD thesis, Heidelberg, (May 10, 2000), pp. 178
7. L. G. Roberts, Machine perception of three-dimensional solids, PhD thesis, MIT, Lincoln Laboratory, (May 22, 1963), pp. 82
8. Open Source Computer Vision Library, Reference Manual, (2014)
9. J. B. Burns, A. R. Hanson, E. M. Riseman, IEEE Trans. on Pattern Analysis & Machine Intelligence **8**, 4, 425-455 (1986)

Hybrid forecasting of PM2.5 using SOFM and ELM

Krzysztof Siwek[1,*], *Tomasz* Grzywacz[1]

IETiSIP, Faculty of Electrical Engeenering, Warsaw University of Technology, Warsaw, Poland

Abstract. The article presents a new approach to atmospheric PM2.5 dust prediction using an Extreme Learning Machine (ELM) neural network with clusterization done by the Self Organizing Feature Map (SOFM). This work is concerned with the calculation of the average level of air particulate matters PM2,5 in Warsaw's Ursynow one day ahead. The brief description of the hazards posed by air pollution is included. The work presents a short description of the SOFM and ELM networks, and their hybridized system used as a prediction tool. The analysis of the obtained results was presented and discussed.

1 Problem statement

We have observed growing pollution of the natural environment in recent years. Water, soil and atmospheric air are polluted. Observing the information provided by the media, and these available directly from the measurement stations, we know this is a serious and global problem.

As a result of civilization progress and industrial development, the impact of humans activities on the natural environment is growing and, unfortunately, in most cases unfavourable for it. The air pollution caused by dust influences human life and health, and can adversely affect the length and quality of human life [1,2,3].

1.1 Particulate matters pollutions

Particulate matters in the atmospheric are classified due to its diameter; the most important are:

• PM10 - dust with a diameter smaller than 10μm, which can reach the upper respiratory tract and lungs,

• PM2.5 - dust with a diameter of less than 2.5μm that penetrates deep into the lungs and enters the bloodstream [2].

The suspended dust consists of an undefined mixture of particles of inorganic and organic substances. It may contain a variety of toxic substances, for example polycyclic aromatic hydrocarbons - benzo(a)pyrene and benzo(e)pyrene, dioxins, furans, heavy metals and many other substances. Air pollution is absorbed by people mainly during breathing and contributes to the development of respiratory and allergic diseases, cancer, as well as heart and blood vessel diseases.

Sources of atmospheric air pollution are of two types: natural and anthropogenic. Natural sources include, among others: volcanic eruptions, wind erosion of rocks, dust blown from deserts, forest and steppe fires.

The second category includes air pollution resulting from human activities: chemical conversion of fuels (combustion), mining, chemical industry, raw and waste landfills, and transport.

Air pollution is usually derived from two sources: combustion of poor quality of coal in old, ineffective boilers and domestic furnaces, and from communication sources (engine exhausts) and the street dust carried from under cars. The exceeding the norms can be serious and good forecasting can help to reduce air pollutions.

2 Database of PM

The measurement data used for experimental research were from the WIOS (Warsaw Inspectorate for Environmental Protection) measurement station located in the residential Ursynow district in Warsaw, Poland measured in the years 2011-2013.

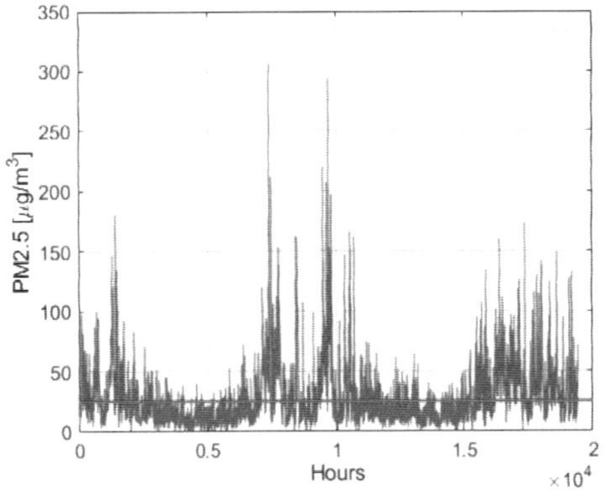

Fig. 1. PM2.5 measured in Warsaw-Ursynow in 2011-2013.

The measurements of PM2.5 are carried out every hour. Additionally the weather conditions (temperature, strength and direction of the wind, humidity, pressure) were recorded at the same time.

* Corresponding author: Krzysztof.Siwek@ee.pw.edu.pl

3 The forecasting system

3.1 The Self Organizing Feature Map (SOFM)

The Self Organizing Feature Map is unsupervised and competitive learning algorithm forming the topological maps, in which the relations of spatially correlated input data in high dimensional space are converted into spatial relationships among the neurons in one or two dimensional grid. In such way the SOFM represents the centres of input data and divides them to separate clusters [4].

3.2 The Extreme Learning Machine (ELM)

The Extreme Learning Machine is a relatively new structure of one-way neural networks, usually with one hidden layer of neurons with non-linear sigmoidal activation function [5]. The main advantage of this neural network is the extremely short learning time, based on random selection of hidden layer weights and calculation of the output layer weights using the SVD decomposition method [6].

3.3 The hybrid forecasting system

The proposed two-stage hybrid system combines the ELM prediction with the SOFM clustering algorithm. In the first stage, SOFM divides the data into clusters. Each cluster contains similar input data. In the second stage, an individual ELM network for each cluster is build. In that way the individual ELM networks are trained only using similar input vectors. In the testing mode the membership to the specific cluster is computed by SOFM firstly, then ELM, associated with this cluster, calculates the final prognosis of the mean value of PM2.5 for the next day.

4 The results

The quality of prediction was assessed using a measure of errors made by the network:

• Average absolute percentage error MAPE

$$MAPE = \frac{1}{n}\sum_{j=1}^{n}\frac{\left|P(j)-\hat{P}(j)\right|}{P(j)}\cdot 100\% \quad (1)$$

• RMSE root mean square error

$$RMSE = \sqrt{\frac{1}{p}\sum_{i=1}^{p}\left|d_i - y_i\right|^2} \quad (2)$$

The input vectors formed from the process features, were the same in each network: 24 previous values of PM2.5 of the following hours preceding the forecast, weather forecast for the next day (temperature, wind power, humidity, pressure – each 24 values), type of the day and season code, totally 171 values. Only those features that are strongly correlated with the destination (the absolute value of Pearson's correlation coefficient above 0.5) were presented to the network input. ELM networks has calculated the mean values of PM2.5 for the next day.

Table 1. Results of numerical experiments.

Number of clusters	MAPE [%]	RMSE [μg/m³]
5	28.14 ± 1.62	11.67 ± 1.22
15	24.94 ± 1.33	10.42 ± 0.88
30	$\mathbf{23.43 \pm 1.29}$	$\mathbf{10.01 \pm 0.81}$
50	25.58 ± 1.39	10.34 ± 0.94
100	26.99 ± 1.40	10.34 ± 0.98

Due to the random initial weight values in the SOFM and random weights generated during learning for the ELM network, 10 learning and testing processes were carried out for each network. Available data of pollution was divided into two randomly selected sets: teaching and testing in 70:30 proportions. After each learning process, MAPE and RMSE errors were calculated, and on their basis the average values of these errors and their standard deviations were computed. Table 1 presents the obtained results for different number of clusters (number of neurons in SOFM).

5 Conclusions

The paper has presented fast hybrid method for PM2.5 forecasting. The complexity of the PM2.5 prediction problem results from the dependence of the local level of atmospheric air pollution on the local weather conditions, which change very quickly and accidentally. The next step of performing a more accurate prediction will be the aggregation of the results of many forecasts calculated using various methods - neural and classical. An interesting approach is also the use of selection of features based on genetic algorithms and not only the Pearson linear correlation coefficient [1].

The numerical results presented in the paper have confirmed efficiency of the proposed method.

References

1. K. Siwek, S. Osowski, Int. J. Appl. Math. Comput. Sci. **26** (2), 467–478 (2016)
2. R. Rückerl, A. Schneider, S. Breitner, J. Cyrys, A. Peters, Inhalation Toxicology, **23** (10), 555–592 (2011)
3. European Environment Agency (EEA) raport, Air quality in Europe (2016)
4. T. Kohonen, *Self organization and associative memory*, 3rd ed., (Springer-Verlag, Berlin, 1989)
5. G. B.Huang, Q. Y. Zhu, C. K. Siew, Extreme Learning Machine: Theory and applications, 1-10 (2016)
6. G. B. Huang, Q. Y. Zhu, C. K. Siew, Extreme learning machine: a new learning scheme of feedforward neural networks, IEEE International Joint Conference on Neural Networks, Budapest, Hungary (2004)

AUTHOR INDEX